Colossus:
The Rise and Decline of US Imperialism

Look back over the past,
with its changing empires that rose and fell,
and you can foresee the future, too.
– Marcus Aurelius

Colossus
THE RISE AND DECLINE OF US IMPERIALISM

John Peterson

Wellred Books
New York

Colossus
The Rise and Decline of US Imperialism
John Peterson

First edition
WR Books, November 2024

marxistbooks.com

USA distribution: Marxist Books, marxistbooks.com
WR Books
PO Box 1575
New York, New York
NY 10013
sales@marxistbooks.com

UK distribution: Wellred Books Britain, wellredbooks.co.uk
books@wellred-books.com

Cover design by Tim LaSalle & Krissy McGonnigle

Layout by Eric Romsted

Proofreading by Steve Iverson

ISBN: 979-8-218-55488-0

Contents

Preface

Imperialism is a vast subject, penetrating virtually every aspect of modern life. It is what lies behind America's trade war with China, its proxy war with Russia in Ukraine, Israel's genocidal slaughter in Gaza, and the living nightmare in countries like Sudan and the Democratic Republic of Congo. Outrage at its cynical cruelty is driving many to become communists today.

Grasping the essence of what Lenin called the highest stage of capitalism is relatively easy. However, it is not enough to know that imperialism is the foreign-policy continuation of capitalist domestic policy, that it arises at a certain stage of historical development, or that it is intimately connected to the national question and racism. While militarism, warmongering, and competing spheres of influence are indeed a big part of it, there is far more to imperialism than that.

As always, to get to the heart of any question, Marxists must base themselves on the fundamentals. When analyzing any phenomenon, our guiding principle is class independence in all things and at all times. This applies also to our analysis of imperialism.

As Marx explained, the nation-state and the market economy based on private ownership of the means of production are the main barriers to human progress, leading to periodic crises of overproduction and social unrest. Imperialism attempts to overcome this by extending capital's power and influence beyond its national borders, whether through the export of capital and commodities, or outright military domination.

However, like the expansion of credit, this can only go so far. No country or politician can indefinitely square the circle of the system's organic contradictions, which are amplified even further on the world arena.

With few exceptions, capital has saturated every corner of the globe. However, like a shark, it must keep moving forward or die. If restricted to the system's limits, this is an insoluble contradiction. Far from a new golden age, deglobalization and the fight over diminishing returns can lead only to rising tensions, crisis, and war. The only way forward is the revolutionary overthrow of the system. Only this can assure our species worldwide harmony and superabundance.

US imperialism is, without a doubt, the world's premiere superpower. But it has reached its zenith in an epoch of terminal systemic decay. It is, as Leon Trotsky wrote, "a colossus with feet of clay." The myth of American exceptionalism had an objective basis, but that basis is now finished. Despite its apparent might on paper, it will crumble to dust before the power of the mobilized working class—but only if it is class conscious and organized in a mass revolutionary communist party.

To this end, the current volume aims to provide the new generation of American communists with a deeper understanding of the country in which we fight for revolution.

Part One establishes a baseline for understanding imperialism by reviewing Lenin's analysis of the question. Then, using facts, figures, and historical examples, we trace the rise and relative decline of American imperialism and its inter-imperialist rivalry with China and Russia. As we will see, the history of the United States is a history of revolution, counterrevolution, and the rise of imperialism.

Part Two is a Marxist primer on imperialist war, with emphasis on the principled position developed by Lenin and Trotsky at the outbreak of World War I.

Part Three recounts the history of the US invasion of Soviet Russia under Woodrow Wilson and Lenin's internationalist appeal to the American working class.

Without the hard work of many comrades, this work would not have been possible. In particular, I would like to thank Pete Walsh, Charlotte Papin, and Fred Weston for their thoughtful edits and suggestions; Steve Iverson for his careful proofreading and comments; Tim LaSalle and Krissy McGonnigle for their creativity and work on the cover; and last but not least, Eric Romsted and Ramneet Manrai for their attention to detail and for running a tight ship at Wellred Books.

As for why this has taken the form of a book, there is a simple explanation. Encouraged by comrades to produce a booklet on the subject, the draft quickly became far too long. Now that the deadline for completing it has arrived, it seems far too short, as there is always more to be said on something as pervasive as imperialism.

In any case, it is my sincere hope that the reader will learn something new and be energized by the ideas and information presented. However, the purpose of this work is not merely to analyze imperialism theoretically, but rather, to understand our class enemy in order to overthrow it.

After all, in the words of Abraham Lincoln, "The struggle of today is not altogether for today—it is for a vast future also."

John Peterson
November 18, 2024

Part 1: The Rise and Decline of US Imperialism

What Is Imperialism?

Force is the midwife of every old society pregnant with a new one. It is itself an economic power.

– Karl Marx, *Capital*, Volume I

We are living through the death spasms of a socioeconomic system in terminal decline. American imperialism's postwar order lies in tatters, and in every country on earth, the capitalists are sitting on a seething cauldron of working-class anger. Neither the liberals nor the conservatives offer a viable way out of the societal impasse, and there is no mass class-independent outlet for the distorted and deepening polarization. This explains the rise of Trumpism, the desperation of the liberals, the intensification of imperialist rivalries—and the rising interest in communism.

As the *New York Times* correctly noted in the aftermath of the 2024 election:

> Mr. Trump's victory amounts to a public vote of no confidence in the leaders and institutions that have shaped American life since the end of the Cold War 35 years ago . . .
>
> If Mr. Trump and his coalition fail to create something better than what they have replaced, they will suffer the same fate they've

> inflicted on the fallen Bush, Clinton and Cheney dynasties. A new force for creative destruction will emerge, possibly on the American left.

For several decades after World War II, the capitalists could afford to buy relative class peace. The prolonged economic upswing accelerated capitalist economic integration, and two mighty superpowers dominated the planet. Despite its enormous power and reach, American imperialism was counterbalanced by Russian Stalinism and the deformed workers' states under its aegis.

However, with the fall of the Soviet Union, US imperialism became the unchallenged master of the "New World Order." Great power politics became obsolete as only one great power remained. Giddy with greed, the US ruling class announced the "end of history." They dreamed of "full-spectrum dominance" and "unipolar hegemony." Some even referred to the US as a "crusader state."

The American bourgeois truly believed they could remake the world, not only in the image of capitalism, but in the image of the United States. With capitalism already dominating half the planet, they thought it would be child's play to impose their institutions and "values" on the rest of it. After all, the "good guys" had won and the "bad guys" had been vanquished. Surely, "democracy" would prevail over "autocracy." This arrogant optimism was reflected in Thomas Friedman's 1996 assertion that "No two countries that both have a McDonald's have ever fought a war against each other."

When institutions like the International Monetary Fund and World Trade Organization proved insufficient, the US Army, Marines, Air Force, and Navy were always held in reserve.

But everything eventually turns into its opposite. The so-called Pax Americana is finished, and the American Dream has been flushed down the toilet. The pace of history has accelerated, and the tectonic plates of world relations have shifted.

In less than thirty years, the post–Cold War order they imagined would last for centuries has unraveled. Instead of the promised "peace dividend" of post-Soviet prosperity, a new arms race has been unleashed and quality of life in the West has plummeted. Once the world's biggest lender, the US is now its biggest debtor, living on borrowed money and time. In fiscal year 2024, the US federal government spent $892 billion on debt-servicing interest payments alone—more than the official military budget.

The productive forces have outgrown the artificial limits of the system and the objective conditions for building a new kind of society are beyond rotten ripe. Due to the belated socialist revolution, many unforeseeable contradictions have been introduced to the equation and humanity has been dragged into a new epoch of war, revolution, and counterrevolution. Trade wars, cold wars, and hot wars are the new normal as China, Russia, and others attempt to expand their spheres of influence at the expense of the so-called collective West.

As Bill Burns, Biden's director of the CIA wrote in April 2024:

> China's rise and Russia's revanchism pose daunting geopolitical challenges in a world of intense strategic competition in which the United States no longer enjoys uncontested primacy and in which existential climate threats are mounting. Complicating matters further is a revolution in technology even more sweeping than the Industrial Revolution or the beginning of the nuclear age.

Robert Gates, who served as Secretary of Defense under GW Bush and Obama, is equally concerned. As he warned in his article, "The Dysfunctional Superpower":

> The United States now confronts graver threats to its security than it has in decades, perhaps ever. Never before has it faced four allied antagonists at the same time—Russia, China, North Korea, and Iran—whose collective nuclear arsenal could within a few years be nearly double the size of its own. Not since the Korean War has the United States had to contend with powerful military rivals in both Europe and Asia. And no one alive can remember a time when an adversary had as much economic, scientific, technological, and military power as China does today.

The Congressional Commission on the National Defense Strategy is also sounding alarm bells over America's lack of preparedness:

> The threats the United States faces are the most serious and most challenging the nation has encountered since 1945 and include the potential for near-term major war.

Even the CEO of JPMorgan Chase, Jamie Dimon, can't see a silver lining in the situation:

> Recent events show that conditions are treacherous and getting worse. There is significant human suffering, and the outcome of these situations could have far-reaching effects on both short-term economic outcomes and more importantly on the course of history . . . several critical issues remain, including large fiscal deficits, infrastructure needs, restructuring of trade, and remilitarization of the world.

And according to the analysts at Verisk-Maplecroft:

> In 2024, the global risk landscape will remain locked in a process of sweeping realignment that is amplifying a complex set of systemic risks that are increasingly transcending borders and sectors.

The top risk they identify is "geo-economic fragmentation"—a fancy word for rising protectionism and a reversal of global economic connections. Or, as some have called it, "slowbalization," a process that has accelerated over the last decade. According to the World Bank:

> This process [of unraveling] encompasses different channels, including trade, capital, and migration flows.

After decades of increasing economic interdependence, we now have "reshoring," "nearshoring," and "friendshoring," as the capitalists balance maximizing profits with risk exposure on their investments. This, in turn, has impacted Foreign Direct Investment (FDI), the lifeblood of imperialist globalization. As *Global Finance* magazine explained:

> As recent history has consistently demonstrated, there is nothing more certain than uncertainty. A pandemic, geopolitical tensions, trade frictions, and even armed conflict have complicated the landscape for global foreign direct investment, leaving business leaders with no clear signals as they set priorities and make critical investment decisions outside their borders.

85% of investors polled said rising geopolitical tensions would impact their investment decisions, with 36% saying the impact would be "significant." An incredible 96% of CEOs polled have reshored already, or are considering doing so.

By some estimates, FDI fell by 12% in 2022 and another 7% in 2023. As of mid-2024, the total remained below pre-pandemic levels. There have also been significant shifts in where FDI is going, with countries like Mexico and Morocco seeing substantial increases due to their proximity to the American and European markets.

The reason is simple enough: the bourgeois invest to make money, not for the sake of it. If the risk is too high and the profits are too low, they will look for safer and more profitable alternatives.

Needless to say, the national capitalists are backed in their foreign ventures by their respective states as they seek to gain an advantage. In pursuit of this, they weaponize trade, offer incentives to friends, and impose penalties on rivals. And when push comes to shove, they rattle their sabers, dispatch assassins, or launch cruise missiles.

That being said, imperialism is neither monolithic nor consistent. While there may be an inherent tendency towards the threat or use of military force at the highest levels of the US government, the bureaucracy of state is riven by conflicting interests and views on how best to navigate the fractious world confronting the bourgeoisie.

The myriad ways in which economics, war, and the class struggle relate to one another—and US imperialism's unique role in all of this—is the focus of what follows.

Concentrated economics

As Marx explained, in the final analysis, it is the economic and class relations of a society that determine its parameters and limits:

> In the social production of their existence, people inevitably enter into definite relations, which are independent of their will, namely relations of production appropriate to a given stage in the development of their material forces of production. The totality of these relations of production constitutes the economic structure of society, the real foundation, on which arises a legal and political superstructure and to which correspond definite forms of social consciousness.
>
> The mode of production of material life conditions the general process of social, political and intellectual life. It is not the consciousness of people that determines their existence, but their social existence that determines their consciousness. At a certain stage of development, the material productive forces of society

> come into conflict with the existing relations of production or—this merely expresses the same thing in legal terms—with the property relations within the framework of which they have operated hitherto.
>
> From forms of development of the productive forces, these relations turn into their fetters. Then begins an era of social revolution. The changes in the economic foundation lead, sooner or later, to the transformation of the whole immense superstructure.

In other words, although there is a dialectical interrelationship between many interlocking parts, it is ultimately the contradictions built into the capitalist economy that lie behind the rising class struggle, instability, and geopolitical tension we see everywhere today.

Lenin concisely summed this up with the profound phrase, "Politics is a concentrated expression of economics."

For Marxists, economics is ultimately an expression of the class struggle. As we will see throughout this book, military power is a function of economic power and the class balance of forces. And as Lenin showed, it is really through finance capital, not overt military might, that imperialism dominates our lives day in and day out.

Capitalist imperialism rests upon the defense of private property of the means of production and the constant expansion of finance capital. It pursues this through a combination of any means necessary: alliances, treaties, embargoes, invasions, occupations, and annexations.

Foreign policy is merely an extension of domestic policy—and vice versa. Just as individual capitalists are compelled, on pain of extinction, to expand their capital and maximize returns on their investments, every imperialist state does the same for its collective national capitalists on the world arena.

In the course of capitalist production and exchange, we see the rise, fall, and interminable changing of place of the petty and big bourgeoisie. Some small companies are transformed into giants, while former Goliaths fall into ruin. Likewise, the imperialist powers exist on a spectrum, and they jockey constantly to shift the balance of power between them. At times, these transitions occur without too much disruption; at others, they lead to all-out war.

All serious imperialists understand that abstract morality has nothing to do with it. Capitalist morality is a cold and calculated question of money, markets, and power, regardless of the human cost. One famous example is the "Great Game" of the mid-19th century, in which the British and Russian Empires fought for supremacy in Central Asia—a "game" that treated millions of people like pawns on a chessboard.

As Lord Palmerston famously stated: "We have no eternal allies, and we have no perpetual enemies. Our *interests* are eternal and perpetual, and those interests it is our duty to follow."

Or, as Winston Churchill put it in 1939:

> I cannot forecast to you the action of Russia. It is a riddle wrapped in a mystery inside an enigma: but perhaps there is a key. That key is *Russian national interests*.

Leonard Wood, who served as Military Governor during the US occupation of Cuba, viewed political stability on the island as a function of "business confidence." As he wrote the US Secretary of War:

> When money can be borrowed at a reasonable rate of interest and when capital is willing to invest in the island, a condition of stability will have been reached.

And as the retired general-turned-anti-war-activist Smedley Butler put it:

> I was a racketeer, a gangster for capitalism. I suspected I was just part of a racket at the time. Now I am sure of it . . .
>
> I helped make Mexico, especially Tampico, safe for American oil interests in 1914. I helped make Haiti and Cuba a decent place for the National City Bank boys to collect revenues in. I helped in the raping of half a dozen Central American republics for the benefits of Wall Street. The record of racketeering is long. I helped purify Nicaragua for the international banking house of Brown Brothers in 1909-1912. I brought light to the Dominican Republic for American sugar interests in 1916. In China I helped to see to it that Standard Oil went its way unmolested.
>
> During those years, I had, as the boys in the back room would say, a swell racket. Looking back on it, I feel that I could have given Al Capone a few hints. The best he could do was to operate his racket in three districts. I operated on three continents.

Marx explained that "the executive of the modern state is but a committee for managing the common affairs of the whole bourgeoisie." And as Engels added, the "bodies of armed men" of the state, including the police and the army, are the enforcers of those common affairs, both at home and abroad.

Concentrated economics and the fundamental unity between foreign and domestic policy are the essence of imperialism, and the US is no exception. As we will see, whether directly or indirectly, the state has played a decisive role in nurturing the development of American capitalism at every stage of its history.

Why we need a class analysis

Capitalism breeds class struggle both at home and abroad, and just as you can't have a revolution without counterrevolution, you can't have imperialism without anti-imperialism. But not all anti-imperialism is equal.

There are reformist "anti-imperialists" of various stripes who believe in a "kinder, gentler" capitalism without militarism. Lacking an understanding of the class basis of imperialism, they view the world through filters such as "periphery versus core" or "Global North versus Global South."

Some, like the late Antonio Negri, explicitly deny the existence of capitalist imperialism in favor of the amorphous concept of "Empire." Instead of a world of inter- and intra-class contradictions, including rivalries between imperialist nation-states, Negri sees a:

> Decentralized network of power that encompasses the entire globe operating through global institutions, corporations, and cultural influences rather than through direct territorial control.

While NGOs, corporations, and culture certainly play a role, imperialist power cannot be divorced from the nation-state. Imperialism's crimes are not the result of bad people or policies in the abstract. They flow from the class divisions inherent to capitalism, the market economy, and the nation-state. They cannot be overcome without understanding their historical context. Moreover, an analysis not rooted in class leads inevitably to class collaboration and illusions in the trap of lesser evilism.

Again, the foreign policy of capitalism is imperialist. Just as you can have capitalists large and small, you can have imperialist powers at different scales in different contexts in different regions, and their relations with each other can be highly contradictory.

New imperialist powers and blocs of powers can emerge while others decline, and even relatively small powers can have an imperialist policy in their near abroad. Remember: the US was also once "merely" a regional power. What matters, above all, is not a country's size, but the class content and intent of its ruling class.

During the Balkan Wars in the early 20th Century, Trotsky even considered countries like Bulgaria imperialist. As he wrote in 1912:

> Bulgarian imperialism is of recent origin but is all the more bellicose and reckless for that. The Bulgarian bourgeoisie came late on the scene and at once began vigorously using its elbows in order to get ahead.

At the time, Bulgaria only had a population of around 4.4 million. How much more "vigorous with its elbows" can a country like China be, with its 1.4 billion people, no matter how late it came onto the imperialist scene? Nowadays, even countries like Sweden and Denmark qualify as imperialist, even if they are only in 23rd and 37th place, respectively, when it comes to world GDP.

Marxists take a *class* position at all times. We are not obliged to "choose sides" when it comes to inter-imperialist conflicts, no matter what the bourgeois media or the so-called left say. As Trotsky emphasized, quoting from Lenin's writings on the question:

> The objective historical meaning of the war is of decisive importance for the proletariat: What class is conducting it? And for the sake of what? This is decisive, and not the subterfuges of diplomacy by means of which the enemy can always be successfully portrayed to the people as an aggressor.
>
> Just as false are the references by imperialists to the slogans of democracy and culture:
>
> "The German bourgeoisie . . . deceives the working class and the toiling masses by vowing that the war is being waged for the sake of . . . freedom and culture, for the sake of freeing the peoples

> oppressed by tsarism. The English and French bourgeoisies . . . deceive the working class and the toiling masses by vowing that they are waging war . . . against German militarism and despotism."
>
> A political superstructure of one kind or another cannot change the reactionary economic foundation of imperialism. On the contrary, it is the foundation that subordinates the superstructure to itself.
>
> "In our day . . . it is silly even to think of a progressive bourgeoisie, a progressive bourgeois movement. All bourgeois democracy . . . has become reactionary."
>
> This appraisal of imperialist "democracy" constitutes the cornerstone of the entire Leninist conception.

In *The Transitional Program*, Trotsky elaborated further on how Marxists must apply a consistent class analysis:

> Imperialist war is the continuation and sharpening of the predatory politics of the bourgeoisie. The struggle of the proletariat against war is the continuation and sharpening of its class struggle. The beginning of war alters the situation and partially the means of struggle between the classes, but not the aim and basic course. The imperialist bourgeoisie dominates the world. In its basic character, the approaching war will therefore be an imperialist war.
>
> The fundamental content of the politics of the international proletariat will consequently be a struggle against imperialism and its war. In this struggle, the basic principle is: "the chief enemy is in *your own* country" or "the defeat of *your own* (imperialist) government is the lesser evil."
>
> However, not all countries of the world are imperialist countries. On the contrary, the majority are victims of imperialism. Some of the colonial or semicolonial countries will undoubtedly attempt to utilize the war to cast off the yoke of slavery. Their war will not be

> imperialist but liberating. It will be the duty of the international proletariat to aid the oppressed countries in their war against oppressors. The same duty applies in regard to aiding the USSR, or whatever other workers' government might arise before the war or during the war. The defeat of *every* imperialist government in the struggle with the workers' state or with a colonial country is the lesser evil.
>
> The workers of imperialist countries, however, cannot help an anti-imperialist country through their own government, no matter what the diplomatic and military relations between the two countries might be at a given moment. If the governments find themselves in a temporary and, by the very essence of the matter, unreliable alliance, then the proletariat of the imperialist country continues to remain in class opposition to its own government and supports the non-imperialist "ally" through its *own* methods, i.e., through the methods of the international class struggle (agitation not only against their perfidious allies but also in favor of a workers' state in a colonial country; boycott, strikes, in one case; rejection of boycott and strikes in another case, etc.)
>
> In supporting the colonial country or the USSR in a war, the proletariat does not in the slightest degree solidarize either with the bourgeois government of the colonial country or with the Thermidorian bureaucracy of the USSR. On the contrary, it maintains full political independence from the one as from the other. Giving aid in a just and progressive war, the revolutionary proletariat wins the sympathy of the workers in the colonies and in the USSR, strengthens there the authority and influence of the Fourth International, and increases its ability to help overthrow the bourgeois government in the colonial country, the reactionary bureaucracy in the USSR.

In contrast to the reformists who would tinker with capitalism while leaving it fundamentally untouched, the comrades of the

RCI are revolutionary anti-imperialists. We understand that only the total overthrow of capitalism through the socialist revolution can liberate humanity from this horror without end.

Lenin's Imperialism

When analyzing any complex social problem, we must start with a theoretical understanding and some historical context. In the case of imperialism, any serious study must start with Lenin's writings on the question.

Lenin has an incomparable way of breaking any theoretical or practical question into its component parts, always from the perspective of the class struggle, and always with a view toward raising the party's political level. By systematically applying dialectics, he is able to examine things from every angle. He then synthesizes and recapitulates everything on an even higher level—all while ruthlessly exposing the shortcomings of his political opponents.

This is why Lenin's works on imperialism and war are essential reading for all Marxists. Part Two of this volume focuses specifically on the war side of the equation. However, for the purposes of Part One, it is necessary to briefly summarize the main points outlined in Lenin's classic, *Imperialism: The Highest Stage of Capitalism.*

Drafted in 1916, during the dark days of World War I, *Imperialism* uses facts, figures, and arguments to analyze what Lenin calls "capitalist imperialism," which he differentiates from the imperialism of societies like Ancient Rome.

Throughout the book, he polemicizes against Karl Kautsky and the petty-bourgeois social-chauvinists who betrayed the interests of the world socialist revolution by supporting "their" ruling class in the war.

As Lenin points out, "the war to end all wars" was all the evidence needed to prove the absurdity of Kautsky's argument that "ultra-imperialism" or "super-imperialism" would lead to a prolonged epoch of peaceful capitalist development and gradual progressive reforms. Kautsky's reformist illusions blinded him to the fact that harmonious imperialist coexistence is impossible on the basis of the nation-state and market economy.

Although Lenin was fully aware of the "inadequate," "conditional," and "relative value" of "all definitions in general, which can never embrace all the concatenations of a phenomenon in its full development," he nevertheless identified five key features for understanding this new stage of capitalist development.

First, the concentration of production and capital has developed to such a degree that it has led to the rise of monopolies, which play a decisive role in economic life.

Second, is the merging of banking capital and industrial capital into finance capital. On this basis, we see the rise of a financial oligarchy, whereby a small group of financial institutions and industrial capitalists wield immense power over the economy. These are fused closely with the state, which, in the final analysis, defends and enforces the interests of the national capitalists on a world scale.

Third, the export of capital—as distinguished from the export of commodities—acquires exceptional importance. As a result, an international network of dependence on finance capital spreads over the entire planet, with banks founded in the colonies playing a crucial role. The export and expansion of capital dramatically accelerates the development of capitalism in those countries to which it is exported.

Fourth is the formation of international monopolist capitalist associations, which share the world among themselves:

> [These] cartels, syndicates, and trusts first divided the home market among themselves and obtained more or less complete

> possession of the industry of their own country. However, under capitalism, the home market is inevitably bound up with the foreign market. Capitalism long ago created a world market. As the export of capital increased, and as the foreign and colonial connections and "spheres of influence" of the big monopolist associations expanded in all ways, things "naturally" gravitated towards an international agreement among these associations and towards the formation of international cartels.

Fifth is the territorial division of the planet among the biggest capitalist powers. To the numerous "old" motives of colonial policy, finance capital adds the struggle for sources of raw materials, the export of capital, spheres of influence, profitable deals, concessions, monopoly profits, and so on. As an example of this, Lenin points out that already by 1900, nine-tenths of Africa had been claimed by one imperialist power or another.

Lenin emphasizes that this division of the world does not preclude its redivision if the relation of forces changes due to uneven development, war, bankruptcy, etc. These redivisions can occur through trade deals, trade wars, proxy wars, direct wars, and so on.

In short, as Marx explained in the *Communist Manifesto,* capitalism "creates a world after its own image"—something even more true in the era of imperialism.

Monopolies and finance capital

However, as Lenin points out, there is an inherent contradiction built into the logic of capitalism, especially in its imperialist stage:

> Free competition is the basic feature of capitalism and commodity production generally; [but] monopoly is the exact opposite of free competition [and negates it].

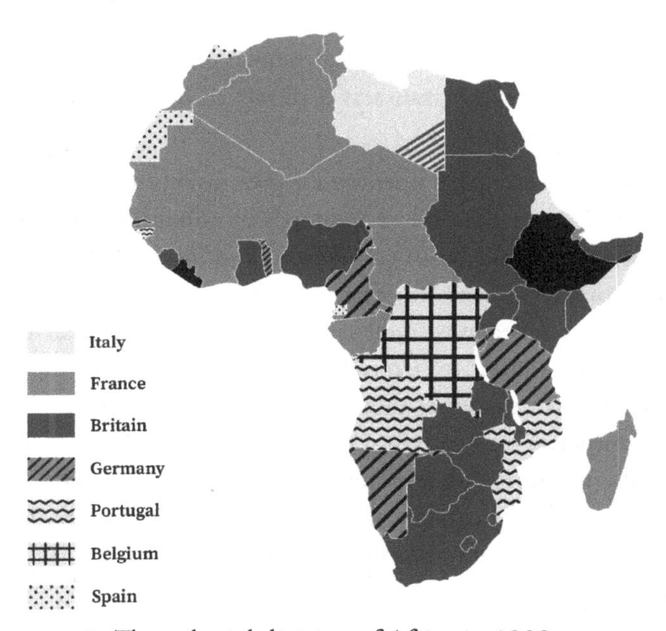

1. The colonial division of Africa in 1900

This leads inevitably to ever larger concentrations of capital, with large-scale industry "forcing out small industry, replacing large-scale by still larger-scale industry."

In the case of banking, Lenin describes how these institutions snowballed over time into a whole far greater than the sum of their parts:

> As banking develops and becomes concentrated in a small number of establishments, the banks grow from modest middlemen into powerful monopolies having at their command almost the whole of the money capital of all the capitalists and small businessmen and also the larger part of the means of production and sources of raw materials in any one country and in a number of countries.
>
> This transformation of numerous modest middlemen into a handful of monopolists is one of the fundamental processes in the growth of capitalism into capitalist imperialism.

> Scattered capitalists are transformed into a single collective capitalist. When carrying the current accounts of a few capitalists, a bank, as it were, transacts a purely technical and exclusively auxiliary operation.
>
> When, however, this operation grows to enormous dimensions, we find that a handful of monopolists subordinate to their will all the operations, both commercial and industrial, of the whole of capitalist society, for they are enabled—by means of their banking connections, their current accounts and other financial operations—first, to ascertain exactly the financial position of the various capitalists, then to control them, to influence them by restricting or enlarging, facilitating or hindering credits, and finally to entirely determine their fate, determine their income, deprive them of capital, or permit them to increase their capital rapidly and to enormous dimensions, etc.

He explains how certain companies, and banks in particular, can dominate other companies by spreading their tentacles like an octopus. In chapter two, "Banks and Their New Role," he details the mechanism for this waterfalling of economic control far beyond their formal market capitalization:

> The big enterprises, and the banks in particular, not only completely absorb the small ones, but also "annex" them, subordinate them, bring them into their "own" group or "concern" (to use the technical term) by acquiring "holdings" in their capital, by purchasing or exchanging shares, by a system of credits, etc.
>
> The Deutsche Bank "group" is one of the biggest, if not the biggest, of the big banking groups. In order to trace the main threads that connect all the banks in this group, a distinction must be made between holdings of the first, second, and third degree, or what amounts to the same thing, between dependence (of the lesser banks on the Deutsche Bank) in the first, second and third degree.

> Altogether, the Deutsche Bank group comprises, directly and indirectly, partially and totally, 87 banks, and the total capital—its own and that of others which it controls—is estimated at between two and three thousand million marks.

To give an updated example, let's look at banking in 2024. All told, there are around 4,500 banks in the US. But just *ten* of these control over *half* of all commercial banking assets. Through their subsidiary connections, they effectively control every other bank in the country and, by extension, virtually all economic activity. At the end of the day, these institutions decide what gets made, bought, and sold, as well as who is housed and employed. This is not some fantastical, shadowy conspiracy theory. Rather, it is a simple fact of economic life in the epoch of imperialism.

A clear example of this pyramid of economic control is BlackRock. By some measures, it is the world's biggest investment management company. Formally, it has "only" $113 billion in assets, with full ownership of companies such as Merrill Lynch Investment Management, Barclays Global Investor, First Reserve Infrastructure Funds, and Kreos Capital. However, it manages a total of $11.5 trillion in assets, giving it tremendous influence over dozens of major companies, including Microsoft, NVIDIA, Apple, Amazon, and Meta.

And BlackRock is just one such company—Vanguard, Fidelity, State Street, Morgan Stanley, JP Morgan Chase, and Goldman Sachs control tens of trillions of dollars more. By one estimate, the financial services sector accounts for as much as 20–25% of the world economy. This includes banking, lending, insurance, and investment companies, which other industries depend on for loans and credit to sustain their operations.

Furthermore, the power of finance capital goes well beyond the official banking entities. "Non-bank" financial institutions provide a wide range of financial services, and include everything from pension funds and insurers to mutual funds and high-risk hedge funds. These "non-banks" had about $239 trillion on their books in 2021, accounting for 49% of the world's total financial assets.

Among these are the so-called "shadow banks," which provide credit just like regular banks but operate without the same level of regulatory oversight and transparency as actual banks. And yet, these shadow banks make up around 14% of the world's financial assets.

Furthermore, it is not only companies that control one another; the web of control can be narrowed down to individual capitalists and CEOs, many of whom are related by blood or marriage.

To give a historical example, J.P. Morgan, the founder of companies like General Electric and US Steel, once sat on the boards of as many as 48 corporations. Today, 746 individuals control 30% of the roughly 5,400 seats in the top 500 companies, often sitting on multiple companies' boards as both competitors and collaborators. This is quite literally the personification of monopoly capital.

And yet, we are constantly told that, despite some regrettable shortcomings, we should feel lucky to live in a "democracy" in which we get to vote for this or that representative of the ruling class. However, it is not publicly elected officials who really call the shots in society, it is the unelected individuals who sit on the boards of the biggest corporations.

Accumulation of capital

As Marx points out in *Capital*, the only source of value is human labor expended upon the products of nature:

> Labor is, in the first place, a process in which both man and Nature participate, and in which man of his own accord starts,

> regulates, and controls the material reactions between himself and Nature. He opposes himself to Nature as one of her own forces.

Throughout his masterpiece, he traces the genesis and metastasis of capital. At a certain stage in the development of human society, it reaches a critical mass and takes on a life of its own. Thereafter, the accumulation of capital by any and all means is the *modus vivendi* of capitalism:

> Within the capitalist system, all methods for raising the social productivity of labor are brought about at the cost of the individual worker; all means for the development of production transform themselves into means of domination over and exploitation of the producers; they mutilate the worker into a fragment of a person, degrade them to the level of an appendage of a machine, destroy every remnant of charm in their work and turn it into a hated toil;
>
> They estrange from them the intellectual potentialities of the labor process in the same proportion as science is incorporated in it as an independent power; they distort the conditions under which they work, subject them during the labor process to a despotism the more hateful for its meanness; they transform their lifetime into working-time, and drag their spouse and child beneath the wheels of the juggernaut of capital.
>
> But all methods for the production of surplus value are at the same time methods of accumulation; and every extension of accumulation becomes again a means for the development of those methods. It follows, therefore, that in proportion as capital accumulates, the lot of the worker, be their payment high or low, must grow worse. The law, finally, that always equilibrates the relative surplus population, or industrial reserve army, to the extent and energy of accumulation, this law rivets the worker to capital more firmly than the wedges of Vulcan did Prometheus to the rock.

> It establishes an accumulation of misery, corresponding with the accumulation of capital. Accumulation of wealth at one pole is, therefore, at the same time, accumulation of misery, agony of toil, slavery, ignorance, brutality, and mental degradation at the opposite pole, i.e., on the side of the class that produces its own product in the form of capital.

Capital never sleeps, and there is no such thing as enough. Unless and until the organized workers consciously overthrow the system, it will continue its destructive course—even when things go badly awry.

In fact, any capitalist worth their salt knows that you should "never let a good crisis go to waste." It is precisely during these periodic episodes of paralysis and dysfunction that the concentration of capital can be accelerated. State handouts to prop up the economy lead to vast transfers of wealth from the majority to an ever smaller minority. As some companies go bankrupt and others are bailed out, investors swoop in to buy up assets at fire-sale prices.

The global pandemic and the accompanying economic meltdown provide an instructive example. Between 2019 and 2021, assets held by US banks grew by $4 trillion. By the end of 2022, American banks owned a combined $22.3 trillion in assets, up 32% over the previous decade after adjusting for inflation.

However, as Lenin explains:

> The monopolies, which have grown out of free competition, do not eliminate the latter, but exist above it and alongside it, and thereby give rise to a number of very acute, intense antagonisms, frictions, and conflicts.

This is a circle that cannot be squared and marks "a new stage of world concentration of capital and production, incomparably higher than the preceding stages." This results "in immense progress in the socialization of production":

> In particular, the process of technical invention and improvement becomes socialized. Production becomes social, but appropriation remains private. The social means of production remain the private property of a few. The general framework of formally recognized free competition remains, and the yoke of a few monopolists on the rest of the population becomes a hundred times heavier, more burdensome and intolerable.

While these contradictions are irresolvable within the limits of capitalism, there is a clear and obvious solution once you look beyond the system's artificial limits. Because what capitalism does, above all, is to lay the objective conditions for socialism.

Today's extreme concentration of capital in the US is a crystal clear example. With a population of around 333 million, there are technically over 30 million companies operating in the country. This helps perpetuate the myth that anyone can make it and be their own boss—even though most of these are sole proprietorships without any employees. The reality is that a mere handful of companies—the Fortune 500—are worth an estimated $33.6 trillion and account for 66% of the entire country's GDP. Between them, they employ some 31 million people worldwide.

As lower wages tend to correspond with higher profits, it is no surprise that the top seven low-wage employers in the US include Amazon, Walmart, Home Depot, Kroger, Target, Walgreens, and Starbucks. Combined, these companies employ 5.6 million workers and profit $268 billion per year. In other words, these companies extract an average of $48,000 in profit from every worker, every year—an astonishing rate of exploitation and a colossal concentration of wealth and the means of production.

However, this also reveals the incredible potential for human progress once these economic levers are nationalized and operated under workers' control, as part of a nationalized, democratically planned economy.

The task of the socialist revolution is precisely to bring production and appropriation into harmony. Instead of *private* appropriation and distribution of the wealth created through socialized production, economic activity will be premised on *social* appropriation and *democratic* distribution of the wealth created through socialized production.

Nothing is permanent, and everything is in flux. Imperialism may be the highest stage of capitalism, but it is also the final stage before it is replaced by socialism. As Lenin wrote:

> Imperialism is that stage of capitalism when the latter, after fulfilling everything in its power, begins to decline.

Trotsky elaborated on this further:

> The cause for decline lies in this: the productive forces are fettered by the framework of private property as well as by the boundaries of the national state. Imperialism seeks to divide and redivide the world. In place of national wars, there come imperialist wars. They are utterly reactionary in character and are an expression of the impasse, stagnation, and decay of monopoly capital.

In other words, imperialism arises when capitalism has reached its peak as a historically progressive force.

For millennia, humanity has endured the exploitation and oppression of class society. But the development of the productive forces this has allowed has laid the material basis for the transition to a higher stage of human existence: communism. Dialectically, imperialism contains within it the seeds for its own destruction and replacement. As Lenin put it, "imperialism is the eve of the social revolution of the proletariat."

This is why, despite the hellscape humanity is passing through today, the Revolutionary Communist International is filled with revolutionary optimism for the future. As the saying goes, "The darkest hour is before the dawn."

From Colony to Colossus: The Meteoric Rise of US Imperialism

With us, expansion means, as it always has meant, peace.
– President Theodore Roosevelt

War is a racket. It is the only one international in scope. It is the only one in which the profits are reckoned in dollars and the losses in lives.
– General Smedley Butler

Humble origins

Now that we have established a theoretical baseline for understanding the essential features of imperialism in general, let's look at the genesis of American imperialism in particular.

For as long as anyone can remember, Americans believed they were God's chosen people, sitting comfortably at the center of the universe. Although by no means directly complicit, American workers benefited from the enormous revenues made possible by global imperialist domination. Under pressure from below, and in the interest of maintaining class peace, certain crumbs could be afforded to certain layers of the workers.

However, as explained above, military power is a function of economic power. US imperialism's economic decline in recent decades has had an inevitable impact on mass consciousness. This is reflected in the growing sense of malaise, falling life expectancy and birth rates, rising rates of depression, suicide, opioid addiction, political instability, and more.

Nonetheless, the US remains the most imposing power on a world scale, and its decline is only relative to the past and to other rising powers. Understanding how this former colonial backwater on the edge of the Atlantic world morphed into the ultimate superpower can help us make better sense of the epoch we live in today. After all, many of the debates still raging today—republicanism vs. autocracy, expansionism vs. isolationism, free trade vs. protectionism—go back to well before the country's founding.

From the very beginning, the corner of the world that would become the United States was shaped by its unique geographical situation. Bounded on two sides by great oceans, by impassable deserts to the south, and endless arboreal forests to the north, it enjoyed an island-like insulation from potentially hostile neighbors. During both world wars, this allowed them to sit safely on the sidelines while the main belligerents exhausted each other—before stepping in to mop up. However, this also means it must transport troops and equipment halfway around the world when it does want to intervene—an expensive and time-consuming process.

It also benefited from a continental expanse with an astonishing array of resources and climates, including navigable rivers, deep natural harbors, vast reserves of timber, minerals, gas, and oil, the Great Lakes, and the bountiful agricultural basin of the Mississippi.

Initially, it was colonized by a diverse range of peoples from across Europe, with some arriving via the West Indies: From the Spanish conquistadors in the Southwest and Florida to the Puritans in New England, the enterprising Dutch in New Amsterdam, pacifist Quakers in Philadelphia, the Tidewater gentry in Virginia, slave lords in South Carolina, the descendants of French fur trappers in Louisiana, and the Scots-Irish borderlanders who populated greater Appalachia.

Almost without exception, they were keen to expand ever-inland, chasing riches and natural resources, and nearly all of them were hell-bent on subjugating or removing the Indigenous peoples who stood in their way. Needless to say, the Native Americans didn't simply roll over.

What are known as the American Indian or American Frontier Wars raged for over three blood-soaked centuries: From the Beaver Wars between the French and Iroquois starting in 1609 to the Pequot War of 1636–38 in Massachusetts, King Philip's War of 1675–76, Pontiac's War from 1763–66, the Trail of Tears and Andrew Jackson's Indian Removal Act of 1830, the Second Seminole War starting in 1835, the Great Sioux War and the Battle of the Little Bighorn in 1876, and the last Apache raid into US territory in 1924.

To this day, there are 574 federally recognized tribes and 326 autonomous Indian reservations in the US, covering 87,800 square miles, or 2.3% of the country's total area. The largest is the 16 million-acre Navajo Nation Reservation spanning Arizona, New Mexico, and Utah.

Already in the colonial era, its expansionist tendencies were evident. But it was the first American Revolution and its aftermath that really set the course for the future imperialist behemoth. In a sublime example of the dialectic of history, the country that fought the world's first successful war of revolutionary national liberation was eventually transformed into its greatest imperialist oppressor.

The Revolutionary War took different forms in different regions, often descending into vicious civil war between the colonists themselves. However, the overarching goal was "life, liberty, and the pursuit of happiness"—though each region's understanding of who these should apply to varied wildly. After seven years and tens of thousands killed, the colonies won their independence from Britain—with a little help from the French.

Out of necessity, thirteen diverse colonies had formed a military alliance to fight the British. However, it was unclear what would follow. Would they form thirteen separate countries, a handful of regional confederacies, or a single united nation-state? How would they deal with external trade, tariffs, taxes, internal improvements, and security? What about the "moral depravity" and "hideous blot" of slavery, as the slaveholder Thomas Jefferson described it? And how best to derail the awakened masses' demand for "democracy"?

In the end, under pressure from events like Shays's Rebellion, they came to a series of ultimately untenable compromises and formed a constitutional federal republic. As a result, this disparate collection of peoples, states, and territories emerged as the only serious power on a vast continent bursting with natural resources. How best to dispense with that land and the peoples living on it would lead to bitter infighting and take more than a century to sort out.

As the reality of independence set in, Presidents George Washington and John Adams each had thorny domestic and foreign policy issues to contend with. But the expansionist tone was set early on. In a letter to the Marquis de Lafayette, Washington referred to his new country as an "infant empire."

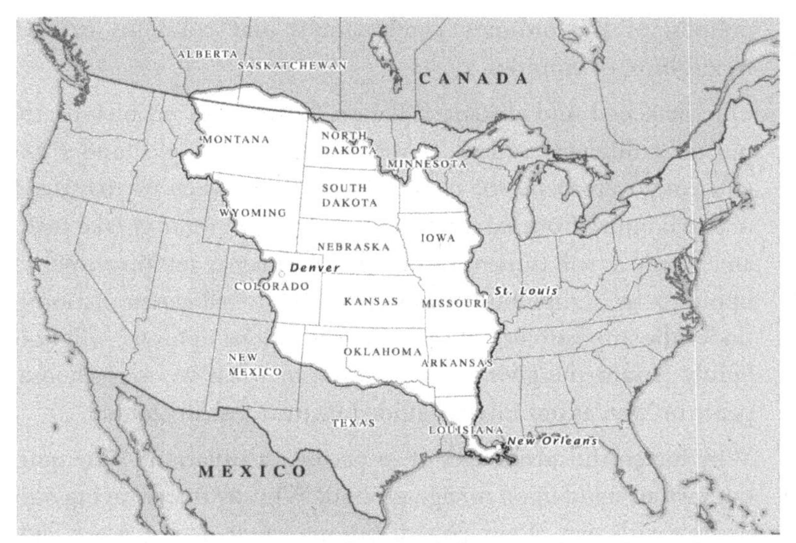

2. The Louisiana Purchase and the states later formed from its territory.

And in his 1796 farewell address, he warned against foreign entanglements, permanent animosities, or alliances:

> The nation which indulges toward another an habitual hatred or an habitual fondness is in some degree a slave . . ..
>
> The great rule of conduct for us, in regard to foreign nations is in extending our commercial relations to have with them as little political connection as possible. So far as we have already formed engagements let them be fulfilled with perfect good faith. Here let us stop.
>
> Europe has a set of primary interests, which to us have none, or a very remote relation. Hence she must be engaged in frequent controversies, the causes of which are essentially foreign to our concerns. Hence therefore it must be unwise in us to implicate ourselves, by artificial ties, in the ordinary vicissitudes of her

> politics, or the ordinary combinations and collisions of her friendships, or enmities.
>
> Our detached and distant situation invites and enables us to pursue a different course. If we remain one People, under an efficient government, the period is not far off, when we may defy material injury from external annoyance; when we may take such an attitude as will cause the neutrality we may at any time resolve upon to be scrupulously respected; when belligerent nations, under the impossibility of making acquisitions upon us, will not lightly hazard the giving us provocation; when we may choose peace or War, as our interest guided by justice shall counsel.
>
> Why forego the advantages of so peculiar a situation? Why quit our own to stand upon foreign ground? Why, by interweaving our destiny with that of any part of Europe, entangle our peace and prosperity in the toils of European ambition, rivalship, interest, humor or caprice?

One lasting legacy of Adams's presidency was the Alien and Sedition Acts. Ostensibly aimed at protecting national security during an undeclared naval war with France, they were primarily used to silence and prosecute critics of the Federalist administration. During World War II, these laws gave legal cover for the harassment, arrest, and internment of thousands of Japanese, Germans, and Italians—most of whom were US citizens. 200 years later, Donald Trump has threatened to revive them in order to combat the "enemy within."

With the signing of the Treaty of Paris of 1783, the colonies' territorial holdings had doubled, stretching westward to the Mississippi. These lands would eventually become the states of Alabama, Mississippi, Tennessee, Kentucky, Ohio, Indiana, Illinois, Michigan, and Wisconsin. But it was Thomas Jefferson and his vision of an "Empire of Liberty" that really got the expansionist ball rolling. In his view, the US "must be viewed

3. Portrait of James Monroe, 1816—John Vanderlyn.

as the nest from which all America, North and South is to be peopled." And as he declared in his first inaugural address, the US was:

> Kindly separated by nature and a wide ocean from the exterminating havoc of one quarter of the globe; too high-minded to endure the degradations of the others; possessing a chosen country, with room enough for our descendants to the thousandth and thousandth generation;

In 1803, Jefferson purchased the Louisiana Territory from Napoleon for $15 million. Overnight, the country doubled in size yet again. This vast tract of land—828,000 square miles west of the Mississippi River—would eventually be divided into all or part of 15 states: Arkansas, Missouri, Iowa, Oklahoma, Kansas, Nebraska, Minnesota, North Dakota, South Dakota, New Mexico, Texas, Montana, Wyoming, Colorado, and Louisiana.

The Monroe Doctrine

Fast-forward twenty years, and the young American republic was still heavily agricultural and economically dependent on exports of raw materials. But it was gradually industrializing, building canals and railroads, and establishing its internal and external markets and relations. By then, the country had fought several wars against various Native American peoples and North African powers. It had also gone to war with Britain in 1812, which resulted in the burning of the president's house and the Capitol in Washington, DC, following the Americans' failed three-pronged invasion of Canada.

It was in this broader context that on December 2, 1823, James Monroe, the country's fifth president, articulated his famous foreign policy principle. The Monroe Doctrine rejected any further colonization or intervention in the Americas by European powers and asserted that any such attempts would be viewed as a threat to the US. It also declared that, in exchange, the Americans would not meddle in European affairs—though that part has been conveniently forgotten.

On the one hand, the doctrine was intended as a paternalistic defense of the newly independent nations dotting the Western Hemisphere; Mexico had won its independence from Spain in 1821, Brazil from Portugal in 1822, and Bolivar's Wars of Independence were still raging in South America.

On the other, the rising American bourgeoisie had its own motives and was claiming its "backyard" for itself. After all, ensuring "national security" requires more than defending against foreign aggression and internal rebellion; one must also have room for territorial and economic expansion.

By all accounts, most Latin American leaders received Monroe's doctrine with sincere diplomatic gratitude. They knew full well there was little the US could do to enforce it since Britain's navy still ruled the waves. Even Simón Bolívar apparently saw it as limited to immediate US national policy, and not as a plan for hemispheric hegemony. However, as the Chilean businessman and minister, Diego Portales, wrote to a friend:

> We have to be very careful; for the Americans of the North, the only Americans are themselves.

The Industrial Revolution was in full swing, and between 1800 and 1840, the country's population more than tripled. Gathering steam on the road to becoming global power, the US economy began to outpace Western Europe, with annual per capita income growing at 1.26%. Internally, things began to differentiate as well, with New England growing at 2.1% per year and the mid-Atlantic region growing at 1.45%, far outpacing the Deep South and Appalachia.

Contributing to the country's growth were grand projects like the Erie Canal. Completed in 1825, it connected the agricultural basin of the Midwest to the Atlantic Ocean via the chain of Great Lakes and the Hudson River. The 363-mile-long waterway dramatically lowered shipping costs and cut travel time between Buffalo and New York City from weeks to days. This revolutionized transportation and trade and cemented New York's status as the country's preeminent port and financial center. Given its success, a series of other canals soon followed.

Meanwhile, in the Southwest, 30,000 Americans were living in Texas by 1835, outnumbering the native *tejanos* by six to one despite a Mexican ban on immigration from the US. In 1836, things came to a head when Texas declared its independence from the government of Antonio López de Santa Anna, who served as president of Mexico 11 times between 1833 and 1855. After existing as an independent republic for nearly a decade, the "Lone Star" state was annexed to the US in 1845, leading to the Mexican-American War of 1846–48.

The Mexican-American War and Manifest Destiny

This was the first serious imperialist foray by the newly minted power as it expanded from sea to shining sea. President James K. Polk had run openly as an annexationist during the 1844 election with the campaign slogan "54°40' or Fight!"—a reference to a heated boundary dispute with Britain over the Oregon Territory. But he also had designs on his neighbor to the south.

To this end, Polk orchestrated an incident of "Mexican aggression" along the Nueces River to justify sending US troops across the border. As he told a joint session of Congress in a classic example of imperialist doublespeak:

> As war exists, and, notwithstanding all our efforts to avoid it, exists by the act of Mexico herself, we are called upon by every consideration of duty and patriotism to vindicate with decision the honor, the rights, and the interests of our country . . .
>
> In further vindication of our rights and defense of our territory, I invoke the prompt action of Congress to recognize the existence of the war, and to place at the disposition of the Executive the means of prosecuting the war with vigor, and thus hastening the restoration of peace.

But not everyone agreed. Even at that time, there was internal opposition. Many saw it as an overtly predatory war and believed pursuing an empire was a mortal danger to the virtues of republican government. As Henry Clay declared, "This is no war of defense, but one of unnecessary and offensive aggression." General Ulysses S. Grant, the future hero of the American Civil War, fought in several battles in Mexico. As he later wrote:

4. General Ulysses S. Grant, Civil War photograph.

> I was bitterly opposed to the measure, and to this day regard the war, which resulted, as one of the most unjust ever waged by a stronger against a weaker nation . . .
>
> I do not think there was ever a more wicked war than that waged by the United States on Mexico. I thought so at the time, when I was a youngster, only I had not moral courage enough to resign.

Henry David Thoreau's influential essay, "Civil Disobedience," was written after his arrest for refusing to pay a poll tax in protest of slavery and the Mexican-American War. As he wrote:

> Witness the present Mexican war, the work of comparatively a few individuals using the standing government as their tool . . . This people must cease to hold slaves, and to make war on Mexico, though it cost them their existence as a people . . .
>
> If all citizens who opposed the Mexican War followed my example and went to jail for their beliefs, the government could be forced to end the conflict.

But the hawks prevailed and US troops eventually marched all the way to the "Halls of Montezuma" in Mexico City. All told, 13,283 Americans and an estimated 25,000 Mexicans died during the conflict, most of them from disease. Along the way, many atrocities were committed by American troops against Mexican civilians, including murder, looting and destruction of property, mistreatment of prisoners, and attacks against Catholic churches, fueled by racism and anti-Catholic sentiment.

The war officially ended with the Treaty of Guadalupe Hidalgo. Under its terms, Mexico was forced to recognize the US annexation of Texas and cede around half of its territory, including the present-day states of California, Nevada, Utah, Arizona, New Mexico, Colorado, Wyoming, and parts of Kansas, Oklahoma, and Texas.

In return, the US paid Mexico $15 million and assumed $3.25 million in debts owed to American citizens. This was a pretty good deal for the gringos, considering that California's GDP alone is now over $3 trillion—more than double the total for modern Mexico.

In 1846, the teeming resources of the Oregon Territory were acquired from Great Britain by treaty, adding present-day Oregon, Washington, Idaho, and parts of Montana and Wyoming. The agreement established the 49th parallel as the border between American and British territories, with the exception of Vancouver Island.

The Gadsden Purchase of 1853 squared things off, with the US purchasing an additional 29,670 square miles of land from Mexico, this time for $10 million. The territory included parts of south Arizona and southwestern New Mexico, with a view towards building a southern transcontinental railroad.

These heady years of constant expansion fed illusions in the not so veiled racism of American exceptionalism. The

American people and their institutions were alleged to possess special virtues and to have been ordained by God to "remake the West" into an agrarian paradise.

As the journalist John L. O'Sullivan wrote in 1845, it was the country's "manifest destiny to overspread the continent allotted by Providence for the free development of our yearly multiplying millions."

However, the new territories stolen from Mexico exacerbated the tensions already straining the sectionally divided country, and debates raged over whether they should become slave states or free. Given the Electoral College and the way seats in Congress are allocated, control over the federal government and all its resources hung in the balance. US imperialism couldn't continue its onward march until the question of the so-called "peculiar institution" was resolved.

The US Civil War and the Gilded Age

A series of crises, near-misses, and untenable compromises over the question of slavery and westward expansion eventually led to the outbreak of open civil war on April 12, 1861. The Second American Revolution is explained in detail in other works, but in the context of the present work, it's worth mentioning that the Confederacy's long standing dream was to build a slave empire across the Southern Hemisphere, starting with Mexico and Cuba.

In 1847, Jefferson Davis had made it clear while fighting in the Mexican-American War that he considered the Gulf of Mexico "a basin of water belonging to the United States." In his considered opinion, "the cape of Yucatan and the island of Cuba must be ours."

Adding to the chaos, in 1861, the Emperor of France, Napoleon III, had installed Archduke Maximilian of Austria as Emperor of Mexico, styling himself Maximilian I. This was a blatant flaunting of the Monroe Doctrine, and at least one prominent Union politician proposed that the North and South should stop fighting each other and instead team up to kick the French out of Mexico.

Once the Confederates had been defeated, Ulysses S. Grant himself proposed using the Union Army—the largest, best-equipped, and most highly trained in the world—to help the Mexicans overthrow Maximilian. In the end, the Mexicans got rid of their emperor the old-fashioned way, with a mass uprising led by Benito Juárez—and a firing squad.

The Civil War marked another nodal point in the unfettered flourishing of American capitalism and imperialism. Over the course of four years, the old United States had been immolated, and a new country rose out of its ashes. Along with tremendous advances in military and related technologies, it accelerated the commercialization of agriculture, industrialization, the building of a continent-wide network of railroads, ports, and canals, and established a national banking system.

Deficit financing through the sale of war bonds, the issuing of the "greenback" paper currency, the establishment of what would become the Internal Revenue Service, and the imposition of the first income tax transformed the country's finances and led to fabulous wealth for those on the inside.

In 1860, the US federal debt totaled $64.8 million. By the end of the war in 1865, it had ballooned to $2.6 billion—a forty-fold increase. Goldman Sachs, JP Morgan, Citi, and Lehman Brothers were among the biggest beneficiaries. What is today the country's biggest bank was named after Lincoln's Secretary of the Treasury, Salmon P. Chase.

The war was followed by the tragic abortion of Southern Reconstruction, aggressive westward expansion into territories still occupied by Indigenous peoples, and the purchase of Alaska from Russia in 1867. This tumultuous period will be

5. The Bosses of the Senate, 1889—Joseph Keppler.

covered in detail elsewhere in the future, but suffice it to say that the capitalists were ruthless and determined, and the economy expanded at a previously unimaginable pace, heavily backed by state intervention, as always.

In just thirty years, between 1860 and 1890, US GDP quintupled from around $12 billion to over $60 billion. By comparison, the GDP of the United Kingdom in 1890 was less than $11 billion. This clearly illustrates the economic basis for the ascent of American imperialism and the decline of its British counterpart. However, the British still had a vast empire and hundreds of millions of colonial subjects to exploit, which prolonged the process of decline.

As Lenin explained, this period saw the initial formation of the capitalist cartels and trusts that would eventually lead to all-out monopoly capitalism:

> The development of pre-monopoly capitalism, of capitalism in which free competition was predominant, reached its limit in the 1860s and 1870s. We now see that it is *precisely after that period* that the tremendous "boom" in colonial conquests begins,

> and that the struggle for the territorial division of the world becomes extraordinarily sharp. It is beyond doubt, therefore, that capitalism's transition to the stage of monopoly capitalism, to finance capital, *is connected* with the intensification of the struggle for the partitioning of the world.

This was the heyday of the Carnegies, Rockefellers, Vanderbilts, and Morgans, of the "robber barons" and "captains of industry" of the Gilded Age. Vast fortunes were made and lost in land and railroad speculation. Corruption was rampant at all levels of business and government, and any remaining illusions in the country's democratic-republican credentials were blown sky high.

The Compromise of 1877 was a dirty deal whereby Rutherford B. Hayes became president in exchange for pulling all federal troops out of the South. Millions of freedmen and women, who had briefly tasted some semblance of freedom during Radical Reconstruction, were abandoned to the tender mercies of Jim Crow and the Ku Klux Klan. Big business now called all the shots. As Hayes later wrote in his diary:

> The real difficulty is with the vast wealth and power in the hands of the few and the unscrupulous who represent or control capital. Hundreds of laws of Congress and the state legislatures are in the interest of these men and against the interests of workingmen.
>
> These need to be exposed and repealed. All laws on corporations, on taxation, on trusts, wills, descent, and the like, need examination and extensive change. This is a government of the people, by the people, and for the people no longer. It is a government of corporations, by corporations, and for corporations.

To further nurture American industry, the Tariff Act of 1890—better known as the McKinley Tariff—was passed, increasing average duties on all imports from 38% to 49.5%. Then serving in Congress, future president William McKinley was known as the "Napoleon of Protection"—a moniker Donald Trump would surely be pleased with today.

However, it was not all smooth sailing for American capitalism, and the boom years were punctuated by a series of devastating slumps, including the Panic of 1873 and the Long Depression, which lasted until 1879.

Needless to say, a massive working class and powerful unions were also forged. From the Great Railroad Strike and the St. Louis Commune of 1877, to the fight for the eight-hour day and the Haymarket Riot in 1886, the Homestead steelworkers' strike in 1892, and the Pullman Strike in 1894, there were many heroic and inspiring class battles.

1898: A Juggernaut is born

However, even the broad expanse of the American nation-state proved insufficient to contain the productive forces that had been unleashed. The US bourgeoisie needed external markets to absorb the growing surplus of commodities and capital. More than that, they wanted their own overseas colonies—never mind that the main European powers had already carved almost everything up.

In 1898, Senator Albert Beveridge put the position clearly:

> American factories are making more than the American people can use; American soil is producing more than they can consume. Fate has written our policy for us; the trade of the world must and shall be ours.

That same year, President William McKinley and the hawks in the US administration picked a fight with the sick and decaying Spanish Empire, which had somehow managed to hold on to a few of its colonies.

In addition to dehumanizing its enemies and using racial epithets such as "kraut," "gook," and "towel head," US

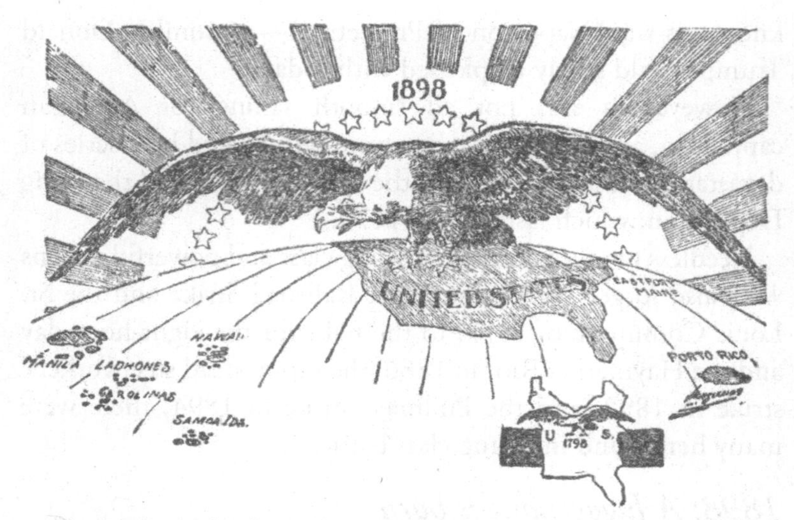

6. 10,000 Miles from Tip to Tip, 1899—Philadelphia Press.

imperialism has also always found convenient pretexts to go to war. It entered World War I after the sinking of the *Lusitania*; World War II after Japan's "surprise" attack on Pearl Harbor; the Vietnam War after the so-called Gulf of Tonkin incident; and after the terrorist attacks on September 11, 2001, it had the excuse it needed to invade Afghanistan and Iraq.

In 1898, the *casus belli* was a mysterious explosion in Havana Harbor that sank an American warship, the USS *Maine*. As always, this was combined with cynical calls for a "humanitarian intervention" to fight tyranny and liberate Spain's colonial subjects. In every theater of the war, US troops fought with the active support of local rebel armies that had been fighting against Spanish occupation for decades or even centuries.

In just a few months, Spain was defeated and the US took possession of the Philippines, Cuba, Puerto Rico, and Guam. $20 million was paid to Spain as compensation for the diverse and fragmented island chain known as the Philippines.

However, far from the freedom they were promised, Spain's former subjects found themselves under the jackboot of a new and often even more oppressive master.

Before the Spanish-American War, there were very few references to the United States as "America." After 1898, the idea of a "Greater Republic" or even "Imperial America" became widespread. There was even a "Greater America Exposition," a world's fair held in 1899 in North Omaha, Nebraska, featuring exotic animals and exhibits from Cuba, Hawaii, the Philippines, and Puerto Rico.

Although the US had long considered itself a beacon of republican freedom, for many, the idea of a grand civilizing mission was intoxicating. Just as the Roman Republic wanted no more kings yet ended up with the Caesars, the US, born as a democratic republic after an anti-imperialist war of liberation, turned very much into its opposite.

It was in this context that the renowned author and apologist for British imperialism, Rudyard Kipling, wrote "The White Man's Burden" in 1899. In it, he oozes open racism as he exhorts the Americans to assume full colonial control of the Filipino people and their country. Here are its opening lines:

> Take up the White Man's burden;
> Send forth the best ye breed;
> Go bind your sons to exile
> To serve your captives' need;
> To wait in heavy harness,
> On fluttered folk and wild;
> Your new-caught, sullen peoples,
> Half-devil and half-child.

But not everyone was convinced. Some objected due to straight-up white supremacism. Certainly, control over new lands and resources was something to celebrate. But having millions of non-whites under US jurisdiction wasn't quite the thing, even if they lived thousands of miles away. The only way to justify the American empire was to argue that these "backward races" were unfit for republican rule. After all, as Woodrow Wilson would put it a few years later, they lived "outside the charmed circle of our own national life."

Others, like W.E.B. Dubois fiercely opposed American occupation of the Philippines for humanitarian and internationalist reasons. Renowned author Mark Twain became a fervent anti-colonialist and joined the Anti-Imperialist League. As he wrote in October 1900, he had once been a "red-hot imperialist":

> I wanted the American eagle to go screaming into the Pacific. It seemed tiresome and tame for it to content itself with the Rockies. Why not spread its wings over the Philippines, I asked myself? And I thought it would be a real good thing to do.
>
> I said to myself, here are a people who have suffered for three centuries. We can make them as free as ourselves, give them a government and country of their own, put a miniature of the American constitution afloat in the Pacific, start a brand new republic to take its place among the free nations of the world. It seemed to me a great task to which we had addressed ourselves.
>
> But I have thought some more, since then, and I have read carefully the treaty of Paris, and I have seen that we do not intend to free, but to subjugate the people of the Philippines. We have gone there to conquer, not to redeem . . .
>
> It should, it seems to me, be our pleasure and duty to make those people free and let them deal with their own domestic questions in their own way. And so I am an anti-imperialist. I am opposed to having the eagle put its talons on any other land.

The philosopher-psychologist William James was also vehemently opposed to American imperial expansion:

> We used to believe then that we were of a different clay from other nations, that there was something deep in the American heart that answered to our happy birth, free from that hereditary burden which the nations of Europe bear and which obliges them to grow by preying on their neighbors. Idle dream! Pure Fourth of July fancy, scattered in five minutes by the first temptation.
>
> In every national soul there lie potentialities of the most barefaced piracy, and our own American soul is no exception to the rule. Angelic impulses and predatory lusts divide our heart exactly as they divide the hearts of other countries. It is good to rid ourselves of cant and humbug and to know the truth about ourselves. Political virtue does not follow geographical divisions . . .
>
> The country has once for all regurgitated the Declaration of Independence and the Farewell Address, and it won't swallow again immediately what it is so happy to have vomited up. It has come to a hiatus. It has deliberately pushed itself into the circle of international hatreds, and joined the common pack of wolves. It relishes the attitude. We have thrown off our swaddling clothes, it thinks, and attained our majority. We are objects of fear to other lands.

"The first Vietnam" and the annexation of Hawaii

Such objections notwithstanding, the Philippines was occupied for nearly fifty years by the Americans, who referred to its inhabitants as "niggers," "barbarians," and "savages." Referred to by some as the "first Vietnam," the imperialist brutality was so extreme that even the British were appalled. As one witness to an early battle to "pacify" the locals noted: "This is not war; it is simply massacre and murderous butchery."

7. Jacob Smith's retalliation for Balangiga, 1902—New York Journal.

A decades-long guerrilla insurgency followed, and as far as the American officers were concerned, there were no neutrals. In the occupiers' view, the best way to combat this "people's war" was to ensure there were no more people. As an example, in early 1901, the entire population of Marinduque Island—51,000 people—was ordered into concentration camps. Anyone who didn't comply "would be considered as acting in sympathy with the insurgent forces and treated accordingly."

According to the American governor of Abra Province:

> Whole villages had been burned, storehouses and crops had been destroyed, and the entire province was as devoid of food products as was the valley of Shenandoah after Sheridan's raid during the Civil War.

An American congressman who visited the Philippines described the "depopulation campaign" as follows:

> You never hear of any disturbances in Northern Luzon because there isn't anybody there to rebel . . . The good Lord in heaven only knows the number of Filipinos that were put underground. Our soldiers took no prisoners, they kept no records; they simply swept the country and wherever and whenever they could get hold of a Filipino they killed him.

And in the words of the "civilizing" General Shafter:

> It may be necessary to kill half the Filipinos in order that the remaining half of the population may be advanced to a higher plane of life than their present semi-barbarous state affords.

In the end, as many as a million Filipinos may have been killed in the first phase of the occupation, from 1899 to 1902, now known as the Philippine-American War.

Under mass pressure from below, the Philippines finally gained independence in 1946. But to this day, the Commonwealth of Puerto Rico, and Guam remain "unincorporated territories" of the US. Or, to call things by their proper name, colonies.

As for Cuba, it was formally released from US control in 1902, but it remained a de facto colony until the 1959 revolution. To this day, it is forced to play host to a US prison camp, 8,500 troops, and a McDonald's at Guantanamo. Although the Cubans formally have "ultimate sovereignty" over the area, the US has "complete jurisdiction and control."

Fired up for further expansion after defeating Spain and drawing on its Texas playbook, the US also annexed Hawaii in 1898. Although the island chain had been recognized as a sovereign nation for nearly a century, it had been under increasing US domination since the 1840s.

In 1887, Samuel Dole had drafted the island's 1887 constitution, disenfranchising many Native Hawaiians. In 1893, a group of white planters and capitalists had overthrown Queen Lili'uokalani in a coup abetted by the US envoy, who threatened an invasion if she resisted. Dole was subsequently "elected" as president of what became the Republic of Hawaii, and he served as the Territory of Hawaii's first governor after annexation. Many readers will recognize Dole's name from the cans of pineapple that line grocery store shelves worldwide.

In short, the Spanish-American War marked another decisive point of inflection in the rise of US imperialism—and it was only getting started.

The early Twentieth Century

Lenin identified the early 1900s as the tipping point for full-fledged monopoly capitalism and imperialism. Following the assassination of President William McKinley by the anarchist Leon Czolgosz in 1901, the first decade of the new century was dominated by the presidency of Teddy Roosevelt.

Roosevelt, who fought with his "roughriders" in Cuba during the Spanish-American War, was an unapologetic imperialist with a special interest in the country's "backyard." These were the years of "gunboat diplomacy" and saw a series of military interventions and occupations in Cuba, Nicaragua, Honduras, the Dominican Republic, Venezuela, Haiti, and beyond. "Might makes right" was on the order of the day, or, as Roosevelt bluntly framed his policy, "Speak softly and carry a big stick."

In 1903, Roosevelt sent warships and orchestrated Panama's independence from Colombia, after it declined to allow the construction of a canal across its narrowest isthmus. Needless to say, the new republic allowed the construction of the Panama Canal, with huge implications for the US economy.

Completed in 1914, it further cemented the US as a rising manufacturing and maritime power. No longer did ships traveling between the Atlantic and the Pacific have to make the long trip around the tip of South America. As Senator S.I.

8. William McKinley.

9. Theodore Roosevelt.

Hayakawa quipped in 1977 during the debate over whether the US should return the canal to the Panamanian people, "We should keep the Panama Canal. After all, we stole it fair and square."

For its troubles, Panama was ruled for decades by a series of oligarchs and dictators, with the US military intervening a dozen times between so-called independence and 1968, followed by the infamous ouster of Manuel Noriega in 1989.

In 1904, the president announced the Roosevelt Corollary to the Monroe Doctrine. At least in words, the original doctrine had been noninterventionist in nature. Roosevelt now asserted that the US had not only the *right* but the *duty* to intervene in Latin America to maintain stability, protect investments in infrastructure, trade routes, and natural resources, and ensure political stability favorable to US interests.

There was big money to be made in the region, especially in the "banana republics." This was the term coined by the American writer O. Henry to describe the United Fruit Company's subjugation of Guatemala and Honduras.

Dependent on exports of natural resources and dominated by strongmen in the pay of American big business, these and other countries were economically vulnerable and politically unstable. A series of "banana wars" waged to defend United Fruit's interests began in that epoch and have continued in one form or another ever since.

For example, consider the "Banana Massacre" of 1928. Tired of being paid in company credits, redeemable only at overpriced company stores, 30,000 Colombian workers struck against United Fruit to demand payment in cash. In response, the company called in the Colombian military, which proceeded to kill between 1,000 and 3,000 workers and their families.

In 1954, United Fruit called in the CIA to overthrow Jacobo Árbenz, who they accused of being a communist for advocating land redistribution and workers' rights.

And in 2024 times, United Fruit—now rebranded Chiquita Brands International—was ordered to pay $38.3 million in damages to the families of those murdered by extreme-right paramilitary groups, hired by the company to terrorize and exterminate Columbians opposed to its low wages and dangerous working conditions.

The turn of the century also saw many attempts by workers to fight back against the growing rapacity of the imperialists. 1906 saw the heroic strike of the copper miners of Cananea, in Northern Mexico, which was put down in blood with help from the paramilitary Arizona Rangers, who crossed the border to defend the interests of the mine's American owners. There was also the Rio Blanco strike of 1907, in which Mexican textile workers in Veracruz rose up against French factory owners, another prelude to the chaotic revolution that would break out in 1910.

These years also saw the US invasion and occupation of several parts of Mexico during its revolution. And let us not forget Pancho Villa's raid on Columbus, New Mexico, the last time an armed force invaded the US. Or that Villa successfully evaded General John J. Pershing and over 10,000 US troops who chased him across Northern Mexico for nearly a year during the so-called Punitive Expedition.

However, it was William Howard Taft, who succeeded Teddy Roosevelt as president, who really leveraged the growing power of US imperialism with what he called "Dollar Diplomacy." As he explained in his December 1912 message to Congress:

> The diplomacy of the present administration has sought to respond to modern ideas of commercial interaction. This policy has been characterized as substituting dollars for bullets. It is one that appeals alike to idealistic humanitarian sentiments, to the dictates of sound policy and strategy, and to legitimate commercial aims.

The US government began actively encouraging American banks and corporations to invest in the development of railways, ports, and other critical infrastructure in foreign countries. This would increase economic and political dependence on the US, thus opening opportunities for further expansion by American finance capital into these strategically important markets.

As we will see, these methods of domination and profit-making were taken to a whole new level in the years after World War I, and ratcheted up even further after World War II.

A world of war, revolution, and counterrevolution

War has been described as the handmaiden of revolution. This was certainly the case across Europe after the slaughter of World War I. It was the war that broke Russian tsarism economically, politically, and militarily, paving the way for the February and

10. Woodrow Wilson.

October Revolutions. The German, Austro-Hungarian, and Ottoman Empires also came tumbling down.

However, risky as they are, wars can also lead to spectacular profits. They also serve as accelerators of technological and social change. World War I not only hastened the collapse of the old Eurasian empires, it provided an opening for US imperialism to climb even higher up the imperialist hierarchy.

While there were plenty of ebbs and flows yet to come, World War I and the presidency of Wilson (1913–21) marked another critical juncture. No longer was the American republic merely a cherished model others were expected to admire and emulate—it was something to be actively imposed. A fervent believer in America's worldwide "Manifest Destiny," Wilson told students at Columbia University in 1907:

> Since trade ignores national boundaries, and the manufacturer insists on having the world as a market, the flag of his nation must follow him, and the doors of the nations which are closed against him must be battered down.

Despite having global aspirations, Wilson was compelled to balance between the isolationist sentiment of the American masses and the opportunities for expanding US power opened by the outbreak of war in 1914. Promising to keep the country out of the conflict, it was Wilson who first popularized the slogan "America First" during his 1916 presidential campaign.

However, with the Allied and Central Powers slugging it out to determine who would rule Europe, the colonies, and the seas, American imperialism couldn't resist putting its increasingly weighty thumb on the scale of world relations.

Wilson eventually found a convincing reason to join the Allies. The kaiser's submarines sank one too many American ships, and the Zimmerman Telegram urging Mexico to invade the US in exchange for some of its lost territories had inflamed public opinion against Germany. On April 6, 1917, war was officially declared. By May 1918, over one million US troops were stationed in France, with half of them fighting on the front lines.

Of course, entering the war had nothing to do with "honor" or "making the world safe for democracy," though that was the official line. As W.E.B. DuBois put it, this was "a war for empire."

The American economy had boomed during the war's early years as it flooded Europe with raw materials, food, and manufactured goods. Now it wanted boots on the ground to consolidate its gains. There was also the small matter of nearly $10 billion in wartime loans made to Britain and France, repayment of which would have been jeopardized by a German victory. As Wilson himself explained:

> Concessions obtained by financiers must be safeguarded by ministers of state, even if the sovereignty of unwilling nations be outraged in the process . . . The doors of the nations which are closed must be battered down.

In total, 53,000 Americans were killed in action, with another 63,000 non-combat deaths due mainly to the influenza pandemic of 1918. When the killing fields were finally quieted by the Russian and German Revolutions, British imperialism was severely weakened and the Continent was in ashes. Meanwhile, the US was virtually unscathed. It emerged as the world's greatest creditor and an economic, technological, diplomatic, military, and cultural powerhouse.

This was evidenced by Wilson's prominent role in negotiating the disastrous Treaty of Versailles, his infamous "Fourteen Points," and US imperialism's humiliating incursions into Soviet Russia, as detailed in Part Three of this volume. And although the US drifted back towards isolationism and didn't end up joining, he played a key role in establishing the "thieves' kitchen" of the League of Nations, as Lenin called it. For good measure, Wilson expanded the Americans' Caribbean footprint further by buying the Virgin Islands from Denmark in 1917.

In another indication of the US's rising interwar prominence, J.J. Pershing was promoted to "General of the Armies" in 1919, thus ensuring he could pull rank on all other Allied generals. The only other six-star general in US history was George Washington—who was promoted posthumously in 1976 to ensure that he, in turn, was never outranked by any other general.

As every Marxist knows, the Russian Revolution was the greatest event in world history. It forever changed the class and geopolitical balance of forces and put the fear of God into the bourgeoisie. Unfortunately, as explained in countless books and articles, due to a lack of revolutionary leadership, the wave of class struggle that followed the Bolsheviks' success crashed on the rocks of counterrevolution, and world capitalism was restabilized.

11. The Cloud, 1919—Lewis Crumley Gregg.

Threatened by the dramatic events unfolding in Russia, Germany, Hungary, and beyond, the US ruling class unleashed the original Red Scare, a blatant political and physical assault on labor rights, civil liberties, and free speech. The attacks included the Palmer Raids, the deportation of hundreds of foreign-born radicals like Emma Goldman and Alexander Berkman, and the trial and eventual execution of anarchists like Sacco and Vanzetti, often on trumped-up charges.

Just weeks before the October Revolution, the Justice Department raided the offices of the anarcho-syndicalist Industrial Workers of the World, leading to hundreds of arrests. Eugene Debs, one of the finest proletarian leaders and orators in American history, was arrested and convicted under the Sedition Act of 1918 for opposing US entry into the war. Despite being in prison, he won nearly one million votes in the 1920 presidential election. Such was the climate of class struggle in the US in the first decades of the 20th century.

The changing balance of power

Leon Trotsky was a gifted Marxist, a keen observer of international politics, and a farsighted thinker and writer. In 1926, he summarized the profound shifts taking place in the years between world wars:

> These last years, the economic axis of the world has been radically displaced. The relations between the USA and Europe have become drastically altered. It is the result of the war. Naturally, this change was prepared long since: there were symptomatic indications of it, but it has become an accomplished fact only recently, and we are now trying to account for this gigantic shift that has taken place in mankind's economic life and, consequently, in human culture.
>
> A German writer has recalled in this connection Goethe's words describing the extraordinary impression made on contemporaries by the Copernican theory according to which not the sun revolves about the earth but, on the contrary, it is the earth, a modest and middle-sized planet, that revolves around the sun. There were many who refused to believe it. Their geocentric patriotism was outraged. The same is true now in regard to America. The European bourgeois does not want to believe that he has been shoved to the background, that it is the USA that rules the capitalist world.
>
> It required the war in order at a single blow to raise America, lower Europe and lay bare the abrupt shift of the world axis. The war, as an enterprise for the ruination and decadence of Europe, cost America around $25 billion. If we recall that American banks now hold $60 billion, that sum of $25 billion is relatively small. Furthermore, $10 billion went as a loan to Europe. With the unpaid interest these $10 billion have now become $12 billion,

and Europe is beginning to pay America for its own ruination. Such is the mechanism whereby the United States was able to rise at one stroke above the whole world as the master of its destinies.

From the power of the United States and the weakening of Europe flows the inevitability of a new division of world forces, spheres of influence and world markets. America must expand while Europe is forced to contract. In precisely this consists the resultant of the basic economic processes that are taking place in the capitalist world. The US reaches out into all world channels and everywhere takes the offensive. She operates in a strictly "pacifist" manner, that is, without the use of armed force as yet, "without effusion of blood" as the Holy Inquisition said when burning heretics alive.

She expands peaceably because her adversaries, grinding their teeth, are retreating step by step, before this new power, not daring to risk an open clash. That is the basis of the "pacifist" policy of the United States. Her principal weapon now is: finance capital backed by its billions of gold reserves. This is a terrible and overwhelming force in relation to all parts of the world and particularly in relation to devastated and impoverished Europe.

To grant or to refuse loans to this or that European country is, in many cases, to decide the fate not only of the political party in power but of the bourgeois regime itself. Up to the present time, the US has invested $10 billion in the economy of other countries. Of these $10 billion, two have been granted to Europe in addition to the $10 billion formerly supplied for its devastation.

Now, as we know, the loans are granted in order to "restore" Europe. Devastation, then restoration: these two aims complement each other, while the interest on the sums appropriated for both keep flowing into the same reservoir. The US has invested the most capital in Latin America which, from the economic standpoint, is becoming more and more a dominion of North America. After South America, Canada is the country which has obtained the most credits; then comes Europe.

However, by accelerating the development of capitalism, US imperialism was merely sharpening the system's internal contradictions. As Trotsky noted in October 1929, just weeks before the Great Crash on Wall Street:

> The prewar power of the United States grew on the basis of its internal market, i.e., the dynamic equilibrium between industry and agriculture. In this development the war has produced a sharp break. The United States exports capital and manufactured goods in ever greater volume. The growth of America's world power means that the entire system of American industry and banking—that towering capitalist skyscraper—is resting to an ever increasing measure on the foundations of the world economy.
>
> But this foundation is mined, and the United States itself continues to add more mines to it day by day. By exporting commodities and capital, by building up its navy, by elbowing England aside, by buying up the key enterprises in Europe, by forcing its way into China, etc., American finance capital is digging with its own hands powder and dynamite cellars beneath its own foundation.

In the 1920s and early 1930s, with Germany ostensibly disarmed and France and Japan lagging behind, the US and UK were the planet's premiere imperialist powers. The question of sea power was decisive, and given America's rapid economic growth, Britain's centuries of naval domination was under threat.

The US was making giant strides forward and the British were feeling the strain. Already in 1902, Joseph Chamberlain, the British colonial secretary, had complained that, "The weary Titan staggers under the too vast orb of his fate."

It is sufficient to note that before World War I, Britain spent $237 million per year on its navy, compared to $130 million for the US. By 1929, the British were spending $270 million per year versus $364 million for the Americans. Treaties to ensure parity between their fleets had been signed in an attempt to rationalize the arms race, but a preemptive strike by the British against the upstart Americans could not be ruled out. As Trotsky explained:

> After the experience of the last war there is no one who does not understand that the next war between the world titans will not be brief but protracted. The issue will be determined by the relative productive power of the two camps. This means among other things that the combat fleets of the sea powers will be not only supplemented and renovated but also expanded and newly created in the very course of the war . . .
>
> In the event of war with America the one theoretically conceivable condition of success for England is to assure herself, before the outbreak of war, a very great military-technical preponderance which would in some measure compensate for the incomparable technical and economic preponderance of the United States. But the equalization of the two fleets prior to the war means that in the very first months of war America will possess an incontestable preponderance. Not for nothing did the Americans threaten several years ago to turn out cruisers in an emergency like so many pancakes . . .
>
> In recent years the US War and Navy departments have applied themselves systematically to prepare the entire American industry for the needs of the next war. Schwab, one of the magnates of maritime war industry, recently concluded his speech to the War College with the following words: "It must be made clear to you that war in the present period must be compared with a great big industrial enterprise . . .
>
> The French imperialist press has naturally done everything in its power to incite America against England. In an article devoted to the question of the naval agreement, *Le Temps* writes that naval parity by no means signifies the equalization of sea power,

> inasmuch as America cannot even dream of securing such naval bases as England has acquired in the course of centuries.
>
> The superiorities of British naval bases are absolutely incontestable. But after all, the accord on naval parity, if it is concluded, will not represent America's last word on the subject. Its slogan is "Freedom of the Seas," that is a regime that must first of all place restrictions on Great Britain's use of her naval bases. No less significant is another slogan of the United States: "The Open Door."
>
> Under this banner, America will act to counterpose not only China but also India and Egypt to Great Britain's naval domination. America will conduct her offensive against British naval bases and points of support not by sea but by land, i.e., through the colonies and dominions of Britain. America will put her war fleet in action when the situation is ripe for it.
>
> Of course, all this is the music of the future. But this future is not separated from us by centuries nor even decades. *Le Temps* need not worry. The US will take piecemeal everything that can be taken piecemeal, altering the relationship of forces in all fields—technical, commercial, financial, military—to the disadvantage of its chief rival, without for a moment losing sight of England's naval bases.

In the end, due to German rearmament, the resilience of the USSR, and the unanticipated course of World War II, the transition from British to American hegemony was effected without a direct confrontation between the two powers. As we will see, Trotsky was extremely prescient about the role played by naval bases in that transition—something that has not gone unnoticed by US imperialism's current imperialist rivals.

All historical analogies have their limitations. Nonetheless, it is for good reason that we point to the centuries-long fall of the Western Roman Empire as an apt parallel for the decline of

12. The Bonus Army on the steps of the Capitol, 1932.

US imperialism. That being said, the relatively rapid decline of British imperialism is perhaps even more appropriate.

Class unrest and state intervention to save capitalism

Underwriting America's rising star was a GDP growth rate of 42% during the decade of the "Roaring Twenties." However, what goes up must come down, and a painful hangover followed the open bar in the form of the Great Depression.

Between 1929 and 1932, global trade collapsed by two-thirds. US industrial production fell 47%, real GDP collapsed by 30%, and unemployment surpassed 20%. The economic dislocation and subsequent working-class radicalization posed a serious threat to American capitalism.

In 1932, some 43,000 people, including 17,000 veterans, formed the "Bonus Army," marched on Washington, DC, and set up a makeshift camp they called "Hooverville" near the Capitol. Their main demand was payment of a deferred bonus promised by the government for their service in World War I. None other than Douglas MacArthur led the charge to violently evict them, with at least two veterans killed and thousands injured.

Due to major mistakes by its national and international leadership, efforts to build a Communist Party in the US had been dysfunctional almost from the outset. Membership hovered below 20,000 until 1933, but based on events, it shot upward, reaching 66,000 in 1939 and peaking at over 75,000 in 1947. However, the extent of labor radicalization in this period is best exemplified by the rise of industrial trade unionism, in which communists and other leftists played a key role.

Between 1930 and 1941, 27,000 work stoppages led to a loss of 172 million work days. Agricultural and manufacturing workers, coal miners, cigar makers, longshoremen, loggers, pilots, truck drivers, cannery, steel, hotel, and textile workers, and many others struck to fight back against the bosses. There were sit-down strikes and city-wide general strikes led by communists and other radicals in Flint, Minneapolis, Toledo, and San Francisco. On this basis, the Congress of Industrial Organizations (CIO), formed in 1935, surged forward.

However, there was no revolutionary leadership worthy of the name, and certainly not one with sufficient roots in the working class. As a result, President Franklin Delano Roosevelt—Teddy's cousin—was able to buy time and take the edge off through a series of programs known as the New Deal. Its $41.7 billion price tag would be the equivalent of nearly $980 billion in 2024 dollars. But even this was not enough to get the economy up and running. FDR only managed to cut

13. Strikers occupy Fisher Body Plant Number Three, 1937.

across the danger of mass social unrest by going to war against Germany and Japan.

The inevitable result of the failed revolutions following World War I and the festering contradictions of the Treaty of Versailles, World War II presented American imperialism with another unmissable opportunity. Whereas World War I was fought mainly in Europe to decide who would rule the colonies, World War II was fought on a world scale to decide who would rule the planet.

America's wartime mobilization was without a doubt the most extraordinary economic turnaround in the history of capitalism. During the course of the war, industrial productivity rose by 96% and 17 million new civilian jobs were created, wiping out the unemployment of the Great Depression. From the dark depths of the 1930s, the economy grew by an average of 11 or 12% per year. In 1932, GDP growth had hit a record low of -12.90%. In 1942, it reached an all-time high of 18.90%.

Millions of Americans left their small towns and farms to join the military or find work in the big industrial centers. More than six million women joined the workforce, three million volunteered with the Red Cross, and over 200,000 served in the military. Between 1941 and the late 1970s, nearly five million Black Americans left the South and migrated to the North, Midwest, and far West, as part of the Second Great Migration.

Despite the many myths to the contrary, this dramatic economic and demographic reconfiguration did not flow from the genius of private enterprise. Rather, yet again, it required massive state intervention and the economies of scale only it can afford to turn things around. As summarized by the economist J.W. Mason, a fellow at the Roosevelt Institute:

> During the Second World War, the United States had a centrally planned economy. Strategic resources were produced in quantities set in Washington and allocated among end users by the public officials sitting on the War Production Board. Key prices and wages were administered, not left to markets. The large majority of investment was directed, financed, and, in most cases, owned by the federal government.
>
> Thousands of private businesses that failed to comply with the planners' instructions were simply taken over by the government—including some of the country's largest corporations, like Montgomery Ward. For millions of Americans, the photograph of Ward's adamantly anti-Roosevelt chairman Sewell Avery being carried from his headquarters by a squad of soldiers crystallized the new relationship between government and capital.

Such centralization and planning was necessary to meet the challenge of fighting an all-out war on two fronts, and to compete with the extraordinary economic achievements of the Soviet Union during that period. Nevertheless, the American war economy remained capitalist in all its fundamentals. By 1944, pre-tax wages in manufacturing were 50% higher than in 1939. However, corporate profits after taxes grew by more than 100%. As Lenin wryly observed, war is not only terrible, it is terribly profitable.

Once the war was won, the capitalists were keen to get things back to "normal"—lest the millions of returning veterans get any ideas about how the economy might be organized differently. As Mason explains:

> This enormous rolling back of public production was not inevitable or driven by concerns of efficiency. It was an ideological project pushed by business leaders. Even in the days after Pearl Harbor, as dozens of government-financed and -owned plants were being authorized, conservatives like Senator Robert Taft were determined to ensure that these taxpayer-funded factories would eventually be "returned" to private business—an outcome that would require Congress to be "constantly on guard, and determined to restore a system of privately owned and operated enterprise."
>
> By the end of the war, the conservatives had largely displaced New Deal economists like Eveline Burns and Alvin Hansen, whose National Resources Planning Board had been developing plans for turning the publicly owned war facilities into Tennessee Valley Authority-style public corporations. Instead, the discussion was dominated by the likes of the Baruch-Hancock report, which took as its starting point that the top priority should be "taking the government out of business."
>
> The 1946 Employment Act, among the crown jewels of postwar Keynesianism, formalized a public commitment to avoid a return to the mass unemployment of the 1930s, but stipulated that full

employment was to be achieved only through policies that "foster and promote free private enterprise."

As is clear from the above, even the American bourgeois understand that in times of acute crisis, centralization is a far more efficient way of organizing the economy. Notwithstanding their avowed commitment to free enterprise, when the going gets rough, the capitalists have no problem begging for hefty public handouts. And in times of prosperity, they compete over whose turn it is to loot the public treasury through other means, including juicy profits from no-bid government contracts.

So while the social and employment programs of the New Deal staved off revolution, it was World War II that bailed US capitalism out of the Great Depression—and launched it into the imperialist stratosphere.

Opening Pandora's Box

Most Americans are led to believe that other than Pearl Harbor, the US wasn't physically touched by the war. Little do they know that the Aleutian Island of Kiska in Alaska was occupied by the Japanese for a year. Nor are they aware that, at the time of the infamous December 7, 1941 attack on Hawaii, the Philippines was also part of the "Greater United States." In fact, Manila was the country's sixth-largest city—bigger than Boston or Washington, DC. In 1940, the colonies accounted for 13% of the US population, meaning you were more likely to be colonized than African-American.

Within hours of the bombing of the US Pacific Fleet, Japan invaded and eventually occupied the Philippines. Following in the tradition of the Spanish and American imperialists, the Filipino people were viewed as subhuman by the occupiers, with 100,000 killed during the "Manila Massacre" of 1945 alone. As the Japanese military orders instructed:

> When Filipinos are to be killed, they must be gathered into one place and disposed of with the consideration that ammunition and manpower must not be used to excess . . . As the disposal of dead bodies is a troublesome task, they should be gathered into houses that are scheduled to be burned or demolished. They should also be thrown into the river.

Although they were not American citizens, Filipinos were considered US nationals. This means that, in terms of American lives lost, the fighting in the Philippines during World War II was even deadlier than the Civil War. And yet, most mainland-born GIs sent to "liberate" the islands from the Japanese had no idea they were fighting on US territory.

The one-time extent of "Greater America" has faded from the country's collective memory. So how is it that the US emerged from the 1940s as the greatest imperialist power in history while also reducing its territorial footprint?

One key fact explains the role played by the war in completing US imperialism's metamorphosis: Of the over 16 million Americans who served during the war, only one in ten saw combat. The rest were part of an enormous logistical octopus that established America's military and economic presence in every corner of the globe.

As the novelist Neal Stephenson described it:

> The United States military is, first and foremost, an unfathomable network of typists and file clerks, secondarily a stupendous mechanism for moving stuff from one part of the world to another, and, last and least, a fighting organization.

As had been the case during World War I, the US was formally neutral when the fighting first broke out. The national mood was isolationist and laws were passed legally barring it from selling arms or offering credit to warring nations. By the war's end, however, US imperialism had embedded itself in the very fabric of the formerly dominant European empires, above all, the British. It did so patiently and deliberately, step by step.

After Hitler invaded Poland in 1939, the Neutrality Acts were replaced by "Cash and Carry," which allowed the sale of war materiel to the belligerents, as long as the recipients paid immediately in cash and arranged for transport using their own ships.

In 1940, the UK was desperately embroiled in the Battle of Britain. The Americans came graciously to the rescue with the "Destroyers for Bases" agreement, which provided the Brits with 50 naval destroyers in exchange for land rights on British possessions. As a result, the US received 99-year leases to set up bases in places like Newfoundland, the Bahamas, Bermuda, Jamaica, and Trinidad.

In these lands, the Americans could fly their flag, confiscate property, and build anything they wanted. Their workers and troops were even immune from British taxes and laws. Formally speaking, these bits of the world were still part of the British Empire. But possession is nine-tenths of the law, and as a high-ranking US official put it after the war: "Nothing is more certain than they could have become American possessions for the asking."

It's not by accident that George Orwell referred to Britain as "Airstrip One" in his dystopian classic, *1984*.

Then came the Lend-Lease Act of 1941, by which the US supplied the UK, China, the Soviet Union, and other Allied nations with food, oil, warships, warplanes, and other weaponry. By the war's end, over $50 billion had been provided to the Allies. However, although this aid was "free," it came with many strings attached, and American commodities made deeper inroads into the world market.

Again, although most people tend to focus on the military side of the equation, the export of commodities and capital has long been the main weapon used by US imperialism to impose its will. As Marx wrote in the *Manifesto*, this is "the heavy artillery with which it batters down all Chinese walls."

As early as the 1850s, the US had started claiming isolated islands from the Caribbean to Oceania as its own. Their original purpose was to mine guano for fertilizer and to establish remote naval relay bases. However, World War II, and in particular, the advent of aviation and the need for refueling stations took things to a whole new level.

During the war, the US set up an estimated 30,000 installations at 2,000 overseas bases. In Panama alone, it maintained 134 bases, not including the facilities of the canal zone itself. Its logistics capabilities were unmatched. In the words of General William Tunner, head of the Air Transport Command: "We can fly anything, anywhere, anytime."

As we will see further on, the importance of the nuts and bolts of warfare should not be underestimated. As General Omar Bradley famously said, "Amateurs talk strategy, and professionals talk logistics."

All told, the US sent 12 million troops to Europe during the war, bringing with them their food, music, sports, and more. Over two million G.I.s—short for "Government Issue"—passed through Britain alone. By the war's end, Churchill grudgingly acknowledged that events had brought US imperialism to the "summit of the world."

Tens of millions of Europeans, Asians, and Africans were killed during the war, as compared to "just" 418,500 Americans. Along with these devastating population losses, European and Japanese industrial capacity had been shattered, while the Americans' was intact and running at full tilt.

In 1945, the US produced more commodities and had more oil, gold, and planes than all other countries combined. It also had more ships and bases than any other power, as well as a brief monopoly on atomic weapons. The US emerged from the conflagration as the world's biggest lender, putting it in an incredibly dominant position. The Americans seemed poised to take direct possession of vast swathes of the planet. Stalin had done his part to facilitate America's postwar domination by unilaterally dissolving the Comintern in 1943, without even consulting its members.

In 1945, the overseas areas under US jurisdiction included 135 million people—more than lived in the mainland United States. At one point during the occupation of Japan, Douglas MacArthur had absolute control over roughly 80,000,000 people across the Pacific. Over just nine days, he personally oversaw the drafting of the still-in-force Japanese Constitution.

With its troops everywhere and its economy in overdrive, there was talk, not only of turning Alaska and Hawaii into states, but also the Philippines, Iceland, and possibly even France and Japan. It was like 1898 on steroids.

Patton, Russia, and Germany

On April 25, 1945, just weeks before the Nazis surrendered, US and Russian troops met at the Elbe River in northern Germany.

After surviving the unspeakable horrors of Operation Barbarossa and the Battle of Stalingrad, the Soviets had turned the tide at the Battle of Kursk in the summer of 1943. Their counterattack swept across the Ukrainian steppes to the Balkans, the Baltic, through Romania, Poland, Hungary, and Czechoslovakia before raising the red flag over the Reichstag in Berlin.

For their part, the Americans had landed on the blood-soaked beaches of Normandy in June 1944 and fought their way across France and over the Rhine. Had he had his way, General George S. Patton would have ordered his troops to push eastward in an attempt to take Berlin and push the Soviets out of Germany altogether—no matter the cost. As he put it in his own racist, reactionary words:

> We may have been fighting the wrong enemy (Germany) all along. But while we're here (on the Soviet border), we should go after the bastards now, 'cause we're gonna have to fight 'em eventually . . .
>
> Let's keep our boots polished, bayonets sharpened and present a picture of force and strength to these people. This is the only language [the Soviets] understand and respect. If you fail to do this, then I would like to say to you that we have had a victory over the Germans and have disarmed them, but have lost the war . . .
>
> The difficulty in understanding the Russian is that we do not take cognizance of the fact that he is not a European, but an Asiatic, and therefore thinks deviously. We can no more understand a Russian than a Chinaman or a Japanese, and from what I have seen of them, I have no particular desire to understand them, except to ascertain how much lead or iron it takes to kill them.
>
> In addition to his other Asiatic characteristics, the Russian has no regard for human life and is an all-out son of bitch, barbarian, and chronic drunk . . .
>
> In my opinion, the American army as it now exists could beat the Russians with the greatest of ease, because, while the Russians have good infantry, they are lacking in artillery, air, tanks and the knowledge of the use of the combined arms, whereas we excel in all three of these. If it should be necessary to fight the Russians, the sooner we do it the better . . .
>
> They are a scurvy race and simply savages. We could beat hell out of them . . .

To be sure, from the perspective of US imperialism, Patton's distrust of the Russians was well founded. And it went beyond his understandable hatred of the USSR and its planned economy.

14. George S. Patton, Omar Bradley, and Bernard Montgomery meeting to discuss the Normandy campaign, 1944.

As we will see, keeping Europe's economic and population powerhouses divided has long been a core component of US foreign policy. It is not by accident that Otto Von Bismarck once quipped: "The secret of politics? Make a good treaty with Russia."

Patton was so keen to ensure the Germans could serve as a long-term bulwark against the Russians that he even opposed de-Nazification after the war:

> I don't like the Nazis any more than you do. I despise them. In the past three years I did my utmost to kill as many of them as possible. Now we are using them for lack of anyone better until we can get better people . . .
>
> More than half the Germans were Nazis, and we would be in a hell of a fix if we removed all Nazi party members from office. The way I see it, this Nazi question is very much like a Democrat and

> Republican election fight. To get things done in Bavaria, after the complete disorganization and disruption of four years of war, we had to compromise with the devil a little. We had no alternative but to turn to the people who knew what to do and how to do it. So, for the time being we are compromising with the devil . . .

Patton was not alone. Incredibly, the British Chiefs of Staff Committee had developed contingency plans for a surprise attack and war against the Soviet Union. The aim of "Operation Unthinkable," as it was called, was to impose "the will of the United States and British Empire upon Russia."

However, the more serious representatives of imperialism understood that the balance of forces that had emerged from the war would allow for none of this. Even then there were limits to US military power. Above all, there were political and economic considerations—including the threat of a new wave of class struggle and revolutions.

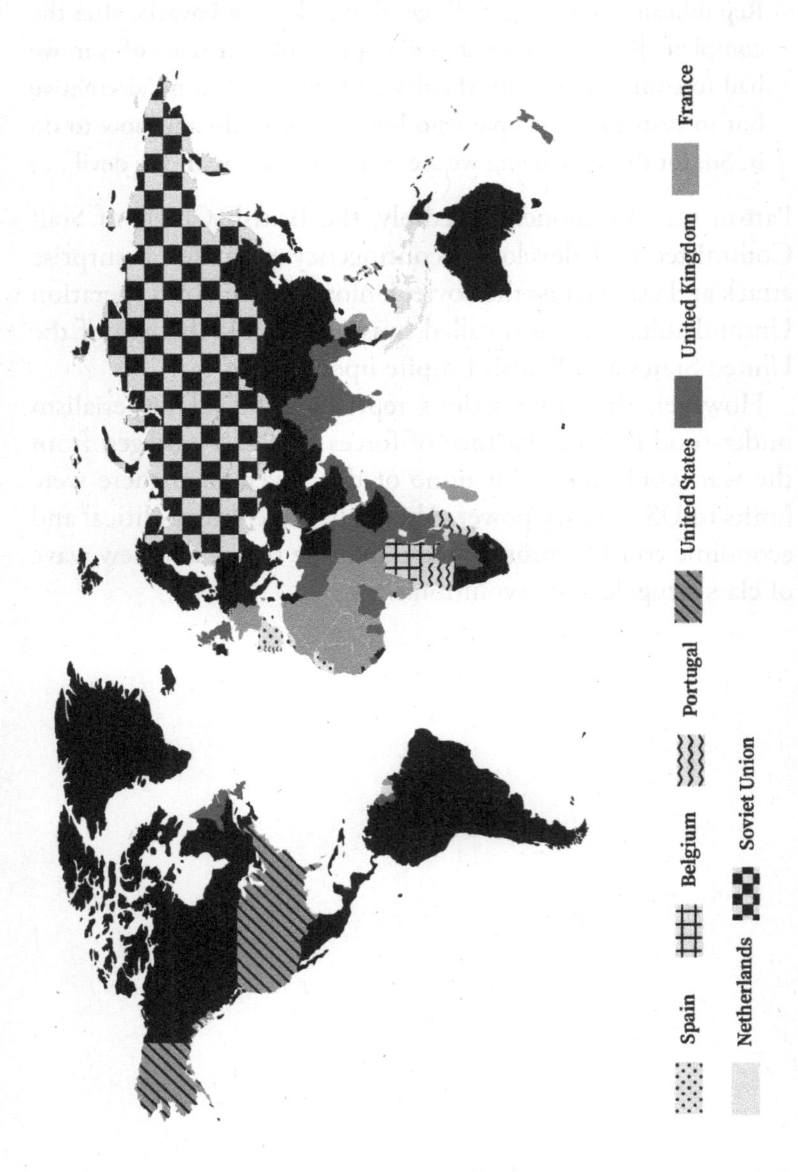

15. Division of the world in 1945.

The Postwar Boom and the Restoration of Capitalism

The day of small nations has long passed away.
The day of Empires has come.
– Joseph Chamberlain

Mutinies and revolutions

With the war winding down and the European empires severely weakened, hundreds of millions were rising up against colonial slavery. As one American general put it, Asia was "an enormous pot, seething and boiling." The entire region, from India to China, was teeming with revolution, as were Africa and Latin America, with nationalist struggles also intensifying in the Philippines and Puerto Rico.

For Marxists, the Chinese Revolution of 1949 ranks as the second-greatest event in human history. Tens of millions fought in an epic struggle against landlordism, capitalism, and Japanese imperialism. The mass struggle to liberate the Indian subcontinent from British domination was also an inspiration, despite the cynical betrayals by Gandhi, Nehru, and Jinnah, and the sickening travesty of Partition.

In 1940, nearly one out of every three people living on the planet was directly colonized. By 1965, it was just one in 50. Between 1945 and 1960, three dozen new states in Asia and Africa achieved autonomy or total independence from their European colonial rulers. These facts alone reveal the enormous power of the aroused masses, even when reformist or Stalinist leaders hijacked their struggles.

But not only that. The US military was also infected with the spirit of rebellion. Millions of Americans had been mobilized to fight for freedom against fascism and empire. Now that the war against Hitler and Hirohito was over, they had no interest in fighting to establish new colonies or to hold on to old ones.

It had taken fully four years to position the 7.6 million American troops still in the field at the end of the war—and all of them wanted to be sent home as soon as possible. Moving that many people halfway across the world quickly was an obvious logistical nightmare. But there was another problem: the military tops wanted to keep 2.5 million soldiers, sailors, and airmen in uniform. Although the war had changed the algebra of imperialist power, George Marshall, the Army Chief of Staff, knew that they needed more than bases and planes to intimidate enemies and put down revolutions:

> We are now concerned with the peace of the entire world, and the peace can only be maintained by the strong.

What resulted was the biggest mutiny in American military history. Mass protests exploded across Asia, Europe, and the continental US. In Guam, they burned the Secretary of War in effigy. 20,000 GIs marched on Manila, proclaiming: "The Filipinos are our allies—we ain't gonna fight them!" Communists were actively involved in the agitation and had a "destructive effect on soldiers' and civilians' morale," according to the authorities.

A unit of Black soldiers stationed in Burma (now Myanmar) wrote to the president to say they were "disgusted with undemocratic American foreign policy . . . We do not want to unify China with bayonets and bombing plans." They were well aware that back at home, they did not have the same rights as white Americans.

The First Lady, Eleanor Roosevelt, tried to brush it all off as no big deal:

> They are good boys, but if they don't have enough to do, they'll get in trouble. That is the nature of boys, I'm afraid.

But the ruling class was definitely afraid. By June 1947, just one million soldiers and sailors remained in uniform, and the US had only the sixth-largest army in the world.

This all coincided with the biggest strike wave in US history. In 1945, there were 4,750 work stoppages, followed by another 4,985 in 1946, involving 4.6 million workers and amounting to 116 million lost work days for the bosses.

Wages were the main issue after years of wartime belt-tightening and pent-up frustration at the no-strike pledges imposed by the labor and Communist Party leaders during the war. Major strikes in coal mining, railroads, and steel production led to significant changes in US labor law as the government struggled to regain control.

Following the Wagner Act of 1935, which established the National Labor Relations Board, the US bourgeois passed the Labor Management Relations Act of 1947, better known as Taft-Hartley. A key element in the state's efforts to tie organized labor's hands, Taft-Hartley prohibits jurisdictional and wildcat strikes, solidarity or political strikes, secondary boycotts, and secondary and mass picketing. It also bans the closed shop, opening the door to "right to work" legislation. Furthermore, it requires union officers to sign non-communist affidavits with the government and allows employers to file lawsuits against unions for contract violations and to engage in anti-union propaganda.

In short, US imperialism was in no position to permanently occupy the lands they held at the end of the war. Occupation is both expensive and politically unpopular. But that didn't mean they didn't plan on dominating the planet.

Finance capital and debt slavery

By 1945, US imperialism realized it didn't have to physically hold entire countries to control them. All they needed was to keep a few hundred military bases, many of them on remote islands. From these points, they could project overwhelming military force and dominate the key hubs of the global economy. With a worldwide logistical network and a commanding position in banking, they could dictate the terms of trade and the flows of currency and capital.

The Marshall Plan was one piece of the puzzle, with $12 billion sent to Western Europe to rebuild after the war, equivalent to $173 billion in today's dollars. The plan was explicitly aimed at countering the weight of the Soviet Union and its Eastern Bloc, whose economies were also recovering and even booming after the war. However, these were loans, not gifts, and the money had to be used to buy goods from US producers. In other words, this was yet another circular handout to private corporations using public dollars, with the added bonus that Western Europe was even further in thrall to the Americans.

An even more important component was the Bretton Woods system, established in 1944 and fully implemented by 1958. The US dollar was officially recognized as the global reserve currency, with exchange rates for all participating currencies pegged to the dollar. The dollar was, in turn, pegged to the price of gold, putting American capitalists and banks in a privileged position on the world market.

Bretton Woods fell apart in the 1970s, but to this day, 37 countries and territories around the world use the US dollar as an official currency. This represents serious economic leverage over the destinies of millions of people in supposedly sovereign countries.

Bretton Woods also gave birth to the International Monetary Fund and the World Bank. Ostensibly, their purpose is to "oversee the international monetary system and promote economic stability and growth." In reality, they exist to impose policies and regimes favorable to Western imperialism. By weaponizing finance capital to achieve political ends, they reinforce inequality and deepen dependency while keeping the major imperialist players on top.

For good reason, some refer to the IMF as the "International Mafia of Finance." But it is only natural that the capitalist cartels would band together to undermine their rivals and prevent the emergence of new competitors. After all, if a country is allowed to develop its own industrial base, it will start using its own natural materials instead of exporting them at rock-bottom prices. It's no surprise, therefore, that with very few exceptions, most "developing" countries remain woefully underdeveloped, despite 70-plus years of "investment" from the West.

Another tactic used by the dominant countries to maintain their competitive advantage is to impose sanctions or otherwise limit the transfer of advanced technologies. In the case of Huawei's Chief Financial Officer, Meng Wanzhou, the US issued an arrest warrant for allegedly violating US sanctions on Iran.

Then there's the question of "brain drain." To keep their edge and dull that of their rivals, countries like the US poach talented engineers, doctors, scientists, nurses, and skilled technicians from around the world. Since 1960, over 150,000 Filipino nurses have immigrated to the US, constituting 33% of all foreign-born RNs. More than 75% of those who emigrate from India to the US have a tertiary education. As for Guyana, more than 70% of the entire population with a tertiary education has left the country to work in the US.

Loans from institutions like the IMF come with harsh conditions attached, usually in the form of compulsory privatization, austerity, tax increases, and cuts to public services and subsidies for essentials like food and fuel. In many countries, these measures have sparked mass protests and even revolutions.

In 1989, the Venezuelan "Caracazo" was sparked after President Carlos Andrés Pérez agreed to implement the IMF's "shock therapy." Ironically, during his election campaign, Pérez had called IMF staff "genocide workers in the pay of economic totalitarianism," and denounced its policies as a "bomb that only kills people." The military was called in to quell mass riots in the capital and other major cities, resulting in as many as 5,000 killed. This was the ember that eventually grew into Hugo Chávez's Bolivarian Revolution.

In recent years, mass unrest has accompanied IMF loans in Argentina, Ecuador, Egypt, Sri Lanka, and Kenya. It has even been reported that, in exchange for billions in loans, the IMF mandated Ukraine's 2014 attack on its Russian-speaking population in the Donbas, part of the West's relentless push to encircle Russia. This was a blatant proxy provocation, leading eventually to the outbreak of open war.

The IMF and other loaning institutions know full well that these loans can never be repaid. They are after more than just money—though they make plenty of that as well. John Perkins provided a blow-by-blow explanation in his whistleblower account, *Confessions of an Economic Hitman.* As one of his handlers candidly told him, his job was:

> To encourage world leaders to become part of a vast network that promotes US commercial interests. In the end, those leaders become ensnared in a web of debt that ensures their loyalty. We can draw on them whenever we desire—to satisfy our political, economic, or military needs. In turn they bolster their political positions by bringing industrial parks, power plants, and airports to their people. The owners of US engineering/construction companies become fabulously wealthy.

Corruption in these deals is rampant. Billions in "loans" intended for infrastructure, defense, and other projects are simply pocketed by top officials or parked in Swiss or offshore bank accounts to be enjoyed once they flee the country and leave the masses to foot the bill. According to the IMF itself, the global cost of corruption and efficiency losses is $4.5 trillion, or about 5% of the world's GDP.

In the US alone, debt servicing on external public debt—i.e., interest payments—reached more than $1 trillion in 2024. That's hundreds of billions in virtually free money for the banks every single year.

As of 2024, worldwide public debt stood at over $100 trillion. Divided by the current population of approximately 8.2 billion people, this amounts to a staggering $12,195 of debt for every man, woman, child, and infant on the planet—and rising. This is roughly equivalent to the average global GDP per capita.

In other words, every human on the planet would have to work for an entire year without consuming or spending anything to pay off their share of debt. Since this isn't physically possible, generational debt slavery is now the norm for most countries and almost all the inhabitants of the planet—with virtually nothing to show for it.

Perhaps the most heinous example in history is the case of Haiti. In one of the most inspiring revolutions ever seen, the Haitian slave masses rose up in 1791 against their French overlords. After winning independence in 1804, the country was forced to pay "reparations" to former slaveholders and the French government for loans and the loss of their slave-plantation assets and revenues. Forced on the Haitians at gunpoint, it was financed by French banks and Citibank. Totalling around $560 million in today's dollars, it took until 1947—122 years—to pay back, with the interest adding up to as much as $150 billion or more.

This is the real face of imperialism. This is why Haiti, a tropical paradise rich in natural resources, is a living hell on Earth for most of its 12 million inhabitants. This is why 712 million people worldwide live on less than $2.15 a day, while we're told there's no money for healthcare and education. This is why 45 million kids across the globe suffer from severe malnutrition—nearly one out of every three children under five years of age.

Public-private partnership and class collaboration

Yet again, we see that it is through the terms of trade, debt, and economic relations generally that imperialism imposes its will, no matter what cost. Those driving this inhuman process have a messianic belief in themselves and their mission to spread capitalism around the planet. For them, the millions of human casualties are mere "externalities." As the impotent neo-Keynesian economist Joseph Stieglitz lamented:

> Modern high-tech warfare is designed to remove physical contact: dropping bombs from 50,000 feet ensures that one does not "feel" what one does. Modern economic management is similar: from

> one's luxury hotel, one can callously impose policies about which one would think twice if one knew the people whose lives one was destroying.

The ruling class's callous attitude toward human life was casually summed up by Allen Dulles at a secret conference held in Princeton, NJ in May 1952:

> After all, we have had a hundred thousand casualties in Korea. If we have been willing to accept those casualties, I wouldn't worry if there were a few casualties or a few martyrs behind the iron curtain . . .
>
> I don't think you can wait until you have all your troops and are sure you are going to win. You have got to start and go ahead . . . You have got to have a few martyrs. Some people have to get killed.

To cover their tracks, governments lean heavily on ostensibly private institutions, including banks, engineering and construction conglomerates, and security contractors to do their dirty work. In this way, they defend the overall interests of the bourgeois and enrich their cronies, while being shielded from direct blame for many of the consequences.

As John Perkins explained:

> Economic hit men are highly paid professionals who cheat countries around the globe out of trillions of dollars. They funnel money from the World Bank, the US Agency for International Development, and other foreign "aid" organizations into the coffers of huge corporations and the pockets of a few wealthy families who control the planet's natural resources.
>
> Their tools include fraudulent financial reports, rigged elections, payoffs, extortion, sex, and murder. They play a game as old as empire, but one that has taken on new and terrifying dimensions during this time of globalization . . .

> For every $100 of crude taken out of the Ecuadorian rainforests, the oil companies receive $75. Of the remaining $25, three-quarters must go to paying off the foreign debt. Most of the remainder covers military and other governmental expenses—which leaves about $2.50 for health, education, and programs aimed at helping the poor.

To this "pound of flesh" must be added terrible working conditions and environmental devastation. And when these mafiosi tactics run their course, the "jackals" are often sent in by the CIA to intimidate, assassinate, and overthrow. From Iran to Guatemala to Chile to Ukraine, one "unfriendly" regime after another has been toppled, with counterrevolution often masquerading as "progressive" intervention and even revolution.

A major feature of this is the revolving door between big corporations, government ministries, elite universities, the media, lobbyists, and think tanks like the World Economic Forum, Brookings Institution, and the Heritage Foundation, which exert an inordinate amount of influence on policy. It's not for nothing that defense contractors spent $70 million on lobbying ahead of the annual defense budget bill in 2023.

Take, for example, Robert McNamara, who served as Secretary of Defense under Presidents Kennedy and Johnson. Best known as one of the key architects of the Vietnam War, he also served as president of the Ford Motor Company and the World Bank.

Or take the billionaire Elon Musk, whose companies SpaceX and Tesla have received billions in public dollars since 2008 ($20 billion and $9 billion, respectively). After pouring $130 million into Trump's victorious campaign, his net worth soared by $70 billion. He now stands to make even more as the federal government is refashioned to suit his interests.

16. Robert McNamara, Secretary of Defense, 1965.

Certain "independent agencies" and "nonprofit" institutions also play a key role. Key among these is the United States Agency for International Development, established in 1961 by John F. Kennedy. Responsible for administering civilian foreign aid and development assistance, its stated mission is "to promote and demonstrate democratic values abroad, and advance a free, peaceful, and prosperous world." Active in over 100 countries, its 2024 budget included $63.1 billion for foreign assistance and diplomatic engagement. As with the IMF, grants from USAID come with plenty of pro-US strings attached.

Then there's the Peace Corps, also established by JFK in 1961. Its stated goals are to "provide technical assistance, help people outside the United States understand American culture, and help Americans understand the cultures of other countries." While plenty of well-intentioned individuals have joined its ranks with a view toward making the world a better place, it too, is a tool for US imperialism.

The Peace Corps is a prime example of US efforts to exert "soft power," i.e., attempting to influence others through attraction and persuasion rather than coercion or force. Other examples include the Carter Center and the Clinton Foundation.

Through cultural exchanges, construction projects, and development aid, initiatives like this seek to win "hearts and minds" in so-called developing countries, often paving the way for American commercial interests. Peace Corps volunteers can also serve as "eyes and ears" for US intelligence services in remote and otherwise inaccessible parts of the world—even if the participants are not consciously aware of it.

Yet another public-private pillar of US imperialism is the National Endowment for Democracy. Funded by Congress through the State Department, it was founded during the Reagan administration, in 1983. Formally, the NED is "a private, nonprofit foundation dedicated to the growth and strengthening of democratic institutions around the world." With an annual budget of over $315 billion, it operates in at least 130 countries to "provide grants to non-governmental groups supporting democracy abroad," with a focus on "promoting free elections, independent media, human rights, and civic education."

In other words, this allegedly "nonpartisan" entity is 100% dedicated to defending and extending American imperialism. Made up of four core institutions, the first is the Center for International Private Enterprise, which is essentially the international tentacle of the US Chamber of Commerce, the world's largest business organization.

Second is the International Republican Institute. Chaired by John McCain for 25 years, this is the international tentacle of the Republican Party. As explained on its website, the IRI:

> [Works] to strengthen civil society, political parties, marginalized communities, and other key areas essential to democratic

> governance. We encourage democracy in places where it is absent, help democracy become more effective where it is in danger and share best practices where democracy is flourishing . . .
>
> Our staff and local partners help legislators enhance transparency, connect policymakers with their constituencies, empower individuals who have previously felt left out of the political process, and we have observed over 200 elections.

Third is the international tentacle of the Democratic Party, the National Democratic Institute. Unsurprisingly, its mission is also to "promote and strengthen democracy globally through citizen participation, openness, and accountability in government" by "supporting elections, strengthening political parties, promoting citizen participation, and enhancing government accountability."

And last but not least, is the ill-named "Solidarity Center." Named after AFL-CIO headquarters—located just one block from the White House—it represents the international tentacle of American organized labor. The result of John Sweeney's 1997 consolidation of four previously existing entities—the American Institute for Free Labor Development, the Asian-American Free Labor Institute, the African-American Labor Institute, and the Free Trade Union Institute—its budget is 95% funded by the federal government.

In its various guises, "Solidarity Center" has intervened in union struggles on behalf of the bosses worldwide. By posing as "labor friendly," it has given left cover to US imperialism for decades.

In Argentina, it backed company unions versus independent ones. In Cambodia, it helped draft labor codes acceptable to the bosses during the transition from autocracy. In the Philippines, it tested industry-approved codes of conduct to ensure unionized workers adhered to them. In Indonesia, it worked with Reebok to offer workers'-rights seminars in the company's sweatshops and child labor. In Iraq, it was involved in efforts to reorganize Iraqi labor unions after the 2003 invasion. And in Venezuela, it made sure the Bolivarian unions didn't go beyond the limits of capitalism. It speaks volumes that Madeleine Albright was one of its biggest supporters.

This all flows organically from the subservient attitude of the labor leaders, most of whom fear the workers more than they fear the capitalists. As Trotsky wrote in the context of 1940:

> There is one common feature in the development, or more correctly the degeneration, of modern trade union organizations in the entire world: it is their drawing closely to and growing together with the state power. This process is equally characteristic of the neutral, the Social-Democratic, the Communist and "anarchist" trade unions. This fact alone shows that the tendency towards "growing together" is intrinsic not in this or that doctrine as such but derives from social conditions common for all unions.
>
> Monopoly capitalism does not rest on competition and free private initiative but on centralized command. The capitalist cliques at the head of mighty trusts, syndicates, banking consortiums, etc., view economic life from the very same heights as does state power; and they require at every step the collaboration of the latter. In their turn the trade unions in the most important branches of industry find themselves deprived of the possibility of profiting by the competition between the different enterprises. They have to confront a centralized capitalist adversary, intimately bound up with state power.
>
> Hence flows the need of the trade unions—insofar as they remain on reformist positions, i.e., on positions of adapting themselves to private property—to adapt themselves to the capitalist state and to contend for its cooperation.
>
> In the eyes of the bureaucracy of the trade union movement the chief task lies in "freeing" the state from the embrace of capitalism,

> in weakening its dependence on trusts, in pulling it over to their side. This position is in complete harmony with the social position of the labor aristocracy and the labor bureaucracy, who fight for a crumb in the share of superprofits of imperialist capitalism.
>
> The labor bureaucrats do their level best in words and deeds to demonstrate to the "democratic" state how reliable and indispensable they are in peace-time and especially in time of war. By transforming the trade unions into organs of the state, fascism invents nothing new; it merely draws to their ultimate conclusion the tendencies inherent in imperialism.
>
> Colonial and semi-colonial countries are under the sway not of native capitalism but of foreign imperialism. However, this does not weaken but on the contrary, strengthens the need of direct, daily, practical ties between the magnates of capitalism and the governments which are in essence subject to them – the governments of colonial or semi-colonial countries. Inasmuch as imperialist capitalism creates both in colonies and semi-colonies a stratum of labor aristocracy and bureaucracy, the latter requires the support of colonial and semicolonial governments, as protectors, patrons and, sometimes, as arbitrators.
>
> This constitutes the most important social basis for the Bonapartist and semi-Bonapartist character of governments in the colonies and in backward countries generally. This likewise constitutes the basis for the dependence of reformist unions upon the state.

Needless to say, "Solidarity Center" represents one of the most egregious examples of class collaboration by American labor leaders.

The mother of invention

In an article titled "The Invention of the War Machine," the historians M. Anthony Mills and Mark P. Mills describe the constant development of the "tools of death" and their impact on the broader economy:

> The many technological innovations most prominently associated with World War I may be grouped into three categories: first, *weapons technologies* invented for, or in most cases improved upon or scaled specifically for, warfighting; second, *medical innovations* occasioned by the war's traumas; and third, *non-weapons technologies* catalyzed by or commercialized because of the war more generally.

In fact, this dynamic can be seen as far back as the 15th and 16th centuries, when the wars that ravaged Europe played a key role in revolutionizing the means of production and giving rise to capitalism. And while World War I offers many excellent examples, the transformation undergone by the US during World War II was truly next-level.

With Europe engulfed in flames, Japan had taken advantage of the chaos at the war's outset to occupy a swathe of European colonies and islands in the Pacific, cutting American industry off from strategically vital natural resources such as tin and rubber.

Rubber was essential not only to keep the economy growing and the population satisfied, but also for warmaking. To build a single military aircraft, roughly 1,000 pounds of rubber was needed; for a tank, 2,000 pounds; and a battleship absorbed a whopping 75 tons. Every US soldier at the time was equipped with footwear, clothing, and equipment requiring up to 32 pounds of rubber.

It was, therefore, worth going to extreme lengths to acquire something as apparently innocuous as rubber—or oil. Faced with rising class struggle and tensions over access to raw materials, FDR deliberately provoked war with Japan.

17. President Franklin D. Roosevelt signing the declaration of war against Japan, 1941.

Japan is a small island nation with far fewer domestic resources than the continent-spanning US, making it even more dependent on imports. In July 1940, in a bid to slow Japan's military buildup, FDR cut off US shipments of scrap iron, steel, and aviation fuel. A year later, after Japan joined the Axis Powers, occupied French Indochina, and prepared to attack resource-rich British Malaya, Roosevelt froze all Japanese assets in the US. This effectively cut it off from three-fourths of its overseas trade and 88% of its imported oil. With sufficient oil reserves for just three years at peacetime consumption levels, the Japanese Empire was boxed into a corner. War was inevitable—and Roosevelt knew it.

But there were other, more far-reaching consequences that went beyond the war itself.

As a result of all of the wartime disruptions, American industry had been forced to make significant readjustments—with heavy state investment and direction. The potentially catastrophic supply-chain restrictions drove revolutionary advances in chemistry and synthetics, including rubber, plastics, explosives, textiles, fertilizers, pesticides, and atomic energy. US imperialism no longer had to depend on access to specific parts of the world to acquire certain essential commodities—it could manufacture artificial versions of them itself.

The knock-on effects were dramatic. For example, due to advances in medicines and antibiotics, American military deaths due to disease during World War II were just 4% of what they had been during World War I. In the case of rubber, it was the first commodity to be rationed in the US in 1942—followed by gasoline, sugar, coffee, meats, fats, canned goods, cheese, and shoes. By 1945, the country was producing over 900,000 tons of synthetic rubber per year.

Another seemingly insignificant change contributing to these rapid advances was the standardization of parts. In the 1920s, Herbert Hoover had pushed to ensure the compatibility of components across industries. In the 1940s, given the need to mobilize industry for the war effort, standardization was expanded further and extended worldwide. It's not by coincidence that the word "global" only came into common usage in the 1940s.

Generously subsidized by the state, US manufacturing went into overdrive during the war years, churning out 84,000 tanks and 6.2 million rifles, and equipping 16 million soldiers. At its peak, the US produced 360 planes a day.

By almost any measure, these are impressive numbers. But the Soviet planned economy achieved even more—despite its Stalinist deformations and the untold death and devastation inflicted by the Nazis. To give just two figures, the Soviet

Union's GDP fell by 34% between 1940 and 1942. Over the course of the war, an astonishing 27 million soldiers and civilians were killed, including two million Jews.

And yet, the Soviet masses rebounded to produce 102,500 tanks and 30.3 million rifles while putting 34 million troops in the field. During the Battle of Stalingrad, Soviet soldiers fought firefights with German soldiers at one end of a factory, while workers produced weapons and supplies at the other. It was this gargantuan effort that broke the Wehrmacht's back and prevented the destruction of the USSR at that time. Despite his paranoia, class collaboration, and incompetence, Stalin emerged victorious and strengthened.

However, American imperialism was by far the biggest winner. By 1946, the US accounted for 60% of world industrial production. Gross National Product, a measure of all goods and services produced, grew by 50% in just ten years, rising from $200 billion in 1940 to $300 billion in 1950. This was the objective basis that drew the postwar world into America's gravitational pull. As Henry Luce wrote in a 1941 editorial for *Time* magazine, this was to be "The American Century."

In the decades that followed, US imperialism tightened its grip on humanity in other ways as well. From Hollywood movies and American music, to the adoption of English as the lingua franca for the internet, computer programming, air traffic controllers, social media, and science, the world was "Coca-Colonized," as one French communist described it.

Bases and bombers

But make no mistake about it, a globe-spanning military presence remains a key component of American imperialism's strategy to this day. It ain't over until it's over, and as we'll see, the neocons haven't given up on recouping their lost ground and influence—as deluded as that may be.

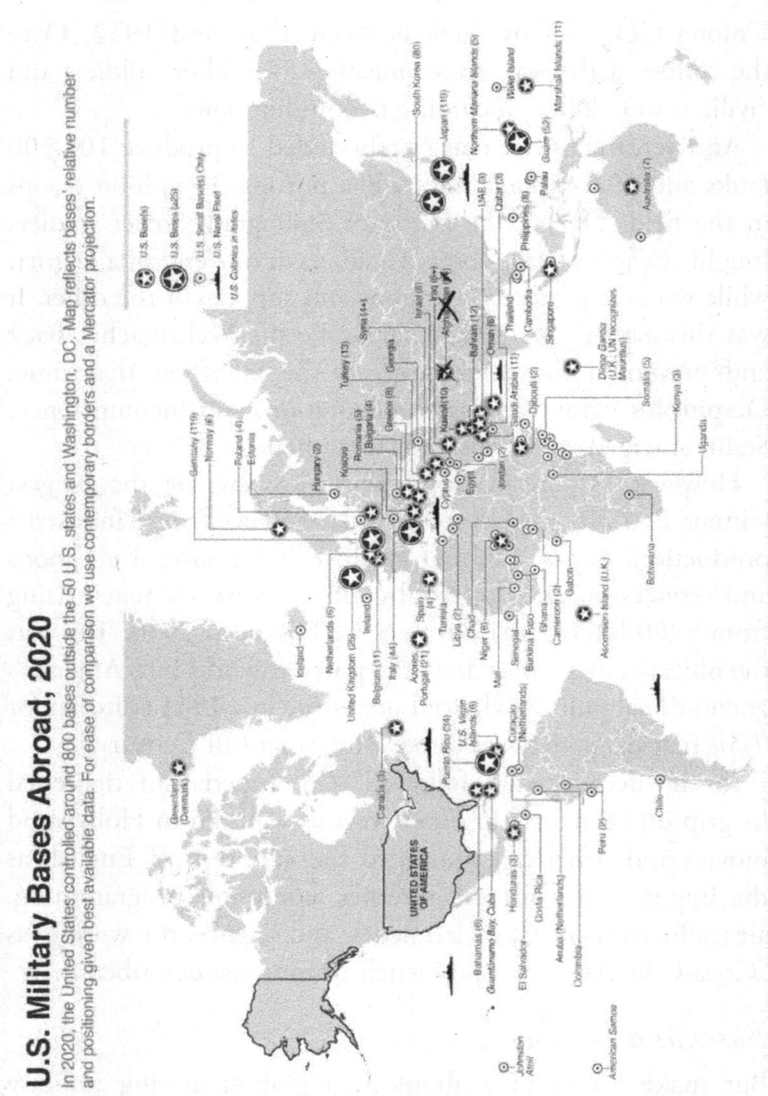
U.S. Military Bases Abroad, 2020
In 2020, the United States controlled around 800 bases outside the 50 U.S. states and Washington, DC. Map reflects bases' relative number and positioning given best available data. For ease of comparison we use contemporary borders and a Mercator projection.
U.S. Base(s)
U.S. Bases (≥25)
U.S. Small Base(s) Only
U.S. Naval Fleet
U.S. Colonies in italics
UNITED STATES OF AMERICA

18. Map of major US overseas military bases in 2020.

Uncle Sam still operates around 800 military bases and related installations around the world, three times more than any other country. Just 60 miles south of the North Korean border lies Camp Humphreys, the biggest foreign military base of all. Home to over 40,000 soldiers, it is a little slice of American heaven—complete with Burger King, Popeye's, Krispy Kreme, and laser tag.

To this day, there are some 36,000 troops stationed in Europe at around 60 military bases. The US also operates 11 nuclear-powered aircraft carriers, each of which is like a floating airbase, armed to the teeth.

Roughly four million people live in the American colonies of Guam, American Samoa, the Northern Marianas, and Puerto Rico. 25% of the island of Guam is a military base. Okinawa was returned to Japan in 1972, yet the US military still controls 20% of the island.

As a bonus, big-name clothing companies like the Gap, Tommy Hilfiger, The Limited, and Ralph Lauren can operate sweatshops using low-wage immigrant labor on Guam and Saipan because, technically, anything produced there is "made in the USA." The same goes for Puerto Rico, which is also forced to host US military facilities. Even the smallest Hawaiian island is a military firing range.

And although the Philippines gained its "independence" in 1946, it was forced to grant 99-year leases to the US military for several military bases. With tensions in the South China Sea rising over Taiwan, the US recently increased the number of bases in the Philippines from five to nine—so much for national sovereignty.

Furthermore, US bases bring with them water, air, and soil pollution from sewage, fuel, lead, construction, and other garbage and waste. Given the relatively high wages received by US service personnel, inflationary pressures are higher than average in many areas surrounding US bases, pushing locals out of their homes.

America's postwar hubris

For the first two decades after the war, world capitalism boomed, driven largely by postwar reconstruction spending and the revival of world trade. Ted Grant outlined the conditions for this exceptional period in his classic work, *Will There Be a Slump?*:

> What, then, are the basic reasons for the developments of the post–Second World War economy?
>
> 1. The political failure of the Stalinists and the social democrats in Britain and Western Europe created the *political* climate for a recovery of capitalism.
>
> 2. The effects of the war, in the destruction of consumer and capital goods, created a big market (war has effects similar to, but deeper than, a slump in the destruction of capital). These effects, according to United Nations statisticians, only disappeared in 1958.
>
> 3. The Marshall Plan and other economic aid assisted the recovery of Western Europe.
>
> 4. The enormously increased investment in industry.
>
> 5. The growth of new industries—plastics, aluminum, rockets, electronics, atomic energy, and by-products.
>
> 6. The increasing output of the newer industries—chemicals, artificial fibers, synthetic rubber, plastics, rapid rise in light metals, aluminum, magnesium, electric household equipment, natural gas, electric energy, building activity.
>
> 7. The enormous amounts of fictitious capital, created by the armaments expenditure, which amount to 10% of the national income in Britain and America.
>
> 8. The new market for capital and engineering products, created by the weakening of imperialism in the undeveloped countries, which has given the local bourgeoisie the increased opportunity to develop industry on a greater scale than ever before.

> 9. All these factors interact with one another. The increased demand for raw materials, through the development of industry in the metropolitan countries in turn, reacts on the undeveloped countries and vice versa.
>
> 10. The increasing trade, especially in capital goods and engineering products, between the capitalist countries, consequent on the increased economic investment, in turn acts as a spur.
>
> 11. The role of state intervention in stimulating economic activity.
>
> All these factors explain the increase in production since the war. But the decisive factor has been the increased scope for capital investment, which is the main engine of capitalist development.

With a world to dominate, profits to be made, and the communists driven out of the unions, American capitalists invested heavily in the so-called "defense" industry. However, as Marx explained, once aggregated and unleashed on the world, capital can escape the control of its masters. This is equally true for militarism. As outgoing president and former general Dwight D. Eisenhower worriedly told Congress in his 1961 farewell address:

> Until the latest of our world conflicts, the United States had no armaments industry. American makers of plowshares could, with time and as required, make swords as well. But we can no longer risk emergency improvisation of national defense. We have been compelled to create a permanent armaments industry of vast proportions. Added to this, three and a half million men and women are directly engaged in the defense establishment. We annually spend on military security alone more than the net income of all United States corporations.
>
> Now this conjunction of an immense military establishment and a large arms industry is new in the American experience. The total influence—economic, political, even spiritual—is felt in every city, every Statehouse, every office of the Federal government. We

19. President Dwight D. Eisenhower delivers his farewell address, 1961.

> recognize the imperative need for this development. Yet, we must not fail to comprehend its grave implications. Our toil, resources, and livelihood are all involved. So is the very structure of our society.
>
> In the councils of government, we must guard against the acquisition of unwarranted influence, whether sought or unsought, by the military-industrial complex. The potential for the disastrous rise of misplaced power exists and will persist. We must never let the weight of this combination endanger our liberties or democratic processes.
>
> We should take nothing for granted. Only an alert and knowledgeable citizenry can compel the proper meshing of the huge industrial and military machinery of defense with our peaceful methods and goals, so that security and liberty may prosper together.

Leaving aside the cynical flourish about liberty, his words have proved more than a little bit prescient.

Along with the military-industrial complex, US imperialism's national security and surveillance state has also mushroomed. These now include: The Office of the Director of National Intelligence, the Central Intelligence Agency, the Defense Intelligence Agency, the National Security Agency, the Federal Bureau of Investigation, the Drug Enforcement Administration, Bureau of Alcohol, Tobacco, Firearms and Explosives, the National Geospatial-Intelligence Agency, the National Reconnaissance Office, Army Intelligence, Navy Intelligence, Air Force Intelligence, Marine Corps Intelligence, Space Force Intelligence, the Department of Energy's Office of Intelligence and Counterintelligence, the Department of Homeland Security's Office of Intelligence and Analysis, US Coast Guard Intelligence, the intelligence divisions within departments like State, Treasury, Energy—and more.

As we've seen, however, there were limits to what US imperialism could do, despite its privileged postwar position. It may have been the biggest capitalist superpower, but it wasn't the only superpower. It still had to account for the resurgent Soviet Union and the growing number of deformed workers' states in Eastern Europe, China, Africa, and beyond.

The first big test came in Korea, just a few years after the end of the second great slaughter. Although there was never a Congressional declaration of war—it was considered a mere "police action"—some 2.5 million people were killed in the fighting, including 36,000 Americans.

In 1945, Korea had been partitioned at the 38th parallel by US imperialism and the Soviet Union. In 1950, the North Koreans invaded the South in an attempt to reunify the peninsula. At first, General Douglas MacArthur, who commanded the troops of the so-called United Nations, succeeded in pushing the North Koreans back to the Chinese border. However, they were met there by the Chinese People's

Volunteer Army, recently victorious in its own revolutionary war of national liberation.

Hundreds of thousands of Chinese soldiers poured across the border, routing the Americans and eventually capturing Seoul. More US troops were landed, and the struggle continued. After two more bitter years, the fighting ended in a stalemate and an armistice, not an actual peace accord. Formally speaking, the war continues to this day, with over a million North Korean, South Korean, and American troops facing off across the mine-filled demilitarized zone between the two countries.

Then came the debacle of Vietnam. After the French imperialists were defeated at the Battle of Điện Biên Phủ in 1954, US imperialism was sucked into the morass. As Robert McNamara told CNN in 1996:

> [The domino theory] was the primary factor motivating the actions of both the Kennedy and the Johnson administrations, without any qualification. It was put forward by President Eisenhower in 1954, very succinctly: If the West loses control of Vietnam, the security of the West will be in danger; "the dominoes will fall" in Eisenhower's words.
>
> In a meeting between President Kennedy and President Eisenhower, on January 19 1961—the day before President Kennedy's inauguration—the only foreign policy issue fully discussed was Southeast Asia. Even today, some question as to exactly what Eisenhower said, but it's very clear that, at a minimum, he said . . . that if necessary, to prevent the loss of Laos, and by implication Vietnam, Eisenhower would be prepared for the US to act unilaterally—to intervene militarily.

Ten thousand days later, despite its overwhelming military superiority on paper, US imperialism suffered a humiliating defeat. Mass protests raged at home, military morale disintegrated, and officers were "fragged" by soldiers under their

20. A National Liberation Front prisoner awaits interrogation, 1967—National Archives.

command. Colonel Harry G. Summers, Jr., who participated in peace talks during the war, summed things up nicely in a 1988 interview with *Vietnam Magazine*:

> "You know, you never beat us on the battlefield," I told my North Vietnamese counterpart during negotiations in Hanoi a week before the fall of Saigon [on April 30, 1975]. He pondered that remark a moment and then replied, "That may be so, but it is also irrelevant."

Roughly three million American soldiers were sent to Southeast Asia to put down the "communists." The costs were tremendous: $176 billion spent, 58,000 Americans dead, and 300,000 wounded and disabled. 830,000 veterans were subsequently diagnosed with post-traumatic stress disorder. Between 1964 and 1969, the US dropped more than nine times the tonnage of high explosives on Vietnam as it did in the Pacific theater during the entirety of World War II. By the time it was all over, as many as four million Vietnamese, Laotians, and Cambodians had been killed, wounded, or gone missing.

In the aftermath, US imperialism was forced to end the draft, retool the military, and hunker down for a generation. Nonetheless, it remained a superpower. Given the overall strength of its economy, it could weather a mistake like Vietnam—though that is not necessarily the case today.

Class struggle and the end of the postwar boom

The mass protests against the Vietnam War movement—including the 50,000-strong "March on the Pentagon"—were just the tip of the iceberg. The postwar years also saw the titanic struggles of the early civil rights movement and the rise of groups like the Black Panthers and Brown Berets. From the "Long Hot Summer" of 1967, to Stonewall in 1969, to the standoff at Wounded Knee in 1973, one oppressed group after another rose up and fought back. In addition, there were significant strikes by teachers, auto, railroad, steel, communications, newspaper, postal, sanitation, and other workers.

The country was roiled by the assassinations of John F. Kennedy, his brother Bobby, Malcolm X, and Martin Luther King, Jr. The brutality of the Chicago Police Department against protesters outside the 1968 Democratic National Convention was broadcast for the world to see. And in 1970, soldiers from the Ohio National Guard fired on unarmed protesters at Kent State University, killing four students and wounding nine.

Needless to say, the boom-slump cycle inherent to capitalism continued during the prolonged postwar expansion. However, the downturns were relatively minor, and the upswings were undeniably strong, at least for capitalism. Wages tracked closely with rising GDP, which grew from $228 billion in 1945 to almost $1.7 trillion in 1975. During that same span, hourly compensation for most workers increased by 91%, not far off from the 97% increase in productivity.

This was the Golden Age of the American Dream. The bitter class battles that gave rise to industrial unionism in the 1930s receded into memory. To be sure, plenty of mass struggles punctuated this period. However, there was a material basis to the illusion that capitalism had resolved its contradictions. This mood infected millions, corroding the so-called left and softening up the unions. Instead of the class militancy that had won important concessions in the past, the labor leaders doubled down on class collaboration.

With rising wages, defined pensions, paid vacation, health care, sick leave, Medicare, Medicaid, and Social Security, it was all but taken for granted that every future generation would have it better than the one that came before. This all changed abruptly in 1973—except, of course, for the class collaboration of the labor leaders and the "left."

With the postwar reconstruction of Europe complete and the "booster" effect of wartime technological advances having run their course, capitalism began to settle back into its "normal" channels. Then, triggered by a sudden disruption to energy prices and supplies, the global economy entered a synchronized slump. The postwar boom was over.

On October 19, 1973, in protest of US imperialism's support for Israel during the Yom Kippur War, the Organization of Arab Petroleum Exporting Countries announced an embargo. By 1974, the price of oil had quadrupled from $3 to nearly $12, leading to fuel shortages and rationing. The US and other advanced Western economies were hit with stagflation, a combination of high inflation and unemployment and slow

21. Bethlehem Steelworks, 2018. Operations ceased in 1995.

economic growth. US GDP growth fell from a robust 5.65% in 1973 to -0.54% in 1974.

Based on the boom, certain concessions had been granted to certain layers of the class, keeping class unrest within manageable limits. Now, to remain competitive vis-à-vis their rivals, the bourgeois had no alternative but to claw back the gains won through workers' struggles in the past—a finished recipe for intensified social crisis and class war.

From 1973 to 2013, productivity increased by 74%, while inflation-adjusted hourly compensation for a typical worker rose by just 9%. Deindustrialization of the American economy began in earnest, with an avalanche of offshoring to countries with lower wages, abhorrent working conditions, and few environmental protections. In June 1979, US manufacturing employment reached an all-time peak of 19.6 million. By 2024, it was down to around 13 million, despite a 50% increase in the US population.

While the percentage of unionized American workers peaked in 1954, at 35%, the highest number of union members was in 1979, at 21 million. The smashing of the PATCO air traffic controllers' union in 1981 led to a decades-long reversal in organized labor's fortunes. From a unionization rate of 20.9% that year, it has fallen to just 10% in 2024.

Since lower wages translate into higher profits, attacking existing unions and preventing new ones from forming has been central to the bosses' all-but-one-sided class war ever since. On average, union members earn 10–20% more than non-union employees doing the same job. The discrepancy is so drastic that men who belong to a union their entire career may earn as much as $1.3 million more than those who never join one.

Cheap oil had been the lifeblood of the postwar boom. Now, it couldn't be taken for granted. Ensuring access to low-cost energy has shaped the domestic and foreign policy of virtually every country ever since. As it happens, the energy business is also highly profitable, with companies like Exxon Mobil raking in more profits than Walmart or Amazon.

The fall of the Soviet Union

The late 1970s and 1980s were the years of Carter, Reagan, Thatcher, and George Bush, Sr. Of Brezhnev, Andropov, Gorbachov, *glasnost*, and *perestroika*. The Cold War rhetoric ramped up and the arms race intensified. Then suddenly, everything was overshadowed by yet another dramatic turning point: the disintegration of the Eastern Bloc and the USSR.

Following the fall of the Berlin Wall in 1989, several Soviet republics declared their independence. The unraveling culminated with the Belavezha Accords of December 8, 1991, which declared that the Soviet Union had ceased to exist. On

22. Crowd standing on the Berlin Wall by the Brandenberg Gate before this section is torn down, 1989.

December 26, the Supreme Soviet formalized the dissolution of the USSR as a state and subject of international law.

For most of its existence, the Soviet Union was a million miles from being a healthy model for a harmonious human future. Nevertheless, despite its Stalinist disfigurement, the collapse of the first consolidated workers' state was a world-historic defeat for the working class.

The reasons for its ignominious collapse are complex and have been detailed at great length in countless articles and books by Leon Trotsky, Ted Grant, and Alan Woods. The short version is this: After decades of stagnation—brought about by bureaucratic mismanagement and the lack of workers' democracy—the system seized up and imploded. As Trotsky explained in his article, "Twenty Years of Stalinist Degeneration," written in 1938:

The incumbent government's tendencies are diametrically opposed to the program of Bolshevism. But inasmuch as the institutions erected by the revolution still continue to exist, the bureaucracy is compelled to externally adapt its tendencies to the old principles of Bolshevism: it continues to swear by the covenants of October; it invokes the interests of the proletariat and invariably refers to the Soviet system as Socialist. One may say without risking a blunder that in the history of mankind there has never been a government so given to lies and hypocrisy as the Soviet bureaucracy of today.

In and of itself the preservation of state ownership of the means of production is of enormous progressive significance, inasmuch as with the aid of planned economy this permits a swift development of the productive forces. True, the economic statistics issued by the bureaucracy do not merit any confidence: they systematically exaggerate successes while concealing failures. It is nonetheless unthinkable to deny the fact that even today the Soviet Union's productive forces are still developing at a tempo that was not and is not known in any other country in the world . . .

The development of the productive forces is the fundamental factor of human culture. Without increasing man's power over nature it is impossible even to think of destroying the rule of man over man. Socialism cannot be erected on backwardness and poverty. The technical premise of Socialism has taken an enormous forward step in the Soviet Union in the course of these twenty years.

However, least of all is this the merit of the bureaucracy. On the contrary, the ruling caste has become transformed into the greatest brake upon the development of the productive forces. Socialist economy must by its very essence take as its guide the interests of the producers and the needs of the consumers. These interests and needs can find their expression only through the medium of a full-flowering democracy of producers and consumers. Democracy, in this particular case, is not some sort of abstract principle. It is the

> one and only conceivable mechanism for preparing the Socialist system of economy, and realizing it in life.

Fast forward a few decades, and the bureaucracy was not only a brake upon the development of the Soviet Union's productive forces, it was an active agent for capitalist restoration. At stake were the enormous resources of the state, which would translate to spectacular wealth, power, and privileges for many of these wolves in sheeps' clothing. In other words, it had virtually nothing to do with the economic or military greatness of American capitalism.

As Max Boot explained in *Foreign Affairs*:

> One of the biggest such myths is that Reagan had a plan to bring down the "evil empire" and that it was his pressure that led to US victory in the Cold War. In reality, the end of the Cold War and the fall of the Soviet Union were primarily the work of Soviet leader Mikhail Gorbachev—two consequences of his radically reformist policies (the former intended, the latter unintended).
>
> Reagan deserves tremendous credit for understanding that Gorbachev was a different kind of communist leader, someone he could do business with and thereby negotiate a peaceful end to a 40-year conflict. But Reagan did not bring about Gorbachev's reforms, much less force the collapse of the Soviet Union. To imagine otherwise is to create dangerous and unrealistic expectations for what US policy toward China can achieve today.

The economic devastation wreaked by capitalist restoration was the equivalent of two world wars. Between 1989 and 1991, the Gross National Product in Soviet countries fell by 20%. In places like Yugoslavia, the breakup resulted in the revival of nationalist poison and fratricidal war. As late as the end of the 1990s, the GDP of countries like Armenia, Azerbaijan, Georgia, Moldova, and Tajikistan remained 30–50% below pre-collapse levels.

Income inequality skyrocketed, and life expectancy dropped precipitously, with death rates rising by 50%. Quality of life plummeted, and infectious diseases eradicated long ago reemerged. The highly educated inhabitants of a once-mighty power were stripped of their dignity and pride.

Russia's state was taken over by gangsters and the planned economy was privatized at fire-sale prices. A former KGB operative and consummate Bonapartist, Vladimir Putin, best reflected the interests of the new oligarchy. Against all odds, he has remained in power for over twenty years. Tapping into the deep sense of national humiliation, he has used his Machiavellian cunning to guide Russia's bumpy rebirth as an imperialist power. While pouring scorn on the legacy of Lenin and the Bolsheviks, he has evoked the alleged glory of the tsarist empire and revived the poison of Russian nationalism.

Despite its many warts, the USSR was a beacon of hope and inspiration for millions worldwide. After its fall, demoralization and confusion reigned in the workers' movement and beyond. The Western bourgeois strutted around like peacocks and rubbed their "victory" in everyone's faces.

The "neoconservative" ideologues, who had been worming their way through the Washington bureaucracy since the 1960s, gleefully seized the reins of US foreign policy. Fanatical belief in American exceptionalism and the superiority of "American values," aggressive military spending, meddling, intervention, and regime change were on the order of the day. As President Obama is alleged to have told his close advisors during a meeting in the Oval Office: "There is a bias in this town towards war."

Paralyzed by their internal sclerosis, the Soviets were forced to watch as an American-led coalition invaded Iraq in 1991. A testing ground for the latest in military technology, the Gulf War showcased the post-Vietnam renewal of the US military.

The Americans enjoyed absolute air supremacy, allowing them to systematically destroy Iraq's military infrastructure. After a months-long build up of troops and war materiel, the ground war against Saddam Hussein's forces lasted just 100 hours.

George Bush, Sr. was kind enough to explain his dystopian vision of American greatness to a joint session of Congress:

> Halfway around the world, we are engaged in a great struggle in the skies and on the seas and sands. We know why we're there: We are Americans, part of something larger than ourselves. For two centuries, we've done the hard work of freedom. And tonight, we lead the world in facing down a threat to decency and humanity.
>
> What is at stake is more than one small country; it is a big idea: a new world order, where diverse nations are drawn together in common cause to achieve the universal aspirations of mankind—peace and security, freedom, and the rule of law. Such is a world worthy of our struggle and worthy of our children's future.

The imperialist pummeling of Iraq wouldn't have happened in a thousand years if the USSR had been a healthy workers' state. Even in its degenerated form, the Soviet Union wouldn't have allowed this just a decade earlier.

The earth-shaking significance of the Soviet collapse and its aftermath cannot be overstated. It fundamentally shifted the balance of forces and gave Western imperialism a new lease on life. The cold and calculated restoration of capitalism in China by its bureaucracy accelerated after Tiananmen in 1989, opening additional vistas for capitalist exploitation and profit making. India, too, offered its vast population and resources to the magnates of world capital.

This was the heyday of "hyperglobalization." Total trade in goods and services rose from 39% to 61% of world GDP between 1990 and 2008. Western imperialism ran roughshod over the world and the "War on Terror" raged. As the petty-bourgeois ex-communist Martin Jacques bemoaned in *The Guardian* in 2006:

> In short, globalization has brought with it a new kind of western hubris—present in Europe in a relatively benign form, manifest in the US in the belligerent manner befitting a superpower: that western values and arrangements should be those of the world; that they are of universal application and merit. At the heart of globalization is a new kind of intolerance in the west towards other cultures, traditions and values, less brutal than in the era of colonialism, but more comprehensive and totalitarian.
>
> The idea that each culture is possessed of its own specific wisdom and characteristics, its own novelty and uniqueness, born of its own individual struggle over thousands of years to cope with nature and circumstance, has been drowned out by the hue and cry that the world is now one, that the western model—neoliberal markets, democracy and the rest—is the template for all.

To be sure, as always under capitalism, only a handful at the top benefited from the rearranged deck chairs. But the class war is far from over, and the accelerating inequality over the last 50 years has only set the stage for new social explosions and revolutions—including in the United States.

The West goes East

The North Atlantic Treaty Organization was formed in 1949 as an alliance for the collective defense of 12 Western European countries. A blatant fig leaf for US imperialism, it implanted the Americans in the heart of Europe, serving as a counterweight to the Soviet Union, and cutting across the potential for strategic unity across Eurasia. In response, the Warsaw Pact—which included the USSR, Albania, Bulgaria, Czechoslovakia, East Germany, Hungary, Poland, and Romania—was formed

23. Boris Yeltsin and Bill Clinton at a summit in 1995.

in 1955 to guarantee the security of the USSR and Eastern Europe.

With the collapse of Stalinism, the Warsaw Pact was formally dissolved on July 1, 1991. However, far from being disbanded once its original *raison d'être* had ceased to exist, NATO was not only maintained, it was expanded and converted into an offensive tool for imposing the Western imperialism's will.

In the immediate aftermath of their "victory" over the Soviets, the Americans held most of the cards. They could have brought the shell-shocked Russians into the fold as subordinates. The anti-communist hacks who had betrayed what remained of the October Revolution were all too willing to become "equal partners" with the American and European capitalists.

As Boris Yeltsin stated during a 1989 trip to the US: "Let's not talk about Communism. Communism was just an idea, just pie in the sky."

In exchange for allowing a reunified Germany to join NATO, the Americans promised the Russians the alliance would not expand eastward. A series of pacts and agreements were signed to facilitate communication and cooperation. Top US officials assured Russia that it would be "a key participant in the process of building new structures in Europe." With a forked tongue, Bill Clinton told Boris Yeltsin in 1994:

> I would like us to focus on the Partnership for Peace program so that we can achieve a united Europe where people respect each other's borders and work together.

Yeltsin—who led the counterrevolutionary charge for capitalist restoration—had deep illusions in peaceful coexistence with the West. As he naively wrote Clinton:

> There should exist a basic understanding that Russian-American partnership constitutes the central factor in world politics.

But the neocons truly believed they had defeated the "evil empire" fair and square, and they claimed the right of the conqueror to impose their terms on the conquered. As the Romans put it, *vae victis!*—woe to the vanquished!

Furthermore, Yeltsin deeply underestimated the depths of Western Russophobia—with or without the nationalized planned economy. As Gorbachev later said:

> The decision for the US and its allies to expand NATO into the East was decisively made in 1993. I called this a big mistake from the very beginning. It was definitely a violation of the spirit of the statements and assurances made to us in 1990.

The example of the Soviet Union's nationalized planned economy—which at the very least provided its inhabitants universal employment, housing, healthcare, education, and food—was anathema to US imperialism. Their number one objective was to dismantle the state-run economies of Russia and Eastern Europe. However, even with privatization well on its way, the Americans needed an excuse to stay in the region.

Given Germany's specific gravity and its role in two world wars, they sought to prevent it from reemerging as the region's hegemon if they withdrew their bodies of armed men.

They also wanted to ensure that Germany and Russia wouldn't draw closer together.

The EU, without Russia, it could handle. However, combined with Russia's 150 million inhabitants and near-limitless natural resources, it would pose a serious competitive threat. As we've seen, far from being an invention of the post-Soviet period, dividing and dominating Europe has been US imperialism's policy since before World War II. As Zbigniew Brzeziński frankly expressed it in 1997:

> It is imperative that no Eurasian challenger emerges, capable of dominating Eurasia and thus also of challenging America.

As charming as a crocodile, Clinton promised Yeltsin:

> NATO expansion is not anti-Russian; it's not intended to be exclusive of Russia and there is no imminent timetable.

Incredibly, the idea that Russia itself might one day join NATO was even floated. However, other, more sober representatives of US imperialism could see where things were headed. Jack F. Matlock, Jr., who served as US Ambassador to the Soviet Union in its final years, told the Senate Foreign Relations Committee in 1997:

> I consider the administration's recommendation to take new members into NATO at this time misguided. If it should be approved by the United States Senate, it may well go down in history as the most profound strategic blunder made since the end of the Cold War. Far from improving the security of the United States, its Allies, and the nations that wish to enter the Alliance,

24. Maidan protests, Kiev, 2014.

> it could well encourage a chain of events that could produce the most serious security threat to this nation since the Soviet Union collapsed.

George Kennan, who helped devise the Americans' Cold War policy of "containment," wrote in his diary against awakening in the Russians "the time-honored vision of Russia as the innocent object of the lusts of a wicked and heretical world environment." Weeks later, he noted that the NATO expansion project was a "colossal blunder" and "the greatest mistake of the entire post–Cold War period."

Nonetheless, NATO's mandate was broadened to include "crisis management and cooperative security operations." This was newspeak for military action in the former Soviet sphere of influence and beyond, including in Afghanistan, Libya, Somalia, and Yemen.

In 1999, Czechia, Hungary, and Poland joined the coalition. Kennan again warned:

> I see nothing in it other than a new Cold War, probably ending in a hot one, and the end of the effort to achieve a workable democracy in Russia. I see also a total, tragic and unnecessary end to an acceptable relationship of that country to the remainder of Europe.

That same year—just 12 days after bringing Hungary into the alliance—NATO launched a 78-day bombing campaign against Yugoslavia. This was yet another humiliating kick in the teeth to the Russians. US imperialism's disdain for China was also on full display when some of their precision-guided bombs "accidentally" hit the Chinese embassy in Belgrade.

In 2004, US imperialism stirred the pot further during the so-called Orange Revolution in Ukraine. Playing on the legitimate discontent of the masses, the ascent of pro-Western Viktor Yushchenko was orchestrated by the US State Department. Bringing countries like Estonia, Latvia, and Lithuania into NATO was one thing. But Ukraine was fundamentally different. Zbigniew Brzeziński understood this perfectly well:

> Ukraine, a new and important space on the Eurasian chessboard, is a geopolitical pivot because its very existence as an independent country helps to transform Russia. Without Ukraine, Russia ceases to be a Eurasian empire.

Eventually, NATO's incremental escalation reached a tipping point. In April 2008, NATO declared it was inviting Georgia and Ukraine into the alliance. That August, the Russians invaded and occupied parts of Georgia, sending a clear message that there were limits to what it would tolerate.

When Yuschenko's successor, Viktor Yanukovych, tried to maneuver Ukraine back toward Moscow, he was toppled with the open participation of neo-Nazi elements in the Euromaidan protests of 2014. The new regime started a civil war by banning the use of the Russian language and sending troops to attack the ethnic Russian majority living in the Donbas, where local militias declared the Donetsk People's Republic and the Luhansk People's Republic.

Putin responded by annexing Crimea, and the Russo-Ukrainian War began. In the years that followed, NATO militarized Ukraine in preparation for a more direct confrontation with the Russians. By the eve of the war, it had the second-largest military in Europe. In telescoped form, these are the events that led to the eventual full-scale invasion of Ukraine by Putin in February 2022.

During the Cuban Missile Crisis of 1962, the US had been willing to go to the brink of nuclear war to prevent Soviet missiles from being stationed 90 miles from the US border. And yet, many wonder why Ukraine's intent to join NATO—which would have led to Western bases and intercontinental ballistic missiles being stationed within range of Moscow—was a red line the Putin regime could never tolerate.

As of today, NATO has expanded to include 32 members, including 15 countries formerly allied with the Soviet Union, many of them directly on its border.

Imperialism Today: Dynamite in the Foundations

Pride goeth before destruction, and an haughty spirit before a fall.
– *The King James Bible*

The "War on Terror"

Voltaire once said that "with great power comes great responsibility." For the neocons, great power has meant great temptation and irresponsibility. US imperialism's bravado in the post-Soviet era knew no limits. But for every action, there is an equal and opposite reaction, and anger against its contemptuous arrogance was simmering worldwide.

Blowback from the Americans' efforts to undermine the Soviets in their ill-fated fight against Afghanistan's *mujahideen* led to the terrorist attacks of September 11, 2001. The audacious strike was masterminded by Osama Bin Laden, the leader of Al-Qaeda and son of a billionaire construction magnate from Saudi Arabia, formerly operating on behalf of US imperialism. The rise of anti-Western Islamic fundamentalism was precisely the pretext the neocon evangelists had been waiting for.

As George Kennan had written in 1984, even if the US succeeded in containing or toppling the USSR, they would need a new boogeyman to take its place:

> The habit of spending from two to three hundred billion dollars annually on preparations for an imagined war with Russia—a habit reaching deeply into the lives and interests of millions of our citizens both in and out of the armed services, including industrial workers, labor-union officials, politicians, legislators, and middlemen: This habit has risen to the status of a vast addiction of American society, an addiction whose overcoming would encounter the most intense resistance and take years to accomplish *even if the Soviet Union had in the meantime miraculously disappeared from the earth.*

The US ruling class has always had internal differences over how best to perpetuate their rule. The rise of the neocons—and the growing pushback against them—is a classic example.

In 1996, the neoconservative thinkers William Kristol and Robert Kagan wrote an article in *Foreign Affairs* titled, "Toward a Neo-Reaganite Foreign Policy." In it, they argued that conservatives needed a "more elevated vision of America's international role," one centered on "benevolent global hegemony." In 1997, they founded the Project for the New American Century (PNAC).

In its founding statement, PNAC committed to help "shape a new century favorable to American principles and interests," to promote "political and economic freedom abroad," and to "challenge regimes hostile to our interests and values." Of the twenty-five people who signed this document, ten went on to serve in GW Bush's administration. PNAC also advocated regime change in oil-rich Iraq—well before 9/11.

After Al-Qaeda's attack, the mood for national unity was overwhelming and GW Bush's lagging popularity rocketed to

91%. Despite campaigning as a noninterventionist during the 2000 election, he and his handlers launched an invasion of Afghanistan, allegedly for harboring Bin Laden. They ramped up the national security-surveillance state further by passing the Patriot Act and forming the Department of Homeland Security. As the president dramatically told the world: "Either you are with us, or you are with the terrorists."

The quick and easy victory over the Taliban further inflated the heads of neocons like Vice President Dick Cheney, Secretary of Defense Donald Rumsfeld, and Deputy Secretary of Defense Paul Wolfowitz. Companies closely connected to them, such as Halliburton and KBR, cashed in and made billions.

The "Axis of Evil" of Iraq, Iran, and North Korea was declared, and a longstanding plan to invade Iraq was set in motion. This time, the excuse was the spurious claim that Saddam Hussein—another former US ally—possessed "weapons of mass destruction." Never mind that Iraq had nothing to do with 9/11 and that Hussein had kept Al-Qaeda out of his country.

After 9/11, American flags were flying everywhere and all internal dissent was to be suppressed. And yet, despite the mass media's patriotic hysteria, only 53% of Americans supported the invasion. On February 15, 2003, up to 30 million people in over 600 cities worldwide took to the streets to protest the impending invasion. Hundreds of thousands joined the protests across major American cities.

But Mr. Bush and his cronies were going to have their war, come hell or high water. The Americans and their "coalition of the willing" unleashed "shock and awe" against the people of Iraq, and Hussein's regime was toppled with relative ease. Just weeks after the fall of Baghdad, GW Bush organized his

25. Car bombing in Iraq, 2005.

infamous "Mission Accomplished" photo op from the deck of the USS *Abraham Lincoln*.

The neocons thought they could do no wrong and imagined they could steamroll right through Syria, Iran, and beyond. As the *Wall Street Journal* commented at the time:

> As he sends American troops and planes into Iraq, President Bush has in mind more than changing a country. His dream is to make the entire Middle East a different place, and one safer for American interests. The vision is appealing.

But consolidating a puppet regime imposed from the outside is never easy. In reality, the Taliban had not been defeated; they had merely melted into the population. In Iraq, tens of thousands of bitter and now unemployed officers and soldiers had done the same. Incredibly, the possibility of a guerrilla insurgency had been discounted by the likes of Rumsfeld because, unlike Vietnam, Iraq lacks tropical rainforests. In their zeal to "export freedom and democracy," they had disregarded Robespierre's maxim that "nobody loves armed missionaries."

The US ended up bogged down in two unwinnable wars. It spilled blood and treasure for nearly a decade in Iraq and two decades in Afghanistan. Despite its overwhelming superiority on paper, it was again exposed as a colossus with feet of clay.

Between 2001 and 2019, The "War on Terror" extended to Iraq, Libya, the Philippines, Pakistan, Somalia, Syria, Sudan, and Yemen, costing American taxpayers over $8 trillion—not including future debt servicing. $160 billion was spent on private security contractors, i.e., mercenary outfits like Erik Prince's Blackwater. In addition, an estimated $2.5 trillion will be required just to care for the wars' veterans. In other words, American workers will be footing the bill for generations to come, with billions in interest enriching the owners of that debt.

Military realism and the madness of the neocons

American generals are often caricatured as rabid attack dogs. In Stanley Kubrick's film, "Dr. Strangelove," General Jack D. Ripper launches a nuclear attack on the Soviet Union, convinced that the Russians are conspiring to pollute Americans' "precious bodily fluids" through fluoridated water.

To prevent such scenarios, civilian control over the military has long been the tradition. It is the civilian leadership's prerogative to set policy and strategic objectives, while the military leaders merely offer their professional advice and execute orders. As explained in legalese by the Congressional Research Service:

> The Founding Fathers designed a system of civilian control of the military in a manner that conformed with the government's overall architecture of checks and balances. An elected President was designated the Commander-in-Chief of the nation's armed forces. This had the dual advantage of ensuring that an elected civilian leader presided over the nation's army while at the

> same time enhancing unity of command over the military. The President was also granted the ability to commission military officers, authority to appoint Secretaries to preside over military services, and the responsibility to regularly report to Congress on the state of the union.
>
> Federalist Papers 46 and 59 show that the Founding Fathers were also concerned about unitary executive control of the military. The desire to ensure that the military reflected, and was subordinate to, the will of the people therefore led to considerable congressional powers on matters concerning the armed services. These include the power to lay and collect taxes for the common defense, the sole power to declare war, the ability to raise and support armies, and the authority to establish rules and regulations for the army, navy, and militias when in service of the United States. To further strengthen civilian control of the military, a provision prohibited the appropriation of money for the army for a period longer than two years.

However, despite the inglorious experience of Iraq, Afghanistan, and now Ukraine, the Wall Street–backed hawks remain dominant in Washington. The fact that Harris was endorsed for president by over 700 current or former national security officials says everything about who she represents. Now that Trump and his MAGA maniacs are back in the White House, things could get very messy, very quickly, as a vicious power struggle over control of Washington breaks out.

Trump has referred to the military's generals as "woke," "weak," and "ineffective leaders." During his first term in office, he threatened to send active duty troops to quell the historic George Floyd protests. He has since said he would have no qualms invoking the Insurrection Act to go after critics and political opponents:

> I think the bigger problem are the people from within. We have some very bad people. We have some sick people, radical left lunatics. And I think it should be very easily handled by, if necessary, by National Guard or, if really necessary, by the military, because they can't let that happen.

Never mind the Posse Comitatus Act of 1878, which restricts using the military for civil law enforcement:

> Whoever, except in cases and under circumstances expressly authorized by the Constitution or Act of Congress, willfully uses any part of the Army, the Navy, the Marine Corps, the Air Force, or the Space Force as a posse comitatus or otherwise to execute the laws shall be fined under this title or imprisoned not more than two years, or both.

However, the Insurrection Act, first formulated in 1807, is full of loopholes that could be used to circumvent this later law. As it clearly states:

> Whenever the President considers that unlawful obstructions, combinations, or assemblages, or rebellion against the authority of the United States, make it impracticable to enforce the laws of the United States in any State by the ordinary course of judicial proceedings, he may call into Federal service such of the militia of any State, and use such of the armed forces, as he considers necessary to enforce those laws or to suppress the rebellion.

All of this has the Pentagon's 24,000 military and civilian employees in a tizzy. As reported by *CNN*:

> Officials are now gaming out various scenarios as they prepare for an overhaul of the Pentagon.
>
> "We are all preparing and planning for the worst-case scenario, but the reality is that we don't know how this is going to play out yet," one defense official said.

> Trump's election has also raised questions inside the Pentagon about what would happen if the president issued an unlawful order, particularly if his political appointees inside the department don't push back.
>
> "Troops are compelled by law to disobey unlawful orders," said another defense official. "But the question is what happens then—do we see resignations from senior military leaders? Or would they view that as abandoning their people?"

In other words, it is the Pentagon that today comes across as the voice of relative reason, at least from the perspective of the best interests of US imperialism. In particular, it is the career military professionals, the lieutenant colonels and colonels, who stand closer to the ranks and understand the strengths, weaknesses, capabilities, limitations, and proper use of military power. By contrast, most of the generals are divorced from reality and have to prove they have drunk the neocon Kool-Aid to earn their stars.

In the case of Ukraine, many mid-ranking officers and even some generals could see that the war was objectively lost after Zelensky's failed 2023 counteroffensive. However, despite having no military experience themselves, the neocons wouldn't listen and insisted that all-out victory was still possible.

Given its geographic placement and specific weight on the international arena, US imperialism has been able to weather many shocks that would have crumbled other societies. As a result, the neocons learn nothing and are never held accountable for their repeated disasters. Blithely confident in the superiority of American power, they cannot fathom that the Chinese, Russians, Indians, and Iranians cannot be bullied as they were in the past, nor that these powers may have a few cards up their sleeves. As a result, they stumble from one strategic error to another, often appearing to play checkers while their opponents play chess.

These are the people who threw ordinary Ukrainians to the wolves by sabotaging the 2014 Minsk agreements and Istanbul negotiations that could have provided a political solution to the conflict in early 2022. Instead, they egged the Ukrainians on, destabilizing the entire world, and by extension, accelerating their own demise. As Sophocles wrote in *Antigone*, "Evil appears as good in the minds of those whom god leads to destruction."

How much of the Washington, DC "swamp" Trump will manage to drain remains to be seen. While they have a terrible track record when it comes to winning actual wars, the neocons are formidable bureaucratic warriors. They will not give up their hard-won—and lucrative—positions without a fight.

They are also deeply intertwined with the ship of state as a whole. The vast bureaucratic machinery of the federal government has ensured remarkable continuity in domestic and foreign policy for decades, no matter who sits in the White House. Some have called it the "permanent state." Trump and his entourage have famously denounced it as the "deep state." And Barack Obama referred to it simply as "the blob."

This is the Gordian Knot that Elon Musk and Vivek Ramaswamy have been tasked with slicing. These and other Trump cabinet nominations and appointments are clearly intended as a battering ram to break "the swamp's" grip on the reins of federal power. The one common denominator they share is their "slavish fealty" to their benefactor, as one retired four-star general put it. However, theory and practice are not always the same thing.

Even if the old guard is roundly defeated, the only thing Trump can replace them with is more scum. Neither the neocons nor the MAGA crowd have the interests of the world's workers at heart. Both are rabid defenders of American imperialism, differing only on how best they can do it. Neither can square the circle of the contradictions inherent to their system.

This is an extremely contradictory situation with many moving parts. But no matter how it all plays out, the laws of economic and political gravity apply to everyone and everything. What goes up must eventually come down and bullies always get their comeuppance. And as everyone knows—the bigger they are, the harder they fall.

America's Asia problem

For millennia, Asia was the wealthiest expanse of the terrestrial globe. Overflowing with people and resources, it was the crown jewel of human civilization and culture.

During the three-century reign of the Northern Song Dynasty (960–1279 CE), China was the wealthiest place on Earth, as measured by GDP per capita. When Western merchants first encountered the Middle Kingdom, there was little of interest they could offer its rulers other than gold. As Alex von Tunzelman wrote in the poignant introduction to her book on Partition, *Indian Summer*:

> In the beginning, there were two nations. One was a vast, mighty, and magnificent empire, brilliantly organized and culturally unified, which dominated a massive swath of the Earth. The other was an undeveloped, semi-feudal realm, riven by religious factionalism and barely able to feed its illiterate, diseased, and stinking masses. The first nation was India. The second was England. The year was 1577.

As late as 1820, Asia still accounted for around 60% of world economic production. By the end of World War II, after decades of colonial exploitation and devastation, it was reduced to just 20%.

Maintaining America's postwar predominance in the Indo-Pacific region has been central to US foreign policy ever since. George Kennan understood the stakes and put it bluntly in an influential Cold War policy paper drafted in 1948. It is worth quoting at length, as it clearly outlines the American capitalists' "US perspectives" for this critical part of the world:

> Furthermore, we have about 50% of the world's wealth but only 6.3% of its population. This disparity is particularly great as between ourselves and the peoples of Asia. In this situation, we cannot fail to be the object of envy and resentment.
>
> Our real task in the coming period is to devise a pattern of relationships which will permit us to maintain this position of disparity without positive detriment to our national security. To do so, we will have to dispense with all sentimentality and day-dreaming, and our attention will have to be concentrated everywhere on our immediate national objectives. We need not deceive ourselves that we can afford today the luxury of altruism and world-benefaction.
>
> For these reasons, we must observe great restraint in our attitude toward the Far Eastern areas. The peoples of Asia and of the Pacific area are going to go ahead, whatever we do, with the development of their political forms and mutual interrelationships in their own way. This process cannot be a liberal or peaceful one. The greatest of the Asiatic peoples—the Chinese and the Indians—have not yet even made a beginning at the solution of the basic demographic problem involved in the relationship between their food supply and their birth rate. Until they find some solution to this problem, further hunger, distress, and violence are inevitable.
>
> All of the Asiatic peoples are faced with the necessity for evolving new forms of life to conform to the impact of modern technology. This process of adaptation will also be long and violent. It is not only possible but probable that in the course of this process,

> many peoples will fall, for varying periods, under the influence of Moscow, whose ideology has a greater lure for such peoples and probably greater reality than anything we could oppose to it. All this, too, is probably unavoidable, and we could not hope to combat it without the diversion of a far greater portion of our national effort than our people would ever willingly concede to such a purpose.
>
> In the face of this situation, we would be better off to dispense now with a number of the concepts which have underlined our thinking with regard to the Far East. We should dispense with the aspiration to "be liked" or to be regarded as the repository of a high-minded international altruism. We should stop putting ourselves in the position of being our brothers' keepers and refrain from offering moral and ideological advice. We should cease to talk about vague and—for the Far East—unreal objectives such as human rights, the raising of the living standards, and democratization. The day is not far off when we are going to have to deal in straight power concepts. The less we are then hampered by idealistic slogans, the better.
>
> We should recognize that our influence in the Far Eastern area in the coming period is going to be primarily military and economic. We should make a careful study to see what parts of the Pacific and Far Eastern world are absolutely vital to our security, and we should concentrate our policy on seeing to it that those areas remain in hands which we can control or rely on. It is my own guess, on the basis of such study as we have given the problem so far, that Japan and the Philippines will be found to be the cornerstones of such a Pacific security system and that if we can contrive to retain effective control over these areas, there can be no serious threat to our security from the East within our time.

But all of this is much easier said than done. Everything changes, as the following figures show:

- Asia's share of world GDP is now approaching 50%—precisely where the US stood in 1945.
- Today, with 4.25% of the world population, the US accounts for around 26% of world GDP—still extremely high per capita, but it represents a significant fall as compared to the past.
- For its part, China had 20% of the world's population in 1950 but just 5% of the world's GDP. Today, it has 17.4% of the population, and accounts for around 18% of GDP.
- In 1980, India's share of world GDP was a mere 1.7%, while the UK's was 5.4%. Today, India's contribution has risen to 3.6%, while the UK's has fallen to 3.2%.
- India and China have a combined population of 2.8 billion, more than a third of the world total.

While not everything can be reduced to GDP percentages and demographics, the above graphically illustrates Asia's rise and the relative decline of what many refer to as the collective West.

The sleeping giant

Trotsky was a master of both short- and long-term perspectives. He predicted that, just as the Atlantic world had once eclipsed the Mediterranean, the center of gravity of world history would eventually shift to the Pacific. He has been proven 100% correct.

In many books and articles, we have detailed the lengthy process that led to capitalism's reemergence as the dominant mode of production in China. In essence, the deformed workers' state and core sectors of the planned economy, inherited from the 1949 revolution, served as a springboard for the relatively cold restoration of capitalism by the bureaucracy. This, in turn, allowed it to develop into a powerful imperialist country over the last 20 years.

The "reform and opening up" of the country, initiated by Deng Xiaoping in 1978, led to a torrent of Western investment, starting with specific sectors and special economic zones. This accelerated after the crushing of the Tiananmen Square movement in 1989, and by 2001, China was a member of the World Trade Organization.

For decades, Western capitalists saw China as a near-infinite pool of cheap labor, a giant *maquiladora* that could assemble Western goods and undercut competitors. By doing business in China, they could evade the tangle of labor and environmental regulations that hampered them in their own countries.

However, as Lenin explained, the export of capital breeds capitalism in the countries where it is exported. After transferring their industrial base to China to maximize profits in the short term, the American imperialists bluster indignantly now that China has developed an advanced economy of its own.

Napoleon Bonaparte, who knew a thing or two about political, military, and economic power, is alleged to have said, "Let China sleep, for when she wakes, she will shake the world."

Two hundred years later, China is no longer sleeping and is not merely producing cheap plastic toys. It now accounts for 31.6% of global manufacturing output, while the US sits at 15.9%. China is a major market and a source of outbound investment in its own right. Its oral care market alone is estimated at around $10 billion, with its auto market worth over $500 billion. By 2030, it is expected to have a billion consumers.

The US still has the world's largest economy when measured by raw GDP. However, when measured by Purchasing Power Parity, China's economy passed the US in 2014, and is now roughly 25% larger. Purchasing Power Parity adjusts for the

26. Chinese goods arrive in Miami, 2006.

differences in price levels by comparing the cost of a "basket" of essential goods and services in different countries.

As for FDI and the export of capital, China is now in second place, with $4.9 trillion in outlays, behind the US, with $8 trillion. It is now Africa's biggest trading partner and source of FDI, edging out both France and the US.

A look at the world's top ten companies by revenue further underlines the dramatic changes seen over the last twenty years. Walmart is first, and the Saudi oil giant Aramco is second. Then comes China's State Grid, the largest electrical utility in the world. Then Amazon, followed by two Chinese oil giants, China National Petroleum and Sinopec. After these are ExxonMobil, Apple, Shell, and United Health Group. In other words, the top ten includes five American companies, three Chinese, one Saudi, and one British-Dutch.

As for the all-important banking sector, the five largest banks in the world by market capitalization are JPMorgan & Chase,

Bank of America, Industrial and Commercial Bank of China, Wells Fargo, and China Construction Bank—three American and two Chinese.

And when banks are ranked by their assets, the top four are Chinese, and the fifth is Japanese. This is not what the world looked like in 1945 or even 2005. In fact, in 2005, the top five banks by assets were all European: one Swiss, one British, one German, and two French.

According to market analyst Standard and Poor's, Chinese banks already account for over a third of all assets held by the largest banks on the planet. Four of the 15 biggest companies in China are banks. The combined holdings of all Chinese banks reached $58.54 trillion by the end of 2023—more than double the total for American banks.

And that's not all. As everyone knows, Artificial Intelligence, 5G, quantum computing, and electric vehicles are the future, and whoever dominates these industries will have a significant competitive advantage on the economic and military fronts. As *Foreign Affairs* noted, China is aggressively positioning itself to:

> Dominate new technologies, exploit US dependencies, and export its excess industrial capacity to put competitors out of business.

Its "Made in China 2025" plan, announced in 2015, aimed to reduce dependence on imports of core materials to transform China into a high-tech manufacturing powerhouse within a decade. By all accounts, the plan has achieved its goals, with nearly $2 trillion invested to develop ten key sectors including information technology, robotics and automated machine tools, aerospace and aviation equipment, maritime engineering equipment and high-tech vessels, advanced rail transportation equipment, new energy vehicles, power generation and transmission equipment, agricultural machinery and equipment, new materials, biopharmaceuticals, and high-performance medical devices.

Or take the company BYD, whose early efforts to build electric vehicles was mocked by Elon Musk. It has now overtaken Tesla as the world's top seller of EVs. Its new hybrid cars cost half the price and can drive twice as far on a single tank of gas as its top competitor in that category, Toyota. BYD has already surpassed Volkswagen as the top seller of cars in China, the world's largest automobile market. Flowing from this and the Germans' disastrous policy in Ukraine, the iconic company may be forced to shutter plants and lay off thousands of workers in its home country for the first time in its history.

By 2030, Chinese automakers are expected to expand well beyond their home market to achieve 33% global automotive market share. And while the US sends tens of billions of dollars to Ukraine and Israel, China has announced a $47.5 billion investment in its semiconductor industry. It aims to become the world leader by 2030, putting Nvidia's dominance under imminent threat. This also raises the stakes around Taiwan, which currently produces nearly 90% of the world's most advanced chips.

Or take an old-school industry like shipping. In 1975, the US shipbuilding industry was ranked number one in global capacity. Fifty years later, the US produces less than 1% of the world's commercial vessels and has dropped to 19th place globally.

Meanwhile, China has tripled its production relative to the US over the past two decades, producing over 1,000 oceangoing ships last year, versus just 10 in the US. This has enormous implications beyond commercial shipping. More than 90% of military equipment, supplies, and fuel travels by sea, the vast majority on contracted commercial cargo vessels.

Then there are the rare earth elements, essential for producing magnets, batteries, phosphors, and catalysts. Although large amounts have recently been discovered in Wyoming, China has the world's largest known reserves of these 17 strategic minerals. According to the neocon Brookings Institution, China currently produces roughly 60% of the world's rare earth elements and processes 85% of them.

All of this, of course, has been possible only due to the brutal exploitation of the Chinese working class. It is the workers of China who are the real "sleeping giant" that will one day shake the world. In the meantime, the strategists of US imperialism are right to be worried.

Competitive pressure and the "Pivot to Asia"

All countries, and especially the major powers, strive to export not only capital, but also crisis, unemployment, class struggle, and social unrest. If fewer profits can be made abroad, more must be squeezed out of the domestic population. Faced with an increasingly competitive world, Trump's "America first" policy aims to achieve precisely this. Instead of being forced to make US workers pay in full for the crisis of capitalism, he wants everyone else to pay their share. Starting with the Chinese, of course, but also the Europeans and anyone else he thinks is getting a "free ride."

American politicians of all stripes are under pressure not to lose more American manufacturing jobs, two million of which succumbed in the early 2000s to the so-called "China shock. They accuse China of not playing "fair," of ruining American industry and stealing jobs. Again, so much for the myth of free trade and competition.

Many in the Rust Belt blame the Democrats specifically for deindustrialization, a sentiment Trump tapped into with his calls for "economic nationalism." As a result, millions of workers have been duped into thinking of the Republicans as the "party of the working class."

This is a perfect example of how the national and the international, the economic and the political, are interconnected, and there can be no decoupling of economies or social contradictions under capitalism. Just as you can't build socialism within the borders of the nation-state, you can't have capitalism in one country.

Since national interests ultimately trump partisan politics, Joe Biden not only maintained but expanded the protectionist measures of his predecessor. Seeking to prop up US producers under Chinese pressure—while also striking blows at Europe—he intensified Trump-era tariffs, export controls, tax incentives, and grants to high-tech manufacturers. This essential continuity in policy led some to refer to it as "MAGA for thinking people."

The pressure is also growing in China. With world capitalism careening towards another massive crisis, there is a desperate struggle for markets, spheres of influence, and raw materials. Like hyenas circling a carcass, the big imperialists must dance around each other, as both collaborators and rivals, maneuvering to get the upper hand.

They must play this risky game without breaching the limits of tolerance. That is, without crossing any "red lines" that could push them into open confrontation and war. As Eisenhower's Secretary of State, John Foster Dulles once said, "The ability to get to the verge without getting into the war is the necessary art." After decades of hyperpower arrogance, the American art of diplomacy is in a parlous state—and it's not always clear where the red lines are.

As it happens, China has the world's largest military, with over two million active-duty troops. It also has increasingly sophisticated weaponry, including hypersonic missiles, hundreds of nuclear weapons, and at least one nuclear aircraft carrier, something only the US and France can match.

US imperialism still has the edge in total naval tonnage—3.6 million versus just over two million—but the Chinese Navy has more individual ships. And while the US fleet is spread around the planet, China's are primarily concentrated in the Pacific. That being said, the US has been a true maritime power for over two centuries, and the Chinese lack the operational experience needed to coordinate large-sale naval maneuvers—for now.

Officially, China has only one military base abroad, in Djibouti. But it is actively seeking access elsewhere—including in Cuba. To this end, it has aggressively occupied and militarized a series of barren islands and reefs in the South and East China Seas, and even built new ones, leading to tensions and territorial disputes with everyone from Vietnam to the Philippines, Malaysia, and Brunei. Following its "nine dash line," it claims roughly 90% of the South China Sea, extending hundreds of miles south and east from China's Hainan province. This is, in effect, a Chinese version of the Monroe Doctrine.

The Senkaku Islands in the East China Sea, controlled by the Japanese but claimed by China, are also particularly contentious.

The changing balance of power has led Japan to gradually remilitarize after being almost entirely disarmed after World War II. In 2014, Japan reinterpreted its pacifist constitution—the one drafted by Douglas MacArthur—to allow for "collective self-defense." It now spends around $50 billion annually on "defense" and is investing in advanced military technologies, including missile defense systems and stealth fighters.

The Chinese have taken another page out of America's postwar playbook. They now own or operate ports and terminals at over 100 locations in over 50 countries as part of its Maritime Silk Road, the oceanic component of its Belt and Road Initiative. This was the name given to its global infrastructure development strategy, launched in 2013.

The aim is to connect Asia with Africa and Europe via land and maritime networks, enhancing regional integration, increasing trade, and stimulating economic growth. It does so through the export of capital, labor, and IMF-style loans to host countries, which end up indebted to the Chinese state. They have also actively projected "soft power" by sending over 600,000 aid workers to nearly 170 countries and international organizations. This is all part of what Robert Blackwill has termed China's "Grand Strategy" to supplant the US and dominate the Indo-Pacific world.

Even the US mainland has been targeted, and not only through Huawei and TikTok. Through its shipping conglomerate, Cosco, China operates terminals at several key US ports, including Los Angeles, Long Beach, Seattle, Houston, and Miami. It has also made significant inroads into Asia and Africa, not to mention the US's "backyard" of Latin America. Responding to critics of a massive new port being built by the Chinese at Chancay, Peru's transport minister, Raúl Pérez-Reyes explained:

> In this case it is an investment of Chinese capital, but it is exactly the same as if it were British or North American capital... in no case is our sovereignty lost.

It was in this rapidly shifting context that Barack Obama billed himself as "America's first Pacific president" and announced the "Pivot to Asia" in 2011. Over his two terms in office, he made 15 trips to East Asia, far more than any other president. After focusing on Europe and the Middle East for decades, the aim was to turn US imperialism's diplomatic and military attention to the Asia-Pacific region.

Concretely, the plan called for increasing America's military presence in the region, strengthening bilateral security alliances with countries like Japan, South Korea, and the Philippines, drawing powers like India closer, and expanding trade and investment through initiatives like the Trans-Pacific Partnership.

The TPP was a proposed trade agreement between 12 Pacific Rim countries, including the US, Japan, Malaysia, Vietnam, Singapore, Brunei, Australia, New Zealand, Canada, Mexico, Chile, and Peru. Notably absent from this list is the most important Pacific power of all, China. After seven years of negotiations, the TPP was finally signed in February 2016—only to be scuttled by Trump when he took office in January 2017. As a result, US imperialism has lost considerable momentum when it comes reestablishing its presence in the region, and many of these countries have since drawn closer to China.

In the final analysis, "economic nationalism" and concerns over "national security" come down to economic competition, and military tensions are merely an extension of this. The reason both the Republicans and Democrats agree on the need to "contain" China is simple: It is now the Chinese capitalists who are "battering down walls" worldwide with the support of their state—and they are gearing up to do even more.

As *Foreign Affairs* summarized an official US government document on National Security Strategy:

> [China is] the only state with the intent to reshape the international order and the economic, diplomatic, military, and technological power to do so.

And in the words of Lee Kuan Yew, the former prime minister of Singapore:

> Why not? They have transformed a poor society through an economic miracle to become the second-largest economy in the world—on track, as Goldman Sachs has predicted, to become the world's largest economy.
>
> They have followed the American lead in putting people in space and shooting down satellites with missiles. Theirs is a culture 4,000 years old with 1.3 billion people, many of great talent—a huge and very talented pool to draw from. How could they not aspire to be number one in Asia and, in time, the world?
>
> It is China's intention to be the greatest power in the world.

In 2020, Robert Blackwill argued for an American "Grand Strategy" to contain China:

> The United States has just entered the fourth phase of its relationship with China since the end of World War II.
>
> In phase one, Mao Zedong's decision to go to war with the United States in Korea in 1950 produced a long period of antagonistic interaction.
>
> Phase two saw Richard M. Nixon and Henry Kissinger open up the relationship to better meet the global Soviet threat and, they hoped, help end the Vietnam War on honorable terms.
>
> In phase three, Washington sought to bring Beijing ever more into the international system, hoping it would eventually become a "responsible stakeholder" and accede to US-fashioned rules of domestic and international order.
>
> Now, in phase four, the United States is beginning to fully digest the aggressive elements of Chinese power projection and take initial actions to deal with it . . .

27. Mao Zedong with Henry Kissinger and Gerald Ford, 1975.

> It was not inevitable that the US-China relationship would evolve into its current adversarial standoff. If Washington, through careful and consistent diplomacy in coordination with its Asian and European allies, had routinely contested Beijing's aggressive policies much earlier, China, then weaker, could have pulled back, and a rough equilibrium could have been established and maintained, with major areas of cooperation.
>
> And if Beijing instead had continued on that confrontational path, Washington would have been in a stronger position to respond than it is at present. But the Chinese leadership, faced with successively acquiescent US administrations that miscalculated China's strategic objectives, went on pushing until it finally provoked the current rhetorical Thermidorian reaction from the United States.

Disentangling from Europe and the Middle East has been complicated, and US imperialism's attention has been divided, to say the least. As Nietzsche said, however, "Forgetting our objectives is the most frequent of all acts of stupidity."

Judging from his picks for various positions in his administration, rectifying this loss of focus will be a major priority of Trump's second term. He has surrounded himself largely with anti-China, anti-Iran, pro-Israel hardliners, who are only slightly softer on Russia. But China is clearly marked as the main geopolitical threat.

The US has not really had a comprehensive national security strategy since the end of the Cold War. As one analyst put it, it has busied itself playing whack-a-mole with terrorists and other non-state actors around the planet.

It is, therefore, not an accident that he has revived the slogan "peace through strength." This is a tried-and-true foreign policy outlook adopted by leaders from Hadrian to Ronald Reagan. As the ancient Romans used to say, *si vis pacem, para bellum*—if you want peace, prepare for war. And as George Washington put it in his 1793 State of the Union Address:

> There is a rank due to the United States among nations which will be withheld, if not absolutely lost, by the reputation of weakness. If we desire to avoid insult, we must be able to repel it; if we desire to secure peace, one of the most powerful instruments of our rising prosperity, it must be known that we are at all times ready for war.

Trump wants to negotiate a "better deal" for American imperialism by basing himself on a powerful military that can intimidate and deter its core adversaries through the threat of overwhelming force—instead of trying to police the entire world. There has been more than a little "mission creep" over the decades, and As Frederick the Great once said, "He who defends everything defends nothing."

However, this is a recipe for a next-level, worldwide arms race and the production of trillions of dollars of expensive scrap metal—money that won't be going to improve the daily lives of the majority.

Regardless of how everything shakes out in Washington, the horse of Chinese imperialism has already bolted the stable. They have been patiently watching and waiting, swooping in to capitalize on American screwups and shortsightedness. After being carved up by the Western imperialists during the "Century of Humiliation," beginning with the First Opium War of 1839, they know all too well what happens to weak countries. If the Americans are not already playing catch-up with them in the Indo-Pacific region, they may well be in the not too distant future. As the American Enterprise Institute wrote in August 2023:

> While the United States still enjoys advantages over China in many key fields of national security competition, recent trends illustrate that American military dominance is stagnating and China is rapidly catching up.
>
> China is successfully leveraging asymmetric structural advantages, such as its authoritarian military-civil fusion and geographical position in the Indo-Pacific, to rapidly reach parity with or exceed the United States' military capabilities.
>
> Further complacency about these issues will only ensure that Chinese capabilities surpass those of the United States sooner than expected.

Wars of attrition and the military-industrial balance

For several decades, US military doctrine was based on the "two-war construct." That is, it was prepared to wage two major wars in two major theaters against two major rivals, for example, against Russia in Europe and China in Asia. That's no longer the case. In the early 2010s, the Pentagon had to formally acknowledge that one major war is all it can handle.

Even then, we've seen how careful they've been not to get into it directly with Russia in Ukraine. Not only would it be a bloody and unpopular mess, it would seriously degrade their ability to confront China over Taiwan—and they might not be able to win.

Back in 2022, however, their confidence was high. Thinking the Russians would be pushovers, US imperialism deliberately goaded Ukraine into picking a fight with its much larger neighbor. The purpose of this was clear: to bring down Putin, or at the very least, to take Russia—and, if possible, also Germany—off the great-power game board. Given the stakes, the Russians couldn't afford to blink.

Biden stated unambiguously that Putin "cannot remain in power." US Secretary of Defense Lloyd Austin said, "We want to see Russia weakened to the degree that it can't do the kinds of things that it has done in invading Ukraine." And Britain's then–Prime Minister, Boris Johnson, bluntly asserted that Russia "must fail and be seen to fail." As always, these creatures were happy to fight to the last drop of their proxies' blood, while committing no combat troops of their own.

But sending weapons to Ukraine was only one part of the plan. Crippling the Russian economy was the other. As President Biden announced on February 24, 2022:

> Today, I'm authorizing additional strong sanctions and new limitations on what can be exported to Russia. This is going to impose severe costs on the Russian economy, both immediately and over time. We have purposefully designed these sanctions to maximize the long-term impact on Russia and to minimize the impact on the United States and our Allies . . .

> It will so weaken his country that he'll have to make a very, very difficult choices of whether to continue to move toward being a second-rate power or, in fact, respond (sic) . . . The sanctions we imposed exceed anything that's ever been done . . . They are profound sanctions. Let's have a conversation in another month or so to see if they're working.

To be sure, it wasn't clear at first how Russia's economy would respond to this pressure, how its population would react, or whether its military would recover from its early missteps. However, nearly three years into the conflict, it is evident that US imperialism lost the bet—bigly. John McCain was woefully wrong when he described Russia as a "gas station masquerading as a country," and predicted its imminent collapse. Despite pouring in billions of dollars and committing a significant portion of its military resources, Western imperialism's aggression has boomeranged back on them.

Far from provoking regime change in Moscow, it is they who are increasingly isolated on a world scale. "World public opinion" used to be a synonym for "Western public opinion." Today, 85% of the world lives in countries that have not imposed sanctions on Russia.Putin has weathered the storm. Not only has Russia militarily defeated Ukraine, it has struck a significant blow against the entire West. With support from China, Iran, and North Korea, Russia has successfully retooled its economy to grind out a classical war of attrition against the combined resources of Western imperialism.

As a former adviser to Russia's Central Bank correctly observed, in a perfect synthesis of Lenin and Clausewitz: "Wars of attrition are won by economics." It's not by chance that Putin replaced his longtime Minister of Defense, Sergei Shoigu, with a civilian economist, Andrei Belousov.

Career military professionals in the West understand this as well—and they are increasingly concerned about where things are headed. The Royal United Services Institute, which describes itself as "an independent think tank engaged in cutting-edge research on defense, security and international affairs," recently produced a paper titled, "The Attritional Art of War: Lessons from the Russian War on Ukraine." It is worth quoting at length:

> Attritional wars require their own "Art of War" and are fought with a "force-centric" approach, unlike wars of maneuver which are "terrain-focused." They are rooted in massive industrial capacity to enable the replacement of losses, geographical depth to absorb a series of defeats, and technological conditions that prevent rapid ground movement.
>
> In attritional wars, military operations are shaped by a state's ability to replace losses and generate new formations, not tactical and operational maneuvers. The side that accepts the attritional nature of war and focuses on destroying enemy forces rather than gaining terrain is most likely to win.
>
> The West is not prepared for this kind of war. To most Western experts, attritional strategy is counterintuitive. Historically, the West preferred the short "winner takes all" clash of professional armies. Recent war games such as CSIS's war over Taiwan covered one month of fighting. The possibility that the war would go on never entered the discussion.
>
> This is a reflection of a common Western attitude. Wars of attrition are treated as exceptions, something to be avoided at all costs and generally products of leaders' ineptitude. Unfortunately, wars between near-peer powers are likely to be attritional, thanks to a large pool of resources available to replace initial losses. The attritional nature of combat, including the erosion of professionalism due to casualties, levels the battlefield no matter which army started with better trained forces.

As conflict drags on, the war is won by economies, not armies. States that grasp this and fight such a war via an attritional strategy aimed at exhausting enemy resources while preserving their own are more likely to win. The fastest way to lose a war of attrition is to focus on maneuver, expending valuable resources on near-term territorial objectives. Recognizing that wars of attrition have their own art is vital to winning them without sustaining crippling losses.

Wars of attrition are won by economies enabling mass mobilization of militaries via their industrial sectors. Armies expand rapidly during such a conflict, requiring massive quantities of armored vehicles, drones, electronic products, and other combat equipment. Because high-end weaponry is very complex to manufacture and consumes vast resources, a high-low mixture of forces and weapons is imperative in order to win.

High-end weapons have exceptional performance but are difficult to manufacture, especially when needed to arm a rapidly mobilized army subjected to a high rate of attrition. For example, during the Second World War, German Panzers were superb tanks, but using approximately the same production resources, the Soviets rolled out eight T-34s for every German Panzer. The difference in performance did not justify the numerical disparity in production. High-end weapons also require high-end troops. These take significant time to train—time which is unavailable in a war with high attrition rates.

It is easier and faster to produce large numbers of cheap weapons and munitions, especially if their subcomponents are interchangeable with civilian goods, ensuring mass quantity without the expansion of production lines. New recruits also absorb simpler weapons faster, allowing rapid generation of new formations or the reconstitution of existing ones.

> Achieving mass is difficult for higher-end Western economies. To achieve hyper-efficiency, they shed excess capacity and struggle to rapidly expand, especially since lower-tier industries have been transferred abroad for economic reasons.
>
> During war, global supply chains are disrupted and subcomponents can no longer be secured. Added to this conundrum is the lack of a skilled workforce with experience in a particular industry. These skills are acquired over decades, and once an industry is shuttered it takes decades to rebuild. The 2018 US government interagency report on US industrial capacity highlighted these problems. The bottom line is that the West must take a hard look at ensuring peacetime excess capacity in its military industrial complex, or risk losing the next war.

Just as Germany managed to rebuild after the calamitous Treaty of Versailles, it was all but inevitable that a country the size of Russia would do the same after the disaster of capitalist restoration. And just as the attritional American Civil War transformed the US into a mighty military-industrial machine, Russia has emerged as the greatest industrial and military power in Western Eurasia. According to both the World Bank and IMF, Russia is now the fourth-largest economy in the world, having surpassed everyone except the US, China, and India. Although they have had to raise interest rates to combat inflation, the Russian government is projected to spend 32.5% of its 2025 federal budget on military spending, a record amount, up from 28.3% in 2024.

Even before the Ukraine War, Russia had a significant military industry—the one key sector that wasn't privatized after the fall of the USSR. Russia ranked second in the world for arms and military equipment exports, with agreements on military and technical cooperation with 85 countries. Now, all of that and more has been harnessed for its "special military operation" to assert control over the regions of Donetsk,

Luhansk, Kherson, and Zaporizhzhia, which it now considers an integral part of Russia.

Russia's military-industrial complex includes some 6,000 companies and employs around 3.8 million people, accounting for roughly 20% of the country's manufacturing jobs. Production costs are one-tenth of what they are in the West—another legacy of the Soviet planned economy.

Russia now manufactures seven times as much ammunition and three times as many artillery shells as all NATO nations combined—an astonishing 250,000 artillery shells *every single month*. It has doubled its annual tank production and tripled rocket production since early 2022. By the end of 2024, Russia was producing 4,000 drones daily—a ten-fold increase over a single year. Furthermore, it has achieved this without having to impose austerity. In fact, as of late 2024, real wages were keeping up with inflation and unemployment was at a record low of 2.4%—far lower than in the US.

For a dramatic counterexample, look no further than Europe's long-time industrial powerhouse, Germany. By all accounts, it will take until 2066 to get the German military's stocks of armaments and equipment back to pre-Ukraine War levels. Meanwhile, the Russians have ramped up production to such a degree that they could stock the entire *Bundeswehr*, from top to bottom, in just six months.

While the situation facing Germany is extreme, US imperialism will also require many years and billions of public dollars to replenish its reserves—and the arms manufacturers are licking their chops. As the Heritage Foundation advised in February 2024:

> Since the end of the Cold War, the US has not bought and built enough munitions to keep pace with the military operations the President and Congress have tasked the Department of Defense with conducting. In 2014, the US discovered that it lacked enough

> precision-guided missiles to take on a non-state actor, ISIS, in a limited campaign.
>
> The problem persists as the effort to arm Ukraine has dangerously depleted America's stores of artillery shells. This deficiency in munitions planning weakens America's warfighting capability, endangering its ability to fight future wars. It is vital that the US remedy this deficiency by increasing munitions spending, coordinating with allies, shoring up industry, and doing a better job of husbanding resources.

In the article, "Overstretched and undersupplied: Can the US afford its global security blanket?" the *New Atlanticist* opined:

> In recent decades, US foreign policy has been beset by visions of the United States ensuring security throughout much of the world, but with little thought to the resources or resolve required or the second-order consequences . . .
>
> While maintaining regional stability across the globe is critical to US defense and national security objectives, simultaneously supplying major arms packages to Israel and Ukraine, at a time when the United States needs to prepare for the possibility of armed conflict with China, will stretch production lines and resources beyond sustainable limits, potentially jeopardizing all US-supported efforts.

Deindustrialization has its consequences. In 1960, the industrial sector contributed 25% of US GDP. It has since fallen to 18.9%. Compare this to Russia's 26.6% and China's even more impressive 38.3%.

So while Russian armaments manufacturers can now produce hundreds of air defense missiles every month, Lockheed Martin expects to produce just 650 Patriot air defense missiles a year by 2027. At $4 million a pop, this is sure to satisfy investors. But it is far from what is needed to meet the demands already imposed by the wars in Ukraine and the Middle East. Wars, it must be said, that are not absolutely essential to US imperialism's core interests.

In short, the war in Ukraine has exposed the limitations of Western power. Even at its postwar height, US imperialism could not impose its will unilaterally; it is absurd to think it can do so now.

Economically and politically unprepared for both peace and war

In the final analysis, every major war, from antiquity to the modern age, has been decided by the military-industrial balance and logistics. Maintaining supply lines and mobilizing labor and resources to support those fighting on the front lines is every bit as important as getting the troops recruited, trained, equipped, and in the field in the first place. As the military adage says, "an army marches on its stomach." And as Eisenhower once noted:

> You will not find it difficult to prove that battles, campaigns, and even wars have been won or lost primarily because of logistics.

As of 2023, manufacturing accounted for a mere 10.1% of nonfarm business sector employment in the US, down from 31% in 1970.

Trump may think it's merely a matter of disrupting the status quo in Washington, but even he can't snap his fingers and take the country back to the postwar boom. That ship has sailed. He may be a force of nature, but the nation-state and market economy are even greater forces. The DC bureaucracy has tremendous inertia on its side and will put up ferocious resistance, despite his efforts to "shock and awe" them into granting concessions.

Even if the US does manage to reindustrialize to some degree, given the tremendous advances in technology and the relentless cutting of corners, it won't bring back the millions of highly paid jobs that sector provided in the past. These are still private companies, after all, and they must satisfy shareholders with maximum profits, which isn't always possible in the US. What is more, those jobs only paid what they did because of the momentous organizing struggles of the 1930s and 40s—and we should anticipate even more massive class struggles in the not-too-distant future.

As we've seen, in the longstanding tradition of military conflict driving innovation, the Ukraine War has pushed the Russians to develop sophisticated, battle-tested technologies, some of which may even surpass the Americans' best, particularly when it comes to drones, precision-guided bombs, electronic warfare, stealth aircraft, and defensive countermeasures.

Accustomed to absolute air superiority in every war fought since World War II, US imperialism would not be in such a privileged position in a direct confrontation with China or Russia. Even Iran, which now has a comprehensive strategic partnership with Russia, would pose plenty of problems. Israel's vaunted "Iron Dome" has already been penetrated by drones and missiles launched by Iran and Hezbollah, a case study in how seemingly invincible technologies can become antiquated virtually overnight.

Furthermore, by giving the Ukrainians access to American weapons systems piecemeal, they have allowed the Russians to develop effective countermeasures one by one instead of having to face them down all at once. They claim it only takes them about six weeks to develop effective counters to new tactics or military hardware once those are introduced on the battlefield. One after another, every "game-changing" weapon system given by US imperialism to Ukraine has failed to have any meaningful impact on the course of the war. More than that, the most expensive military in the world has proved to be among the least effective.

Compounding the economic and logistical problems US imperialism faces is a political one. Following the disastrous adventures in Iraq and Afghanistan, public enthusiasm for the neocons' "forever wars" has plummeted. This allowed Trump to cash in as the "anti-war" candidate with the campaign slogan: "no more stupid wars." In another example of the intimate foreign-domestic policy connection, most if not all of the 206 "pivot counties" that propelled him to power in 2016 had higher than average casualty rates in the "War on Terror." Every one of those counties had opted for Obama in 2008 and 2012.

Not only would US imperialism be hard pressed to put large numbers of boots on the ground almost anywhere in the world, but the military is mired in a severe recruitment crisis. Unfortunately for the neocons, fighting wars requires more than generals and fancy weapons systems. You also need willing troops, whether volunteers or conscripts. The Army, Navy, and Air Force all failed to recruit enough servicemembers in 2023. The Army missed its 2023 target by 10,000 soldiers, a 20% shortfall.

In the aftermath of Vietnam, the draft via the Selective Service System was ended and an all-volunteer military was established. But the "backdoor draft" has taken its place. Today's military remains disproportionately proletarian, poor, Black, and Latino, especially among enlisted personnel, as soldiers sign up out of economic necessity.

The US military looms large in the American consciousness, and almost everyone has at least one relative or acquaintance who has served or is on active duty. It has long been the most popular institution of bourgeois rule. However, it, too, has experienced a statistically significant drop in public confidence, from 90% in 2021 to 81% in 2023. More worryingly, from the military's perspective, only 9% of 16-to-21-year-olds say they would consider joining.

And yet, some deluded souls in Washington think the US should have a *three-theater strategy* to fight simultaneous wars in Asia, Europe, and the Middle East. This is a ridiculous fantasy. As the top Republican Senator on the Armed Services Committee wrote in the *New York Times*, "America's Military Is Not Prepared for War—or Peace."

Let's not forget what happened in Afghanistan. After spending $2.3 trillion and sending as many as 100,000 troops at a time, US imperialism was forced into a humiliating withdrawal. This was the longest war ever waged by US imperialism. And although they claimed to have learned the lessons of Vietnam, everything collapsed overnight as the Taliban rolled back into Kabul.

The hard truth facing US imperialism is that, while it remains the greatest military power on the planet as a whole, it is not necessarily the greatest power in every region. Furthermore, having power on paper is very different from being able to use it in practice. Long gone are the days when the US could respond to every crisis by sending in the Marines. This has far-reaching repercussions.

Just look at countries like Israel, Turkey, Saudi Arabia, or even tiny Qatar, formerly pliable proxies of US imperialism, all aggressively pursuing their interests and ignoring Washington when it suits them. They are like little gangsters trying to get away with as much as possible without getting into too much trouble with the padrone. In fact, in the cases of Ukraine and Israel, it has often been *they* who determine US policy, rather than the other way around.

It is also a question of confidence. With so many zigzags in the White House and State Department, how can any country be sure there will be continuity in US foreign policy? After the Ukraine debacle, can Taiwan, the Philippines, Indonesia, or even Japan and Australia be 100% sure the US will be able to defend them if things heat up with China? As things currently stand, the US military would quickly run out of air defense missiles, artillery shells, and ammunition, let alone troops.

As we've seen, in the pursuit of short-term gains, the Western imperialists accelerated the development of Chinese manufacturing. As a result, the military-industrial balance has shifted dramatically towards China and, to some degree, Russia.

In the article, "China Is Ready for War," published in *Foreign Affairs*, Seth Jones of the Defense and Security Department at the Center for Strategic and International Studies comments:

> Indeed, China is rapidly developing and producing weapons systems designed to deter the United States and, if deterrence fails, to emerge victorious in a great-power war. China has already caught up to the United States in its ability to produce weapons at mass and scale. In some areas, China now leads: it has become the world's largest shipbuilder by far, with a capacity roughly 230 times as large as that of the United States.
>
> Between 2021 and early 2024, China's defense industrial base produced more than 400 modern fighter aircraft and 20 large warships, doubled the country's nuclear warhead inventory and more than doubled its inventory of ballistic and cruise missiles, and developed a new stealth bomber. Over the same period, China increased its number of satellite launches by 50%.
>
> China now acquires weapons systems at a pace five to six times as fast as the United States. Admiral John Aquilino, the former commander of the US Indo-Pacific Command, has described this

> military expansion as "the most extensive and rapid buildup since World War II."
>
> China is now a military heavyweight, and the US defense industrial base is failing to keep up.

As detailed above, the war in Ukraine catalyzed big advances in Russia's military capability. However, China's potential to ramp up production if it were compelled to go on a war footing like the Russians is even more breathtaking. Its industrial capacity is so vast that analysts estimate that it could produce as many as 10,000 cruise missiles per week—roughly the equivalent of the entire US arsenal. While this may well be an exaggeration, it is probably not too far off the mark.

And yet, the neocons wallow in denial, and Trump thinks he can simply bulldoze, bluff, or tariff his way out of the hole.

We will touch on perspectives for Trump's second administration further down. But it's worth noting that Trump's hardline approach the first time around only pushed many countries further into the arms of Beijing. The Chinese saw his deliberate disengagement with the world as an opportunity to encroach even further on US spheres of influence. When Trump pulled the US out of the Trans-Pacific Partnership trade pact, China intensified its efforts to dominate the region's economies.

Already, China's diplomatic stature has risen. For example, it played a crucial role in brokering a deal between Iran and Saudi Arabia to restore diplomatic ties and reactivate a 2001 security cooperation agreement. They achieved this while completely bypassing the US—something that would have been unthinkable even a decade ago.

"Multipolarity" and the changing world order

Water will always seek its level, and as the US and its allies have retreated, others have moved in to fill the gap.

The US is no longer a "hyperpower," China and India are no longer backward semicolonies, and Russia is no longer on its knees. It is only natural that the ruling classes of these countries want power and prestige commensurate with their rising influence on the world stage. The treaties and systems of the past reflect an outdated balance of forces and must be burst asunder—one way or another. In their view, a new equilibrium must be set. In short, the so-called collective West is no longer the only sheriff in town.

In 1994, at the height of what some have called "the unipolar moment," Henry Kissinger wrote:

> None of the most important countries which must build a new world order have had any experience with the multi-state system that is emerging. Never before has a new world order had to be assembled from so many different perceptions, or on so global a scale. Nor has any previous order had to combine the attributes of the historic balance-of-power system with global democratic opinion and the exploding technology of the contemporary period.

For thirty years, countries large and small dreamed of a new world system that could counterbalance the Americans' dominance. However, far from being truly "multipolar," the economies of scale and stakes are such that the world is coalescing into two great imperialist blocs.

On the one side are the US, most of Europe, Canada, Australia, Japan, and South Korea; on the other, China, Russia, and Iran. Meanwhile, countries like India, Brazil, Indonesia, South Africa, and Saudi Arabia are trying to split the difference. Countries like Australia are between a rock and a hard place. In recent years, they have tried to play both sides—leaning towards the US for security and towards China for economics—but that kind of a balancing act can't be sustained indefinitely, since security ultimately flows from economics.

After decades of accumulated contradictions, the Ukraine War served as an accelerator for this reconfiguration. In this sense, it was a Hegelian accident expressing a deeper necessity. As described above, in the years following the Soviet collapse, the Russian oligarchs tried to reach an accommodation with the US. Once they did the dirty work of restoring capitalism, they thought they deserved a seat at the table. After all, Russia is the largest country in Europe.

Instead, they were shunned, humiliated, and kept out in the cold. They failed to understand that what the Western imperialists wanted was not a "partner," but unrestrained access to the country's extensive natural resources and labor.

The Chinese bureaucracy also tried to integrate into the Western-dominated system of trade and finance. But as its economy grew, so did its power, and it was increasingly viewed as a threat to be "contained." Starting in the mid-2010s, the US essentially copied its Cold War blueprint for Russia and applied it to China. However, by the 1980s, the Soviet Union was a deformed and dysfunctional workers' state—China in the 2010s was no such thing.

In *The Grand Chessboard: American Primacy and its Geostrategic Imperatives,* Zbigniew Brzeziński warned against the consequences of poking the bear and the dragon once too often:

> A coalition allying Russia with both China and Iran can develop only if the United States is shortsighted enough to antagonize China and Iran simultaneously.

Subsequent events have shown just how shortsighted the neocons have been.

Given their size, history, and 2,600 miles of shared border, China and Russia maintained a respectful distance from each other for decades. However, when confronted with the insufferable arrogance of the Americans, drawing closer eventually became a no-brainer. According to the Council on Foreign Relations:

> China and Russia are not formal treaty allies and are not bound to come to the other's defense. Nevertheless, their emerging strategic partnership has caused alarm in Washington. During a state visit to Stockholm, Sweden in September 2023, US House Foreign Affairs Committee Chairman Michael McCaul (R-TX) called the burgeoning China-Russia security alliance the most "large-scale" threat that Europe and the Pacific have faced since World War II. At a meeting in February 2022, days before Russia invaded Ukraine, Chinese President Xi Jinping and Russian President Vladimir Putin said their partnership has "no limits" and vowed to deepen cooperation on various fronts.

In recent years, the Russians have provided the Chinese with important technical and military assistance, along with access to their huge reserves of natural resources. But it is the Russians who are more dependent on the relationship, given the disparity between their economies. For example, in 2023, 90% of Russia's micro-electronics imports came from China, which it uses to produce missiles, tanks, and aircraft. And as reported in the *New York Times*:

> Russia now depends on China for trucks, drones and other supplies for the war, and has become less of a counterweight to China in struggles for regional influence. As ties have warmed between the two countries, even including many joint military exercises lately in the Sea of Japan and elsewhere, Moscow has been giving more diplomatic support to Chinese projects, notably on the short Russian border with North Korea.

As will be explained below, this growing closeness culminated in the agreements made at the October 2024 summit of the BRICS countries, hosted by the Russians in Kazan.

But first, let us be clear. Far from celebrating "multipolarity" in the abstract, Marxists understand that both of these emerging camps are based on the exploitation, oppression, and rapacity that accompanies all imperialism.

For revolutionary communists, there is no "lesser evil" when it comes to the major and minor imperialist powers. We oppose them all, on a class basis, whether they be American, French, Russian, Chinese, or anything in between. As many countries have already found out, it makes little difference whether your debt repayments are due to the Americans or the Chinese.

The rise of BRICS and the decline of the EU

One example of China's multipronged strategy to counter the specific weight of US imperialism and its allies is the Shanghai Cooperation Organization, founded in 2001. Intended to facilitate security and economic cooperation in the region, its members now include China, Russia, India, Pakistan, and several Central Asian countries.

However, the most significant threat to continued Western dominance worldwide is the evolution of BRICS, which intends to supplant what remains of the 1944 Bretton Woods agreement by the victorious World War II imperialist powers for the postwar capitalist world order—including the IMF.

The acronym "BRIC"—standing for Brazil, Russia, India, China—was first coined by Goldman Sachs economist Jim O'Neill as a shorthand for the economies that could, in his view, dominate the global economy by 2050. At the 2006 meeting of the UN General Assembly, informal discussions to explore greater cooperation between these nations were initiated. In 2009, the first BRICS summit was held in Yekaterinburg,

Russia. In 2011, South Africa joined the formation, thus adding the "S."

The emerging bloc now includes Saudi Arabia, Iran, the UAE, Egypt, and Ethiopia, and accounts for over 37% of world GDP and 45% of the world population. With the EU now generating just 15% of world GDP, even NATO-member Turkey has applied to join, as it can see that its interests lie more in the resurgent East than in the declining West. As for the G7 countries—the US, Canada, France, Germany, Italy, Japan, the UK—their share of world GDP is projected to drop to 27% by 2029.

With others like Algeria, Azerbaijan, and possibly Pakistan, Nigeria, Uganda, and Bolivia also jumping on the bandwagon, its gravitational pull in world economic and diplomatic affairs continues to grow. Throughout history, profits, science, technology, and culture have followed in the wake of trade. As it contributes roughly 60% of the grouping's total GDP, China is by far the heavyweight in what is now becoming known as BRICS+.

BRICS+ provided Russia with an essential lifeline in the face of Western sanctions over Ukraine. As a result, after some initial disruptions, it was business as usual for the Russian economy. Imports and exports of arms, fuel, essential commodities, and even luxury goods have continued almost as if nothing happened. However, instead of coming from the US, Germany, or France, they are produced in China or India, or are acquired on the booming black market, which by some estimates may account for as much as 30% of world GDP.

Western sanctions have served only to push Russia and China closer economically and militarily, while undermining economic and political stability in Western Europe. According to the former chief of the European Central Bank, Mario

Draghi, Europe faces an "existential" crisis. As reported by the *New York Times:*

> If Europe cannot effectively compete and, in turn, provide its people with security and prosperity, [Draghi] said, "it will have lost its reason for being."

The European bourgeois once dreamed of "superpower Europe." Instead, there has been a dramatic realignment and they and the British have been brought fully to heel by US imperialism.

The truth is always concrete. In 1960, at the height of the postwar boom, the 28 countries currently in the EU accounted for more than a third of the world's GDP. In 1980, its share remained high, at 29.8%. But by 2023, it had fallen to 14.5%. And by 2100, it is expected to account for just one-tenth of world economic activity, according to a forecast by the Pardee Center of the University of Denver.

As they become increasingly irrelevant, the Europeans will be sidelined as US imperialism is compelled to focus on the heavy hitters of the new world order: China, India, and Russia.

The nation-state and the market economy, integral to the capitalist mode of production, are the main fetters to generalized human progress. In a vain attempt to work around this, the EU was conceived to aggregate Europe's atomized economies, peoples, and political systems into a semi-centralized semi-state with standard rules, open internal borders, and, for most, a common currency. This was the only way they could hope to compete globally with the continental populations, resources, and economies of the US, China, Russia, and India.

However, without a fully centralized economy, political system, and military, the EU is a Frankenstein's monster that can't escape its inherent contradictions. On their own, the European states cannot compete with the big players. But being tied into knots by the EU bureaucracy in Brussels only gums things up in other ways. All of this has been exacerbated by the neocon liberals' disastrous commitment to bringing Ukraine fully into the EU and NATO fold.

The reality is that for the imperialists, countries like Ukraine are seen as disposable. As we've seen, Ukraine was pushed into the line of fire to further the interests of the NATO neocons. Far from gaining greater security and "democracy," Ukraine may well end up reduced to a dysfunctional rump state, or be dissolved altogether. Like the good comprador he is, Zelensky has offered Ukraine up as a Western colony in all but name. So much for the sacred right of nations to self-determination that the West claims to defend.

The Europeans have fallen into mutual recriminations over the impasse of their failed experiments. The crisis is especially acute in Germany, which for decades based its industrial strategy on cheap energy from Russia. Things have gotten so bad that they joined Austria, France, Denmark, and others in imposing border controls—so much for the Schengen border-free zone. If the largest economy in the EU can't keep up, the entire project will unravel. Given the revolutionary traditions of the European proletariat, this must keep policymakers in Brussels up at night.

And yet, the EU, and Germany in particular, could have pursued a different course. Had they followed the *realpolitik* approach of their not-too-distant past, the Germans would have ruthlessly prioritized their national interests over liberal ideological or abstract moral concerns. Even though they share a continent with Russia and China, which should facilitate organic cooperation, they felt compelled instead to follow orders from their big brother across the pond. By sacrificing their industrial base in a vain attempt to topple Putin, they cut off their nose to spite their face. They even turned a blind eye to the Ukrainians' sabotage of the Nord Stream pipeline, which has accelerated what will be a painful process of deindustrialization.

While the Ukraine War has been a total disaster in almost every respect, the Americans at least succeeded in breaking the Russian-German connection. Europe is now effectively an economic and military vassal of the US. It is more dependent on US imperialism for its security than ever, as it can't possibly contend with the massive Russian military machine that has been built up on its Eastern border.

As for the UK, they used to say that "the sun never sets on the British Empire." The sun has most definitely set on it now. The British bourgeois used to measure their plans for world domination in decades and even centuries. Now, they cannot even see as far ahead as next week.

Once upon a time, they were treated as near equals and had a "special relationship" with the US. Today, Britain is no longer "Great" and has been reduced to an insignificant collection of islands at the edge of world power, and its leaders are viewed with contempt by their American masters.

When the knives come out, it's every imperialist for himself, and even former world powers are treated like mere pawns by Washington. As Henry Kissinger once told Nixon, "It may be dangerous to be America's enemy, but to be America's friend is fatal."

Trump 2.0 and the future of world relations

Much is up in the air as this book goes to press, so the content in this section is highly conditional out of necessity. Nonetheless, it is worth outlining some broad-stroke perspectives for world relations in the coming period.

To begin, we must understand that "America first" economic nationalism is a de facto recognition that US-dominated

28. President Trump meets with NATO Secretary Jens Stoltenberg, 2019.

globalization has reached its limits. However, isolationism is no solution either. Trump's efforts to have the best of both worlds will only introduce new instability and convulsions into the system.

Now that he has secured a second term in the White House, all bets are off when it comes to American engagement with the alliance system that has defined its foreign policy since the end of World War II. Let's not forget that in his initial response to Russia's 2022 invasion of Ukraine, Trump said: "This is genius. Oh, that's wonderful . . . You gotta say that's pretty savvy."

He has since said that if NATO members don't pay what he considers to be their "fair share," he would encourage the Russians to do "whatever the hell they want" to them. In 2017, Fox News's Bill O'Reilly informed the president that "Putin is a killer," to which Trump answered, "You think we're so innocent?"

And as he told a Michigan crowd during his last week on the 2024 campaign trail: "In many cases, our allies are worse than our so-called enemies."

His pick for National Security Advisor, Mike Waltz, is a China hawk and the first Green Beret elected to Congress. Following in the spirit of Trump's first-term complaints, Waltz has repeated that when it comes to strategic alliances, Americans have had to foot "the bill for far too long . . . It's time for allies to invest in their own security."

Trump has made similar complaints about Taiwan, telling Bloomberg Businessweek that "Taiwan should pay us for defense . . . [The US is] no different than an insurance company."

To be sure, there is an essential continuity in US foreign policy, regardless of who is in power. And that is to prevent any serious strategic rivals from emerging. But there's more than one way to skin a cat. Although it may seem counterintuitive at first, when it comes to the long-term interests of American imperialism, Trump may actually have a more realistic foreign policy than the neocons who have dominated Washington for decades. He may be unpredictable, impulsive, and mercurial, but as Shakespeare's Polonius put it, "Though this be madness, yet there is method in't."

A master of political psychology, Machiavelli observed that it can be "a very wise thing to simulate madness." Richard Nixon was an enthusiastic advocate of this approach. According to his chief of staff, H.R. Haldeman, Nixon once told him:

> I call it the Madman Theory, Bob. I want the North Vietnamese to believe I've reached the point where I might do anything to stop the war. We'll just slip the word to them that, "for God's sake, you know Nixon is obsessed about communism. We can't restrain him when he's angry—and he has his hand on the nuclear button"

and Ho Chi Minh himself will be in Paris in two days begging for peace.

Of course, things didn't work out particularly well for Nixon, but it remains a recognized negotiating technique. According to the *Journal of Experimental Social Psychology*:

> Usually people don't like uncertainty, so when the recipient sees that you are behaving in an unpredictable way, they feel that they're not in control of what is happening in the negotiation.

Despite his many failures, Trump is a businessman, pragmatist, and gangster at heart. He has a hypertransactional approach to everything he does, and especially if it boosts his personal brand. After having his wings clipped due to his first-term inexperience, he has nothing but scorn for neocon ideologues like John Bolton. And compared to last time, he will have even fewer guardrails to prevent him from following his instincts.

Trump's *modus operandi* is to bully and bluster—starting with his handshake—to intimidate his opponents into caving to his demands. Like Nixon, Trump thinks that by overwhelming his opponents and threatening Armageddon, they will find it reasonable to accept a 70/30 split instead of the 90/10 they thought was coming.

For a classic example of this technique, look no further than his dealings with nuclear-armed North Korea. After threatening "little rocket man" with "fire and fury" in 2017, it was all smiles and embraces when he actually met Kim Jong-Un the following year. As Trump explained in his inimitable way:

> I was really being tough—and so was he. And we would go back and forth. And then we fell in love, okay? No, really—he wrote me beautiful letters, and they're great letters.

Already, there are reports that Trump advisers are assuring Wall Street that his threatened 60% tariffs on Chinese goods is more of a negotiation tactic than a serious plan.

A true "America first" policy would mean turning US imperialism's back on the "Old World" of Europe, and to some degree, the Middle East. Only this can allow it to pivot fully towards Asia. To this end, he may try to come to mafia-like agreements with certain leaders, allowing them to do as they please on "their" turf—as long as they pay their respects to the Godfather. This was essentially his relationship with Putin, Netanyahu, Modi, and the Saudis during his first term.

However, making deals in business is not at all the same as making deals in international relations. Driving hard and imposing terms instead of negotiating in good faith can backfire and lead to lasting distrust and resentment. Trump's foreign policy advisors may also have a hard time abandoning pet obsessions like Iran and Israel in favor of a focus on the Far East.

If he follows in his predecessors' footsteps and lets the neocon tail keep wagging the dog, his administration may well get bogged down somewhere unanticipated, making things even worse for the US ruling class in the long run. It also remains to be seen how much his domestic battles will distract him from attending to foreign policy.

Most importantly, the US is no longer the only game in town. The balance of geopolitical forces has changed significantly since 2020 and the world's major powers are fully aware of how Trump operates.

After being double-crossed yet again by the Americans during the Biden years, the Russians are in no rush to reestablish relations. With the rise of BRICS+ they don't need to accommodate the Americans unless it is on their own terms.

Russia is a true great power, and as long as imperialism rules the world, its national interests will always trump those of small nations like Ukraine. Putin's terms are nonnegotiable and clear: Recognition that the four Donbas regions plus Crimea are now part of Russia; the demilitarization of Ukraine and a permanent ban on NATO membership; full rights and protections for Ukraine's ethnic Russian minority.

The neocons and Europeans have boxed themselves into a corner by insisting that the only acceptable outcome is total capitulation by the Russians, or better yet, regime change. Zelensky even signed a decree ruling out negotiations as long as Putin remains in power. But the Russians hold all the cards in this situation, and it is Zelensky who may be shown the door in the near term. After years of merciless missile and drone strikes, Ukraine's economy and energy grid are on life support, and its military cannot hold out indefinitely.

The Russians don't trust and don't need a negotiated diplomatic solution involving Western imperialism to secure their southwestern border. Freezing the conflict in place without a decisive resolution will no longer suffice. Given the geography of the Eurasian steppe, ensuring Ukraine is a friendly or at least neutral buffer state is an existential question for Moscow. Since multiple rounds of negotiations over nearly two decades failed to achieve this, they have concluded that only a military solution can do the trick.

Biden's decision to authorize Ukrainian long-range strikes into Russia—a clear "red line" tantamount to an act of war, since ATACM missiles can only be fired with US technical assistance—will only muddy the waters further. Russia is the largest country on the planet, has the world's most sophisticated air defense system, and its most valuable assets are safely beyond where these missiles can reach. The Pentagon was against the decision for good reason, and everyone acknowledges that such strikes cannot alter the war's eventual outcome.

In other words, this was clearly a "f*ck you" parting gift from Biden to his successor, a not-so-subtle thank you for saddling him with the disastrous withdrawal from Afghanistan. The implications of this fateful decision will be worldwide and wide-ranging.

In response, Russia successfully tested a new intermediate-range ballistic missile, hitting a Ukrainian missile factory in Dniepro—a clear signal of what it is capable of doing to Western assets worldwide. The Oreshnik is a multi-warhead, hypersonic weapon flying at Mach 10—an incredible 7,000 miles per hour. As such, it cannot be stopped by any existing air defense systems. In a televised speech just hours later, Putin made it forcefully clear that the Russians are not bluffing:

> The escalation of the conflict in Ukraine, instigated by the West, continues with the United States and its NATO allies previously announcing that they authorize the use of their long-range high-precision weapons for strikes inside the Russian Federation. Experts are well aware, and the Russian side has repeatedly highlighted it, that the use of such weapons is not possible without the direct involvement of military experts from the manufacturing nations.
>
> On November 19, six ATACMS tactical ballistic missiles produced by the United States, and on November 21, during a combined missile assault involving British Storm Shadow systems and HIMARS systems produced by the US, attacked military facilities inside the Russian Federation in the Bryansk and Kursk regions. From that point onward, as we have repeatedly emphasized in prior communications, the regional conflict in Ukraine provoked by the West has assumed elements of a global nature. Our air defense systems successfully counteracted these incursions, preventing the enemy from achieving their apparent objectives . . .

I wish to underscore once again that the use by the enemy of such weapons cannot affect the course of combat operations in the special military operation zone. Our forces are making successful advances along the entire line of contact, and all objectives we have set will be accomplished . . .

We believe that the United States made a mistake by unilaterally destroying the [Intermediate-Range Nuclear Forces] Treaty in 2019 under far-fetched pretext. Today, the United States is not only producing such equipment, but, as we can see, it has worked out ways to deploy its advanced missile systems to different regions of the world, including Europe, during training exercises for its troops. Moreover, in the course of these exercises, they are conducting training for using them.

As a reminder, Russia has voluntarily and unilaterally committed not to deploy intermediate-range and shorter-range missiles until US weapons of this kind appear in any region of the world.

To reiterate, we are conducting combat tests of the Oreshnik missile system in response to NATO's aggressive actions against Russia. Our decision on further deployment of intermediate-range and shorter-range missiles will depend on the actions of the United States and its satellites.

We will determine the targets during further tests of our advanced missile systems based on the threats to the security of the Russian Federation. We consider ourselves entitled to use our weapons against military facilities of those countries that allow the use of their weapons against our facilities, and in case of an escalation of aggressive actions, we will respond decisively and in mirror-like manner . . .

I would like to emphasize once again that it was not Russia, but the United States that destroyed the international security system and, by continuing to fight, cling to its hegemony, they are pushing the whole world into a global conflict.

> We have always preferred and are ready now to resolve all disputes by peaceful means. But we are also ready for any turn of events. If anyone still doubts this, make no mistake: there will always be a response.

All things considered, the Russians were relatively calm, cool, and collected in their response to this new escalation. Trump's transition team signaled their anger at Biden's reckless decision and made it clear they were willing to discuss with the Russians. However, Putin is under increasing domestic pressure to respond aggressively to the constant provocations. Contrary to how he's portrayed in the American media, he is actually on the moderate side of the Russian political spectrum.

Despite everything, after Trump's reelection, Putin made it clear that he was open to negotiations. True to his tough guy persona, he praised Trump for his conduct after the first assassination attempt:

> He behaved, in my opinion, in a very correct way, courageously, like a real man. I take this opportunity to congratulate him on his election.

As for US-Chinese relations, things are even more complicated as there is far more overlap in their core interests and spheres of influence. Whether Trump likes it or not, the US and Chinese economies are highly interdependent. Here are just a few examples:

- Between 2000 and 2024, China's ownership of US Treasury debt grew from $105.6 billion to $749.0 billion, second only to Japan's holdings.
- Between January and November 2023, US exports to China totalled $135.8 billion, with imports of $393.1.

- That same year, Chinese companies invested $28.04 billion in American companies, while US firms invested $126.91 billion in China.
- As for the three most valuable companies in the US, roughly 95% of Apple's products, and 70% of Amazon and Walmart's products are made in China.

Trump may want an "economic divorce," but decoupling the US and Chinese economies would be messy, to say the least.

To be sure, Trump has surrounded himself with plenty of anti-China hawks. However, even this doesn't necessarily mean an all-out trade war is imminent—though it is a slippery slope that could quickly get out of control. To give just one example of the many contradictions at the heart of his inner circle, *Financial Review* reports:

> Tesla's Shanghai Gigafactory—which accounts for almost 23% of the company's overall revenue—was built with significant support from Chinese authorities, including expedited permits and loans from state banks, as well as tax breaks.

And if Trump does follow through with draconian tariffs, it could have unintended consequences. As Engels explained:

> Protection is at best an endless screw, and you never know when you have done with it. By protecting one industry, you directly or indirectly hurt all others, and have therefore to protect them too. By so doing you again damage the industry that you first protected, and have to compensate it; but this compensation reacts, as before, on all other trades, and entitles them to redress, and so on *ad infinitum*.

To be clear, as Marxists, we are neither for nor against free trade or protectionism in the abstract. We are for revolutionary internationalism and an end to all national borders. But it is important to be aware of the contradictions faced by the imperialists as they try to have their cake and eat it too.

Just as the pressure of Western sanctions stimulated big changes in the Russian economy, raising barriers to the US market might do the same for the Chinese economy, even if it causes some initial discomfort. It would force them to focus on developing their domestic and regional markets, instead of relying on the US and Europe. As reported by *Nikkei Asia*:

> Former US President Donald Trump's pending return to office has fueled a major rally among semiconductor stocks in China, with tougher American policies seen accelerating Beijing's push to bolster its domestic chip industry.
>
> China's CSI Semiconductor Index gained for six straight sessions through the Monday following the Nov. 5 American presidential election, won by Trump. The index has risen 26% since the beginning of the year, outperforming the 12% increase in the broader Shanghai Composite Index and the 20% gain in the Philadelphia Semiconductor Index, or Sox, which tracks major US–listed shares in the field.

Already in 2023, the ten ASEAN member countries overtook the US as China's most important export market. Furthermore, there is no guarantee that production of all these goods would come back to the US, where production costs are much higher.

To at least some degree, the relative class peace seen in the US over the last few decades was predicated on cheap imports from China, which helped take the edge off skyrocketing inequality. Access to smart phones, OLED TVs, and other consumer goods fed the illusion that "life is materially a little bit better," when in reality, the share of social wealth accruing to the masses has been shrinking since the 1970s. Eventually, this contradiction will come to a head, leading to a dramatic upsurge in the class struggle.

In other words, Trump and his supporters should be careful what they wish for.

Nonetheless, the Chinese take a long view of history. They may consider some kind of mutually acceptable deal if only to avoid the chaos of an all-out trade war in the short term. After all, continued access to the US market is good for business. This would give them space to build an even stronger position before a decisive confrontation with the Americans becomes inevitable. After Trump's victory over Harris, Xi Jinping congratulated him and offered an olive branch:

> [China and the US would] benefit from cooperation and lose from confrontation. A stable, healthy and sustainable China-US relationship is in the common interests of the two countries and the international community's expectations. It is hoped that the two sides will uphold the principles of mutual respect, peaceful coexistence and win-win cooperation, strengthen dialogue and communication, properly manage differences, expand mutually beneficial cooperation, and find a correct way for China and the United States to get along.

In the long run, inter-imperialist rivalries cannot be overcome within the limits of capitalism without friction, and this is by no means the most likely scenario. However, a temporary truce and rebalancing cannot be categorically excluded.

As for the Russians, far from planning to march on Western Europe, they are pursuing their own pivot to Asia. To this end, they are deliberately developing the economy and infrastructure of the country's Far East. With a trans-Siberian pipeline from Russia to China slated to cross Mongolia, that country has also been invited to join BRICS+.

Putin has also nurtured Southeast Asia ties with his visits to Thailand and Vietnam. Malaysia, a major computer chip producer, has also expressed interest in joining the BRICS+

bloc, with Indonesia, the fourth most populous country in the world and a potential Pacific power in its own right, being courted as well.

A BRICS+ currency for trade within the bloc has also been proposed, which would further reduce dependence on US imperialism and the dollar. According to *Foreign Policy*, the threat is real, and "de-dollarization's moment might finally be here."

For decades, the Americans have weaponized the dollar and the international banking system by imposing sanctions or seizing the assets of regimes they don't like. In the case of Russia, it froze $300 billion held in European and American bank accounts when it invaded Ukraine. There has even been talk of using the accruing interest from these frozen funds to fund Zelensky's war effort. The hypocrisy of US imperialism's selective enforcement of the "rules-based order" is evident for all to see, with "friends and family" getting a blank check to do what they please.

Given the problems faced by the Euro—whereby a common currency attempts to accommodate economies moving in different directions—an actual BRICS+ currency may not materialize. However, an interbank payment system to circumvent the Western-controlled SWIFT system is well underway. Already, 90% of trade between China and Russia is denominated in rubles or renminbi. So while "slowbalization" may cripple the economies of the West, trade between BRICS+ countries may actually increase in the years ahead.

As a result of all these changes, it will also be much harder for the West to strangle or isolate Iran or North Korea through "maximum pressure" and sanctions. Nor will they easily be able to drive a wedge between China and Russia. Brzeziński's 1997 prediction has come true, and the US no longer has unilateral clout.

The way things are going, the Iranians may take a cue from the North Koreans and develop a nuclear weapons program after all. The deterrent effect of such weapons has been proven, and if they are going to be sanctioned no matter what, they may conclude they have nothing to lose either way. Not only would a nuclear-armed Iran upend the imperialists' calculations, it would almost certainly compel the Saudis and possibly others in the region to follow suit, despite their warming relations with Teheran.

While the interests of the BRICS+ countries may converge on a wide range of issues, however, they diverge on many others. The system they are working to establish cannot overcome the nation-state any more than the US-dominated system could. And, of course, these countries must contend with their own internal contradictions.

In the case of China, its leaders are sitting on the dynamite of the world's largest working class. Its economy and political set up have their own limitations and contradictions, and it is by no means guaranteed that it will eventually surpass the US, as the US once surpassed the UK. In fact, GDP growth in China has halved in recent years, falling from over 10% per year for nearly three decades, to just 5.2% in 2023.

To all of the above, we can add the race for the Arctic, including the fight to control Greenland's rare earth deposits, which may account for 25% of the world's total. This explains Trump's interest in buying the island and its 57,000 residents from Denmark: "Essentially, it's a large real estate deal."

Everything seems to point toward a new Cold War. We can be sure there will be plenty of "hot" episodes as proxy wars rage over the new division of the planet and smaller powers try to balance between the big players.

In short, US imperialism is in uncharted waters. However, as we have emphasized throughout this book, its decline is only relative, and it is far from being out for the count. It still has significant reserves with which to push back. An aging lion like the US can be even more dangerous than a young one.

Imperialism in Latin America and the World Revolution

> We see that imperialism, which seemed such an insuperable colossus, has proved before the whole world to be a colossus with feet of clay.
> – Leon Trotsky

Imperialism and Latin America

As we have seen, the US has always considered everything south of its border part of its "backyard." After a period of overt imperialist intervention and economic domination in the late 19th and early 20th centuries, it shifted gears temporarily in the 1930s with FDR's "good neighbor policy."

Fearful of unrest in the hemisphere with wars raging in Europe and the Pacific, Roosevelt emphasized "respect for sovereignty, economic cooperation, and the peaceful resolution of conflicts." Some naive souls on the left sincerely imagined the US really could truly be a "good neighbor" and that it would defend Latin America from the Nazis and Japan—all in the name of liberty and democracy.

However, once World War II was over and American control over the hemisphere was reconsolidated, it embarked on a new wave of open and covert interventions in the region: Costa Rica in the late 1940s; Guatemala in the 1950s; Cuba and the Dominican Republic in the 1960s; Chile and Argentina in the 1970s; Central America and Grenada in the 1980s; Haiti in 1994, not to mention the decades-long harassment and sabotage of the Cuban and Venezuelan Revolutions.

To give a flavor of US imperialism's attitude in the postwar period, look no further than Secretary of State John Foster Dulles's speech after the CIA deposed Jacobo Árbenz and installed Colonel Carlos Castillo Armas in June 1954:

> Tonight I would like to talk with you about Guatemala. It is the scene of dramatic events. They expose the evil purpose of the Kremlin to destroy the inter-American system, and they test the ability of the American states to maintain the peaceful integrity of this hemisphere. For several years international communism has been probing here and there for nesting places in the Americas. It finally chooses Guatemala as a spot which it could turn into an official base from which to breed subversion which could extend to other American Republics.
>
> This intrusion of Soviet despotism was, of course, a direct challenge to our Monroe Doctrine, the first and most fundamental of our foreign policies . . .
>
> In Guatemala, international communism had an initial success. It began ten years ago, when a revolution occurred in Guatemala. The revolution was not without justification. But the communists seized on it, not as an opportunity for real reforms, but as a chance to gain political power. Communist agitators devoted themselves to infiltrating the public and private organizations of Guatemala. They sent recruits to Russia and other communist countries for revolutionary training and indoctrination in such institutions as the Lenin School of Moscow.

> Operating in the guise of "reformers" they organized the workers and the peasants under communist leadership. Having gained control of what they call "mass organizations" they moved on to take over the official press and radio of the Guatemalan government. They dominated the social security organization and ran the agrarian land reform program. Through the technique of the "popular front" they dictated to Congress and the President . . .
>
> If world communism captures any American State, however small, a new and perilous [dangerous] front is established which will increase the danger to the entire free world and require even greater sacrifices from the American people.

Eager to please his paymasters, Castillo imposed a regime of military-police mass murder that would last for decades. In addition to laying the basis for what would come to be known as the "Guatemalan" or "Maya genocide," he rolled back the progressive reforms implemented by his predecessor, outlawed over 500 labor unions, and handed more than 1.5 million acres of land back to United Fruit Company and other major landowners. As it happens, John F. Dulles's law firm represented the United Fruit Company. His brother, Allen Dulles, the director of the CIA, owned shares in it.

In 1946, to further their aims in the region, the US established the Western Hemisphere Institute for Security Cooperation, better known as the "School of the Americas." Located until 1984 in the Panama Canal Zone—along with seven 18-hole golf courses—it is currently based at Fort Benning in Georgia.

At this "school," tens of thousands of elite military officers and police from 23 Latin American countries have been trained in the art of counterinsurgency—i.e., commando tactics, sniper training, psychological warfare, military intelligence, and "enhanced interrogation." The infamous death squads that have terrorized millions for decades were trained at this US school. Many of its top graduates went on to illustrious careers as sociopathic coup leaders, dictators, torturers, and heads of narcotrafficking cartels.

As part of its worldwide network of information gathering, graft, and domination, US imperialism maintains 271 diplomatic posts worldwide, including embassies and consulates in 173 countries. Across Latin America, these are widely reviled as hotbeds of espionage and counterrevolution. It also operates dozens of military bases across the region and spends more than ten times as much on "defense" as the whole of Latin America combined.

So-called free trade is another weapon in US imperialism's arsenal. In an attempt to at least partially overcome the limits of the nation-state, the US has comprehensive free trade agreements in force with 20 countries, including 11 in Latin America—Chile, Colombia, Costa Rica, Dominican Republic, El Salvador, Guatemala, Honduras, Mexico, Nicaragua, Panama, and Peru.

Inspired by Milton Friedman, envisioned by Ronald Reagan, negotiated by G.H. Bush, and signed by Bill Clinton, the North American Free Trade Agreement was in effect for 26 years. This, despite being opposed by two-thirds of Americans when it was ratified. NAFTA has since been replaced with the United States-Mexico-Canada Agreement, with terms even more favorable for US imperialism. It's no accident that Trump called it "the best and most important trade deal ever made by the USA."

From food and beverages to retail, automotive, consumer goods, and technology. From Coca-Cola to McDonald's, Walmart to Procter & Gamble, Ford, General Motors, IBM, and Microsoft, US corporations have a considerable presence in Latin America and dominate critical sectors of the economy.

Then there are the *maquiladoras*, 90% of which are along the US-Mexican border. Most of the 3,000-plus industrial plants are owned by US companies operating under preferential trade agreements. Every year, they import billions of dollars worth of raw materials into Mexico duty-free, to be assembled or processed by workers who are paid low wages and offered few protections, with the finished products exported back to the US. As many as one million workers are employed in these plants, many of which are run like military prisons.

As one female maquiladora worker earning just 600 pesos (less than $30) per week explained:

> We just have enough money to eat soup and beans. We don't eat meat. No one can live on this. A fair wage would be 250 pesos a day. In the United States people make in one hour what it takes us all day to earn.

Maquiladoras first appeared in the 1960s. But with the passage of NAFTA, the temptation of superprofits just south of the border led to a restructuring of the American economy, with massive outsourcing of formerly well-paid union jobs from the so-called Rust Belt.

At the same time, Bill Clinton and his neocon buddies fused with Wall Street, and the Democrats stopped paying lip service to blue-collar union workers. It took a few electoral cycles for these shifts to reach their logical conclusion, but the chickens have now come home to roost. Chuck Schumer summed up his party's strategy in 2016:

> For every blue-collar Democrat we lose in western Pennsylvania we will pick up two moderate Republicans in the suburbs in Philadelphia, and you can repeat that in Ohio and Illinois and Wisconsin.

This cynical approach blew up in the Democrats' face as first a significant layer of white, blue-collar workers, and then even broader segments of the working class abandoned them in favor of Donald Trump in 2016, 2020, and 2024.

The fight for America's backyard

Formally speaking, all Latin American countries are independent. However, the mighty dollar can subvert and corrupt almost anyone or anything. Even if they are compelled to maintain a low public profile, the imperialists can always find comprador capitalists or other local agents to further their interests. As James Connolly famously wrote in the context of Ireland:

> If you remove the English Army tomorrow and hoist the green flag over Dublin Castle, unless you set about the organization of the Socialist Republic, your efforts will be in vain. England will still rule you. She would rule you through her capitalists, through her landlords, through her financiers, through the whole array of commercial and individualist institutions she has planted in this country and watered with the tears of our mothers and the blood of our martyrs.

As for finance capital, that all-important element in Lenin's conception of imperialism, US banks account for about 40% of total banking assets in Latin America.

According to the Economic Commission for Latin America and the Caribbean, the region received $224.579 billion dollars in Foreign Direct Investment in 2022, which was 55.2% above 2021 and the highest levels on record. US imperialism accounted for 38% of the total, with the EU at 17%.

However, Russia has also been chipping away in the region, with investment not only in Cuba and Venezuela, but also in Guatemala, Mexico, Peru, Brazil, and Ecuador. In fact, Russia's exports of goods to Mexico increased by more than 20% during the first six months of 2022. However, it will come as no surprise that Chinese imperialism also has a significant presence, accounting for 9% of FDI sent to the region.

According to *China Daily*:

> In 2022, China's direct investment in Mexico rose 48% year-on-year. Chinese companies now represent the fastest-growing source of foreign investment in Mexico. The trend of Chinese investment in Mexico started around 2019 and will likely continue as the US imposes more tariffs on Chinese products and industries.

The speed at which China has embedded itself in the Western Hemisphere has been nothing short of astonishing. In 2000, just 2% of Latin America's exports went to the Chinese market. By 2022, it had risen to nearly 13%. Between 2020 and 2008, trade with China grew at an average annual rate of 31%, reaching $180 billion in 2010. By 2021, it totaled $450 billion. Some economists predict it could exceed $700 billion by 2035.

China is now South America's top trading partner and the second-largest for Latin America as a whole, after the US. China's main imports from the region are soybeans, copper, petroleum, oil, and other raw materials. In return, it exports higher-value-added manufactured products, i.e., cheaper goods that ultimately undermine local industries—a classical imperialist relationship.

As of 2023, Beijing had free trade agreements with Chile, Costa Rica, Ecuador, and Peru. Twenty-one Latin American countries have signed on to China's Belt and Road Initiative. In addition to FDI, Chinese banks loaned $137 billion to Latin American governments between 2005 and 2020, mainly to fund energy and infrastructure projects, often in exchange for oil.

In 2022 alone, loans to the region from China totaled $813 million. Venezuela is the biggest borrower, with an estimated $60 billion in Chinese state loans, nearly double the amount owed by Brazil. Countries like Chile are also increasingly dependent on Beijing, with $36 billion in exports in 2022—around 38% of its total.

Beijing's efforts to penetrate the region intensified during the pandemic through what some have called "Covid-19 diplomacy." During the crisis, China distributed ventilators, test kits, and masks, and offered billions in loans for the purchase of hundreds of millions of vaccines.

China has also exported millions of dollars in military aircraft, ground vehicles, air defense radars, and assault rifles to Venezuela, Argentina, Bolivia, Ecuador, and Peru. It is also strengthening its ties with Cuba, which is desperate for a lifeline after decades of US sanctions. It has even invested in the space and satellite race through joint projects with Brazil, Argentina, Bolivia, Brazil, Chile, and Venezuela.

With US imperialism spread thin across East Asia, Europe, and the Middle East, China is gaining ground in its backyard. It speaks volumes that along with the US, China is a voting member of the Inter-American Development Bank and the Caribbean Development Bank—even though China is located nowhere near the region.

In 2021, ahead of an important summit hosted by the US, Marco Rubio, Bob Menendez, Tim Kaine, and Jim Risch introduced legislation titled, "Countering Chinese Communist Party Malign Influence Act." As Risch told the media:

> As the United States prepares to host the Ninth Summit of the Americas, we must recommit ourselves to the promotion of economic and political freedom for all in the Western Hemisphere. This summit offers a unique opportunity for democratically-elected leaders of the Americas to support long-term policies

> that lead to greater economic opportunity, democratic stability, and the rule of law. Working with our regional partners, we can meet emerging challenges and curb the malign influence of undemocratic actors such as Russia, China, Cuba, and Venezuela in the region.

And Admiral Craig Faller, the former head of US Southern Command offered this stark assessment of the shifting situation:

> We are losing our positional advantage in this Hemisphere and immediate action is needed to reverse this trend.

Many hawks in the US establishment would prefer to accelerate a direct confrontation with China, believing they can strike a preemptive blow before it's too late. Instead of trying to manage the inter-imperialist competition, they think they can win it outright.

However, most American strategists take a longer, more cautious view. They still think they can rebuild America's industrial base and establish a regional coalition to blunt China's growth. By whatever means, the US seeks to "Taiwan-ize" China instead of allowing China to impose its will on Taiwan. Yet again, however, this is much easier said than done.

Immigration and imperialism

Immigration is a global phenomenon, intimately connected with imperialism. In 2021, there were around 281 million international migrants, a 27% increase from 2010. Immigrants now account for 3.5% of the global population. By the end of 2022, there were an estimated 35.3 million refugees and 5.4 million asylum-seekers globally.

As with everything else under capitalism, immigration is ultimately a function of economics. As Lenin explained:

> One of the special features of imperialism . . . is the decline in emigration from imperialist countries and the increase in immigration into these countries from the more backward countries where lower wages are paid.

Since capitalism as a world system cannot provide enough jobs, healthcare, education, or security for everyone, the human drive to acquire these basic needs inevitably spills over the artificial borders of the capitalist nation-state. Between 2000 and 2022, remittances from immigrants to their countries of origin increased by 650%, from $128 billion to $831 billion.

At the time Lenin wrote *Imperialism*:

> In the United States, immigrants from Eastern and Southern Europe are engaged in the most poorly paid jobs, while American workers provide the highest percentage of overseers of the better-paid workers.

Since then, Latin America has become the number one source of immigration, often undocumented, with Mexico, Central America, and, increasingly, South America as the main places of origin. The number of undocumented immigrants from India and China has also risen in recent years.

Remittances from immigrant workers sent back to Latin America and the Caribbean are a significant source of income for the region, with over $156 billion sent back in 2023 alone, a 7.7% increase from 2022. In the case of Mexico, the $66.2 billion sent that year in remittances accounted for 4.2% of total GDP. As for El Salvador, remittances accounted for more than 24% of GDP.

Forced from their homes largely due to the economic and foreign policies of imperialism, millions risk their lives to pursue the "American Dream." To make the dangerous and expensive crossing, they are prey to corrupt government officials, human smugglers, narcotraffickers, and common criminal gangs. Thousands have died attempting the journey, and countless others have fallen victim to harassment and violence, including sexual violence. For those who do make it more or less safely, the reality of life as an undocumented worker is more like a living nightmare—and the stress and terror is about to be multiplied with Trump back at the helm.

Wage theft is rampant for all low-wage workers in the US, with as much as $50 billion stolen by the bosses every year. With no legal status and few protections, undocumented workers are hit the hardest. Even when they are paid the legal minimum wage of $7.25 per hour, inflation has risen by at least 40% since that level was set in 2009.

Despite the cynical scapegoating by politicians of both parties, low-wage immigrant labor is essential for the functioning of the US economy. Access to this enormous pool of desperate laborers drives down wages for all workers and boosts profits for the capitalists, who use xenophobia and racism to divide and rule.

Trump whipped up votes by claiming the US has been "occupied" by job-stealing, pet-eating immigrants. But he exploited the labor of at least 100 undocumented immigrants to build his Bedminster golf course, and in 2023, hired 136 foreign seasonal workers through legal channels to work at Mar-a-Lago. According to the Department of Labor, this included 53 waiters and waitresses, seven hotel desk clerks, 17 housekeeping cleaners, five first-line supervisors of food preparation and serving workers, 24 cooks, and five bartenders.

As of June 2024, documented and undocumented immigrants made up over 19% of the US labor force—over 32 million workers out of a total of 169 million. Without immigration and births among recent immigrants, the US would be facing a labor shortage and demographic crisis similar to China, Russia, the EU, and Japan. And as reported by the *Financial Times*:

> In a period in which aging populations are gutting workforces worldwide, migrants also provide a practical, much-needed boost in labor terms. Thanks to both immigrants and more Americans returning to work [after the pandemic], the US labor force in 2023 grew three times faster than the underlying population. This helps explain why the widely expected recession never arrived.

It is estimated that undocumented workers paid $96.7 billion in federal, state, and local taxes in 2022 alone—although they are often deemed ineligible for many of the benefits their contributions fund.

Both major parties are enthusiastic supporters of militarizing the border to defend the country from an alleged immigrant "invasion." The US currently has roughly 735 miles of fencing across its 1,954 miles of border with Mexico—which means there are plenty more profits to be made by the private companies doing the construction.

According to the American Immigration Council:

> Since 1994, when the current strategy of concentrated border enforcement was first implemented along the US-Mexico border, the annual budget of the US Border Patrol has increased dramatically. It rose from $400 million in 1994 to over $7.3 billion in FY 2024, a nearly 20-fold increase. Even when adjusted for inflation, this represents an increase of over 765%.

Since establishing the Department of Homeland Security in 2003, the federal government has allocated an estimated $409 billion in tax dollars to agencies responsible for enforcing immigration laws.

US Customs and Border Protection and Immigration and Customs Enforcement now employ a total of 88,000 agents.

While the Border Patrol mainly covers US ports of entry, ICE's mission is:

> To apprehend noncitizens in the interior of the country, detain or monitor those undergoing removal proceedings, and deport those ordered removed.

This, too, is a reflection of American imperialism's decline. Just a few generations ago, when the US economy could absorb any number of immigrants, it emblazoned these words on the Statue of Liberty:

> Give me your tired, your poor,
> Your huddled masses yearning to breathe free,
> The wretched refuse of your teeming shore.
> Send these, the homeless, tempest-tossed to me,
> I lift my lamp beside the golden door!

Between 1892 and 1954, Ellis Island ushered over 12 million immigrants into the country. Now, it welcomes them with attack dogs and drones and locks their children in cages before sending them to slave away in meatpacking plants instead of going to school. As of 2024, the US operates over 200 immigration detention centers, jails, and prisons.

The idea that the US can insulate itself from the world by building an impregnable wall is reactionary political theater. As every revolutionary Marxist knows, you can't build socialism in one country. Nor can you limit capitalism to the borders of a single nation-state, even if it is as big and powerful as the US. The reversal of globalization and revived illusions in isolationism merely confirm that the system has reached its limits and must be overthrown.

With Mexico cracking down on immigrants on behalf of US imperialism, stricter rules for asylum seekers, and mass deportation, the flood of migrants crossing the border may

29. "A Day without Immigrants," Los Angeles, May Day, 2006.

eventually be slowed. However, this is a double-edged sword. Not only do entire US industries depend on this vulnerable workforce, but without the escape valve of emigration to the US, these countries will be under even more economic pressure, and we will see even more explosions of the class struggle.

US imperialism has a long and contradictory relationship with Latin America, going back to before the Mexican-American War. As of July 2023, the Hispanic population in the US was 65.2 million, accounting for 19.5% of the total population, making it the largest racial or ethnic minority in the country.

The Hispanic population of California alone was over 15.76 million people—around 40% of the total—more than the state's non-Hispanic white population of 12.96 million. Based on current trends, they may make up nearly 50% of the state's population by 2060. At over 12 million, they also make up the largest percentage of the population in Texas.

Approximately 41 million people in the US speak Spanish as their primary language, around 13% of the total population. Nearly five million Latinos live in Los Angeles County alone, close to half the city's total population. Of these, some 3.6 million are of Mexican origin, making the City of Angels the second-largest "Mexican" city in the world, after Mexico City itself.

There are roughly 11 million undocumented immigrants in the US, most of them with jobs, accounting for over 5% of the total workforce. This is a tremendous social force, and many of them bring traditions of struggle from their home countries. As Lenin noted, however, many workers can be susceptible to the chauvinism injected by the ruling class, especially during times of economic hardship:

> Imperialist ideology also penetrates the working class. No Chinese Wall separates it from the other classes.

Communists strive to raise the class unity, confidence, and consciousness of the entire working class. To achieve this, we must fight a ruthless battle against the poison of alien class ideas in the workers' movement, including xenophobia and racism. Through common struggle against their common enemies, workers will learn through experience that they have everything in common with their fellow workers, no matter their origins, and nothing in common with the capitalists.

The Mexican dictator, Porfirio Diaz, is alleged to have said: "Poor Mexico; so far from God, so close to the United States."

Over 100 years later, the US and Mexican economies and peoples are more intimately connected than ever. Mexican food, music, and culture are increasingly integrated into American life, especially, but by no means exclusively along the border. While it may seem merely anecdotal, it is telling that Millennials are the first generation to prefer Mexican food over Italian.

Like wildfires and capital, revolutions do not respect borders, and with the advent of social media, ideas and inspiration can disseminate in an instant. What happens on one side of the Rio Grande can and will impact events on the other—and vice versa.

The main enemy is at home!

Imperialism may be a worldwide phenomenon, but US imperialism is by far the most reactionary variant in human history. It flows from this that American communists have an essential duty in the worldwide struggle to overthrow it.

All told, the US has been involved in some 400 military interventions since 1776, half of them since 1950, and half of those since the fall of the Soviet Union. And this doesn't include the innumerable coups, assassinations, acts of sabotage, sanctions, and embargoes it has orchestrated and imposed around the world: From Mosaddegh in Iran, to Castro in Cuba, Lumumba in Congo, Diệm in Vietnam, Allende in Chile, Ortega in Nicaragua, Chavez in Venezuela, and many more.

Far from these being the aberrant actions of rogue agents, Allen Dulles, the first Director of Central Intelligence, explained the truth with admirable candor:

> The CIA has never carried out any action of a political nature, given any support of any nature, to any persons, potentates or movements, political or otherwise, without appropriate approval at a high potential level in our government outside the CIA.

In addition to regime change, the authoritarian, anti-worker, and anti-communist strongmen US imperialism has backed at one time or another is a rogue's gallery of the 20th Century, including, but not limited to:

- Jorge Rafael Videla in Argentina
- Pol Pot in Cambodia
- Augusto Pinochet in Chile
- Fulgencio Batista in Cuba
- Rafael Trujillo in the Dominican Republic
- Hosni Mubarak and Abdel Fattah el-Sisi in Egypt
- Haile Selassie in Ethiopia
- Adolf Hitler in Germany
- Georgios Papadopoulos in Greece
- Efraín Ríos Montt in Guatemala
- François Duvalier in Haiti
- Suharto in Indonesia
- Mohammad Reza Pahlavi in Iran
- Saddam Hussein in Iraq
- Benjamin Netanyahu in Israel
- Hassan II in Morocco
- Anastasio Somoza in Nicaragua
- Sani Abacha in Nigeria
- Muhammad Zia-ul-Haq in Pakistan
- Manuel Noriega in Panama
- Ferdinand Marcos in the Philippines
- António de Oliveira Salazar in Portugal
- Tsar Nicholas II in Russia
- The House of Saud in Saudi Arabia
- P.W. Botha in South Africa
- Park Chung-hee in South Korea
- Francisco Franco in Spain
- Chiang Kai-shek in Taiwan
- Turgut Özal in Turkey
- Idi Amin in Uganda
- Ngô Đình Diệm in Vietnam
- Mobutu Sese Seko in Zaire

The US is the only country ever to use nuclear weapons, having dropped atomic bombs on the defenseless Japanese cities of Hiroshima and Nagasaki, leading to at least 200,000 civilian deaths—all to send a message to the Soviet Union. Also during World War II, the US and its allies firebombed historic cities like Hamburg and Dresden, killing tens of thousands of German civilians. The war correspondent Edgar Jones described US actions in the Pacific during those years:

> We shot prisoners in cold blood, wiped out hospitals, strafed lifeboats, killed or mistreated enemy civilians, finished off the enemy wounded, tossed the dying into a hole with the dead, and in the Pacific boiled the flesh off enemy skulls to make table ornaments for sweethearts, or carved their bones for letter openers.

An estimated 882,000 Vietnamese men, women, and children were killed during the Vietnam War. Over half a million Iraqi children died due to sanctions imposed by the US in the 1990s. The price was "worth it," in the considered opinion of then–Secretary of State Madeleine Albright. Hundreds of thousands more were killed when the US invaded Iraq outright in 2003.

According to the latest estimates, as many as 4.5 million people were killed during US imperialism's "War on Terror," with another 38 million people displaced as a result. As we've seen throughout this book, however, imperialism's biggest impact is economic, and US imperialism has been in the driver's seat for decades.

The effects of this exploitation and domination are cumulative and generational. The poorest half of the world's population now holds less than 2% of the global wealth, while the richest 1% holds nearly 50%. The billionaires practically live on another planet, in gated communities and private islands, while building Armageddon-proof luxury bunkers.

The global luxury yacht market, estimated at $8.75 billion in 2024, is expected to rise to $17.33 billion by 2032. Meanwhile, 25,000 people die worldwide each year from hunger and related causes, including more than 10,000 children. Some 854 million people around the planet are undernourished, with inflationary food prices threatening to push another 100 million into poverty and hunger in the near term. Providing universal access to safe drinking water and sanitation for every inhabitant in the 140 poorest countries would cost just $114 billion annually—less than half of Elon Musk's net worth.

This is what the sociopaths who run society call "survival of the fittest"—never mind that civilization as we know it may not survive their criminal mismanagement of the planet's resources, waterways, and atmosphere.

The all-important question of climate change is directly related to the fight to end imperialism. For starters, the US military is the world's number one polluter, emitting more than 50 metric tons of CO_2 annually.

In wartime, entire regions are devastated and polluted. During World War I, 250,000 acres of farmland were shelled and trenched into wasteland, with the scars still visible today. US imperialism poured 20 million gallons of herbicides on Vietnam, turning jungles and rice paddies into mudflats, and inflicting cancer and birth defects on generations of Vietnamese. Poland alone has removed 100 million unexploded munitions from both world wars. According to the UN, as many as 100 million live landmines lay in wait in war zones past and present—with another 100 million sitting in warehouses just waiting to be planted.

No war but the class war: Death to imperialism!

That everything is connected and in flux is a fundamental premise of dialectics. There are no permanent borders, empires, or dominant powers. A glance at any world map from a hundred years ago makes this abundantly clear. This applies also to the US, no matter how large it looms in recent memory, or how strong it looks on paper relative to most other nation-states today.

Foreign and domestic policy are deeply intertwined, and the contradictions of a system in terminal decline have a colossal impact on mass consciousness. Though there will be ebbs and flows, the next major economic crisis will only further undermine the old norms and accelerate the process toward revolution. As Trotsky wrote in *Marxism in Our Time*:

> The life of monopolistic capitalism in our time is a chain of crises. Each crisis is a catastrophe. The need for salvation from these partial catastrophes by means of tariff walls, inflation, increase of government spending and debts lays the ground for additional, deeper and more widespread crises. The struggle for markets, for raw material, for colonies makes military catastrophes unavoidable. All in all, they prepare revolutionary catastrophes.

A recent poll found that nearly 70% of Americans think the US is in "rapid decline." Millions of young people see it as "a dying empire led by bad people." 65% agreed strongly or somewhat that "nearly all politicians are corrupt, and make money from their political power." Only 38% say they are "extremely proud" to be American. This is a far cry from the American exceptionalism and optimism that prevailed for centuries.

This is why slogans like "Make America Great Again" and "Make America Rich Again" resonate with millions—and why the Democrats' rebuttal that "America is Already Great" falls flat. However, the revival of cringey American nationalism is a sign of fear and weakness, not strength. Trump may promise everything to everyone, but he can't magically bring back the postwar boom. The capitalists can neither fix nor abolish their own system. The only way forward is class struggle and revolution.

As revolutionary communists, we take a keen interest in world affairs and offer solidarity to the workers in every struggle. But we should never lose sight of the fact that *our main fight is right here at home*. This is where we can have a meaningful impact in the fight against imperialism. This is where we can actually stop the genocidal war in Gaza and the killing in Lebanon, Ukraine, and Sudan.

69% of Israel's arms come from the US, all of it authorized by Congress and the president. Since October 7, 2023, at least $23 billion in "security assistance" has been drained from public funds to enable Netanyahu's murderous onslaught. Far from increasing the security of the Jewish people, the pummeling of Gaza and Lebanon has led to skyrocketing anti-Semitism and may yet lead to an existential crisis for the state of Israel.

Trump has raised the specter of the "enemy within." However, the real enemy within are the capitalists and imperialists. The only way to keep US hands off the rest of the world is to ensure its hands are those of the working class. Only the mass action of class-conscious and organized workers can paralyze the economy and establish a workers' state. By expropriating the top 500 companies, a workers' government would control the key levers of the country's economic life, and by extension, its foreign policy.

The contest between imperialism and the working class cannot be reduced to the number of tanks or fighter jets each side possesses. It ultimately comes down to the overall class balance of forces. This is a function, not only of raw demographics, but of the workers' class consciousness, confidence, unity. Above all, it is a question of leadership.

The ruling class may put on a brave face for the broader public, but they are deeply concerned about the future. According to the annual threat assessment of the US intelligence community, published in February 2024:

> In the coming year, the United States faces an increasingly fragile global order strained by accelerating strategic competition among major powers, more intense and unpredictable transnational challenges, and multiple regional conflicts with far-reaching implications. An ambitious yet anxious China, a confrontational Russia, regional powers like Iran, and more capable non-state actors are challenging longstanding rules of the international system as well as US primacy within it.
>
> Simultaneously, new technologies, vulnerabilities in the public health sector, and environmental changes are more frequent, often have a global impact, and are harder to predict. One only needs to look at the Gaza crisis—triggered by a highly capable non-state terrorist group in HAMAS, fueled in part by a regionally ambitious Iran, and exacerbated by narratives encouraged by China and Russia to undermine the United States on the global stage—to see how a regional crisis can have widespread spillover effects and complicate international cooperation on other pressing issues.
>
> The world that emerges from this tumultuous period will be shaped by whoever offers the most persuasive arguments for how the world should be governed, how societies should be organized, and which systems are most effective at advancing economic growth and providing benefits for more people. It will be shaped by the powers—both state and non-state—that are most able and willing to act on solutions to transnational issues and regional crises.

The problem they face is that "persuasive arguments" aren't enough. Capitalism is no longer "effective at advancing economic growth and providing benefits for more people." American imperialism has neither enough carrots nor sticks to keep us all in line, all the time.

They can't even produce enough arms and ammunition to keep the Ukrainians, Israelis, and themselves sufficiently stocked. As for the military, workers in uniform are also affected by the generalized crisis and radicalization. Let us not forget that fraternization, mutinies, and splits along class lines are integral to every revolution, from the Paris Commune to the Russian, German, Portuguese, and Venezuelan Revolutions.

In the absence of a revolutionary solution, the current impasse can continue for longer than most people might think. However, even the most robust and resilient system can be overwhelmed by too many inputs—and US imperialism is running out of runway. We shouldn't be surprised if its relative decline accelerates relatively quickly.

As Trotsky wrote in the context of 1939:

> Partial reforms and patchwork will do no good. Historical development has come to one of those decisive stages when only the direct intervention of the masses is able to sweep away the reactionary obstructions and lay the foundations of a new regime. Abolition of private ownership in the means of production is the first prerequisite to planned economy, i.e., the introduction of reason into the sphere of human relations, first on a national and eventually on a world scale.
>
> Once it begins, the socialist revolution will spread from country to country, with immeasurably greater force than fascism spreads today. By the example and with the aid of the advanced nations, the backward nations will also be carried away into the mainstream of socialism. The thoroughly rotted customs toll gates will fall. The contradictions which rend Europe and the entire world asunder will find their natural and peaceful solution within the framework of a Socialist United States in Europe as well as in other parts of the world. Liberated humanity will draw itself up to its full height.

The last few years have seen revolutionary explosions around the planet, and even more are on the agenda. If we succeed in building a revolutionary leadership in the next historical period, one country after another will fall to the socialist revolution, like dominoes.

Communists in power will dramatically transform human relations, which will be based on genuine cooperation and solidarity between the peoples. A workers' government will have a fundamentally different attitude towards foreign relations, war, and immigration. Along with the rest of the state apparatus, the military will be transitional in nature. Like the early Red Army built by Trotsky, it will be democratized and committed to defending the interests of the world's workers.

Internationalism in practice will end the hellish conditions that force people to leave their homes and loved ones. The artificial borders that disfigure our world will be abolished. Rational planning of the world economy will provide everyone with an incredible quality of life, no matter where they were born or where they choose to live.

Instead of studying the history of the rise and decline of US imperialism, future generations will look back at the rise and fall of all imperialisms. This is the perspective the Revolutionary Communists of America fights for.

To paraphrase the ancient Romans, if you want peace, prepare for revolutionary class war.

Workers of the world, unite!

Part 2: A Marxist Primer on Imperialist War

> The redeeming feature of war is that it puts a nation to the test. As exposure to the atmosphere reduces all mummies to instant dissolution, so war passes supreme judgment upon social systems that have outlived their vitality.
>
> – Karl Marx

> War is just which is necessary, and arms are hallowed when there is no other hope but in them.
>
> – Machiavelli, *The Prince*

Introduction

For thousands of years, many great minds have theorized about the nature, causes, conduct, and art of war, and many classic works have been written on the subject. However, as in all other domains of human investigation, without a consciously materialist and dialectical analysis, the result can be a mess of empty platitudes and confusion. This is especially true in the epoch of imperialism.

Whether we like it or not, we live in an age of crisis and war, revolution and counterrevolution—you can't have one without the other. It's not a question of nationalism or militarism in the abstract, but of politics and economics. Our analysis must, therefore, begin with the inescapable fact that *you can't have capitalism without war*.

The cynical brutality and hypocrisy of the imperialists can be enraging, but for Marxists, it is not enough to be enraged. As Spinoza famously said, "I have striven not to laugh at human actions, not to weep at them, nor to hate them, but to *understand* them."

To cut through the fog, we must scientifically analyze every war concretely, without emotion, always starting from a class perspective. Because despite the death and cruelty that accompanies all wars, not all wars are equal. As we will see, while most wars are indeed reactionary, some are progressive and revolutionary.

Wars are a classic example of the transformation of quantity into quality. The inter- and intra-class contradictions accumulated in the depths of society suddenly explode to the surface, violently upending the status quo and calling into question all assumptions about how society has been run until then.

As Trotsky wrote in *My Life* about the mood in Vienna at the outbreak of World War I:

> The people whose lives, day in and day out, pass in a monotony of hopelessness are many; they are the mainstay of modern society. The alarm of mobilization breaks into their lives like a promise; the familiar and long-hated is overthrown, and the new and unusual reigns in its place. Changes still more incredible are in store for them in the future. For better or worse? For the better, of

> course—what can seem worse [to ordinary people] than "normal" conditions?
>
> Like revolution, war forces life, from top to bottom, away from the beaten track. But revolution directs its blows against the established power. War, on the contrary, at first strengthens the state power which, in the chaos engendered by war, appears to be the only firm support and then undermines it.

As Lenin explained, wars can generate vast fortunes. But they are also extremely risky, as they exacerbate the contradictions of peacetime and test all leaders, parties, tendencies, and ideas:

> War equals the greatest possible crisis. *Every* crisis means (with the possibility of *temporary* delay and regression): A) acceleration of development; B) sharpening of contradictions; C) their exposure; D) collapse of all that is *rotten*.

This is precisely what happened to the Romanov, Hohenzollern, and Hapsburg dynasties during the course of the first worldwide imperialist war, which is why we say that war is the "handmaiden of revolution."

Wars, therefore, represent not only a colossal complication for revolutionaries, but dialectically, a remarkable opportunity that must be seized with both hands.

But if we are going to get organized to defeat our class enemy, we must first *understand* it. Especially when that enemy dominates the planet, sits on hundreds of trillions of dollars, commands tens of millions of soldiers, and is armed to the teeth with the most advanced weaponry—including enough nuclear weapons to destroy all biological organisms on earth 55 times over.

This is the grim reality of our world due to the belated nature of the socialist revolution. However, we must never forget that the class-conscious and organized working class is a far more powerful force. All of the armaments, surveillance, repression, and propaganda are really signs of weakness, not strength. The ruling class is absolutely terrified of the unstoppable power of the class-conscious and organized working class once it moves into action. This is why they move might and main in their efforts to divide, confuse, and turn us against each other—instead of against them.

However, that game won't last forever, and millions of people are already drawing radical conclusions from their experience of life under this murderous and inhumane system. Our task is to help them draw fully revolutionary and communist conclusions, and to do that, we must be armed with Marxist theory, perspectives, and a dialectical understanding of history—and war.

War is terrible—and terribly profitable

As we've seen in Part One of this book, imperialism is a complex question involving far more than militarism and war. But militarism and war are most definitely part of it—an incredibly important part. In the final analysis, all serious social questions are ultimately decided by force. As Otto Von Bismarck put it:

> The position of Prussia in Germany will not be determined by its liberalism but by its power . . . Not through speeches and majority decisions will the great questions of the day be decided—but by iron and blood.

Or, in the words of the Nazi Minister of Propaganda, Joseph Goebbels: "We can do without butter, but, despite all our love of peace, not without arms."

Since 1800, an estimated 37 million uniformed soldiers have been killed fighting in wars, with over 28 million combatants killed in both world wars alone. And this doesn't include the untold millions of civilians who have also been killed in the crossfire.

Since World War II, there have been major wars in Korea and Vietnam, Iraq, and Iran, and America's longest-ever war, in Afghanistan. By some counts, there are 110 armed conflicts raging around the world this very day. Most of them are proxy wars, with the belligerents backed by this or that major imperialist power, in places like the Democratic Republic of Congo, Sudan, Syria, Libya, Ukraine, and Gaza.

And yet, we are fed the lie that war is an abnormality, a disruption of "peaceful" capitalism, a necessary evil resorted to only when human rights and democracy are under threat. But the "new normality" of imperialist devastation and dislocation is merely a return to the old capitalist normality, on a higher, more devastating level.

Any war is disastrous for the people caught up in them, even if they are considered "small" by modern standards. Over 114 million people around the world have been forcibly displaced in recent years as a result of persecution, conflict, and violence, the highest levels on record.

In the words of the American Civil War general, William Sherman, "War is hell. War is cruelty, and you cannot refine it."

However, as Lenin once quipped, war is not only terrible, it is terribly profitable! As Trotsky put it, "War is a gigantic commercial enterprise, especially for the war industry."

Because even relatively minor wars require weapons, ammunition, equipment, food, fuel, and other supplies. Arms manufacturing and export is big business, and the government and private sector "defense contractors" work together closely to maximize profits. It is, in effect, a colossal money-laundering scheme, with billions in public tax dollars going straight into the pockets of big business.

When sales or grants of weapons systems to other countries are authorized, it is often older stocks that are sent, with huge sums of taxpayer money handed to the arms manufacturers to produce new ones for use by the national military. On other occasions, the "aid" comes in the form of loans that can only be used to buy arms from companies based in the country making the loan, which means even more built-in profits for private corporations. According to the Department of Defense, in 2022, it purchased $44.5 billion from Lockheed Martin, $25.4 billion from Raytheon, and $21.5 billion from General Dynamics Corporation.

The world's biggest arms manufacturer, Lockheed Martin, raked in nearly $8.5 billion in profits in 2023. That's equivalent to the GDP of Togo, a country of nearly nine million people. The company's *F-35* fighter jet cost $1.7 trillion and came in 80% over budget and a decade late. Despite billions in taxpayer dollars, it has been plagued with performance issues. According to *Defense News*, the *F-35* program currently has 857 deficiencies, but thankfully, "only" seven are considered critical—including its inability to fly in the rain.

With rising instability and tensions worldwide, a new arms race has been unleashed. Even countries like Germany and Japan, which were demilitarized after World War II, now spend tens of billions of dollars on the military each year.

In 2023, total global military expenditure on the "death industry" reached a record high of $2.44 trillion—a 6.8% increase over the year before. US spending dwarfs the rest of the world, accounting for nearly 40% of the global total, with China, Russia, and India trailing far behind. But even a country like Saudi Arabia spends more than the UK, Germany, or France, which indicates just how insecure the House of Al Saud really feels in its position.

30. A Goverment-Fed Baby—Robert Minor, *The Daily Worker.*

Adjusted for inflation, US military spending has increased by over 62% since 1980. Between 2014 and 2022, the US spent more than twice as much on the military as did all other NATO members combined. And although the official federal military budget is around $877 billion, in practice, through various channels, an estimated $2 trillion goes to the so-called Department of Defense.

When it comes to arms exports, it will surprise no one that the US has accounted for over 41% of arms exports since 2019. In 2023 alone, sales of US military equipment to foreign governments rose 16% to $238 billion, an all-time record. Number two in exports isn't Russia or China, but France—an allegedly "kinder, gentler" capitalist country.

As for the US military, it maintains hundreds of bases and installations in at least 55 countries around the world. With 1.3 million troops on active duty, it has the world's third-largest military, behind only China and India, countries with much larger populations.

It is now more than three decades since the end of the Cold War, and yet, fifteen countries including Israel and North Korea have an estimated 12,000 nuclear weapons between them—all in the name of "deterrence." In 2023, an estimated $91.4 billion was spent on the world's nuclear weapons programs—the equivalent to $2,898 per second, with the US accounting for 80% of the increase in spending from 2022 to 2023.

According to the *New York Times,* over the next 30 years, the US plans on spending an estimated $1.7 trillion revamping its nuclear arsenal. For the sake of comparison, the Manhattan Project during World War II cost "only" $30 billion in inflation-adjusted dollars. Now, *nearly double* that amount is to be spent each year.

For its part, Russia has updated its nuclear doctrine in light of the Ukraine War, and currently has the world's largest nuclear arsenal. This is not merely a Soviet inheritance. In 2022, Russia spent an estimated $9.6 billion to maintain and modernize its nuclear capacity, while China spent an estimated $12 billion to expand its arsenal even further.

With North Korea showing that nuclear weapons do, in fact, serve to deter aggression, the Iranians may yet restart their nuclear program, which would uncork a nuclear arms race in the Middle East and beyond.

Military spending, especially on nuclear weapons, is a colossal waste of resources that could be used instead to improve billions of lives. As Ted Grant once wrote:

> Vast amounts of money are being squandered every year on arms expenditure, which under modern conditions is mainly the production of expensive scrap metal.

Research shows that tax dollars poured into the military-industrial complex creates fewer jobs than money invested in sectors such as education or green energy. For every $1 billion spent on the military, 11,200 jobs are created, as compared to 26,700 in education, 17,200 in healthcare, and 16,800 in clean energy. During the course of the 2001–19 "War on Terror," more than 2.9 million more jobs could have been created if the money had instead been invested in these socially useful fields.

As for the prospect of World War III, this remains highly unlikely, at least in the next period. This is due, in part, to the deterrent effect of nuclear weapons, but above all, to the class balance of forces, which is overwhelmingly in favor of the workers, who have no interest in repeating the horrific mass slaughters of the past.

However, if the Western imperialists keep poking the Russian bear, or if Netanyahu succeeds in goading Iran into an all-out regional war, all bets are off. As one diplomat put it, Putin is bluffing—until he isn't. The same same can be said about the Iranians, who are also playing the long game of a medium-sized regional imperialist power.

As a result, the chances of "mutually assured destruction" have ticked somewhat upward in the recent period. This is yet another reason we need a sense of urgency when it comes to building the forces of revolutionary communism. Only the socialist revolution can disarm the warmongers and beat swords into plowshares once and for all.

Clausewitz and class independence

Carl von Clausewitz was a Prussian military officer who studied Hegel and applied dialectics to warfare in the Napoleonic era. As he wrote in his celebrated book, *On War*:

> War is a mere continuation of policy by other means . . . War is not merely a political act, but also a real political instrument, a continuation of political commerce, a carrying out of the same by other means . . . The political view is the object, war is the means, and the means must always include the object in our conception

> . . . Since war is not an act of senseless passion but is controlled by its political object, the value of the object must determine the sacrifices to be made for it in magnitude and also in duration.

In other words, there is an organic unity between domestic and foreign policy. Military force is not an end in itself, but rather, as one Clausewitzian theorist put it, an "instrument of power pursuing purpose."

This dovetails perfectly with Lenin's idea that "politics is a concentrated expression of economics." Under capitalism, this means maximizing profits and defending the interests of the national bourgeoisie—by any means necessary. As with all investments, the imperialists calculate their risks and attempt to get more out than they put in.

Likewise, communists approach everything from the perspective of furthering the collective interests of the working class.

As Lenin explained, our program in wartime is fundamentally the same as our program in peacetime. We reject both imperialist war and so-called imperialist peace. We stand for class struggle, class independence, and the revolutionary overthrow of the capitalist order by the organized and mobilized working class, both at home and abroad.

It flows from this that Marxists are not pacifists, and do not oppose all wars, regardless of time and place. As Trotsky explained in 1938:

> In order to determine in each given instance the historic and social character of a war, we must be guided not by impressions and conjectures but by a scientific analysis of the politics that preceded the war and conditioned it.

As with any social phenomenon, we must always proceed from the following rule of thumb: Does a particular convergence of factors raise or lower working-class consciousness, confidence,

31. Carl von Clausewitz—Karl Wilhelm Wach.

and unity? As there can be powerful crosscurrents and countervailing tendencies—not to mention pressure from the state and its media mouthpieces—it is not always easy to work this out. However, if you stick to the principle of class independence, you can't go too far wrong.

The fundamentals of a class analysis

The foundations for understanding war from a class perspective were laid by the founders of scientific socialism, and in particular, by Engels. Nicknamed "The General" by Marx's daughters, he was an active participant in the 1848 Revolution and lifelong student of military history, strategy, and tactics.

As he emphasized, if we are to understand imperialist war and the states that wage them, we must first have a clear conception of the state in general. As Engels wrote in his classic work, *The Origin of the Family, Private Property, and the State*:

> The state is, therefore, by no means a power forced on society from without; just as little is it "the reality of the ethical idea," "the image and reality of reason," as Hegel maintains. Rather, it

> is a product of society at a certain stage of development; it is the admission that this society has become entangled in an insoluble contradiction with itself, that it has split into irreconcilable antagonisms which it is powerless to dispel.
>
> But in order that these antagonisms, these classes with conflicting economic interests, might not consume themselves and society in fruitless struggle, it became necessary to have a power, seemingly standing above society, that would alleviate the conflict and keep it within the bounds of "order"; and this power, arisen out of society but placing itself above it, and alienating itself more and more from it, is the state . . .
>
> The second distinguishing feature is the establishment of a public power which no longer directly coincides with the population organizing itself as an armed force. This special, public power is necessary because a self-acting armed organization of the population has become impossible since the split into classes . . .
>
> This public power exists in every state; it consists not merely of armed men but also of material adjuncts, prisons, and institutions of coercion of all kinds, of which gentile [clan] society knew nothing.

The military is the "institution of coercion" or body of "armed men" par excellence. In *Anti-Dühring*, Engels put forward the following brilliant analysis of the contradictions and dangers to bourgeois rule inherent in the arms race then consuming Europe:

> Militarism dominates and is swallowing Europe. But this militarism also bears within itself the seed of its own destruction. Competition among the individual states forces them, on the one hand, to spend more money each year on the army and navy, artillery, etc., thus more and more hastening their financial collapse; and, on the other hand, to resort to universal compulsory military service more and more extensively, thus in the long run

> making the whole people familiar with the use of arms, and therefore enabling them at a given moment to make their will prevail against the warlords in command.
>
> And this moment will arrive as soon as the mass of the people—town and country workers and peasants—will have a will. At this point the armies of the princes become transformed into armies of the people; the machine refuses to work and militarism collapses by the dialectics of its own evolution . . . And this will mean the bursting asunder from within of militarism and with it of all standing armies.

Based on the seeds of discord planted by the Franco-Prussian War, which saw Germany occupy the region of Alsace-Lorraine, Engels even predicted World War I and anticipated the difficulties Marxists would face under such conditions—as well as the revolutionary wave that would follow:

> No war is any longer possible for Prussia-Germany except a world war—a world war of an extent and violence hitherto undreamed of. Eight to ten million soldiers will massacre one another and in doing so devour the whole of Europe until they have stripped it barer than any swarm of locusts has ever done.
>
> The devastations of the Thirty Years' War compressed into three or four years, and spread over the whole continent; famine, pestilence, general demoralization both of the armies and of the mass of the people produced by acute distress; hopeless confusion of our artificial machinery in trade, industry and credit, ending in general bankruptcy; collapse of the old states and their traditional state wisdom to such an extent that crowns will roll by dozens on the pavement and there will be nobody to pick them up; absolute impossibility of foreseeing how it will all end and who will come out of the struggle as victor;

> Only one result is absolutely certain: general exhaustion and the establishment of the conditions for the ultimate victory of the working class.
>
> This is the prospect when the system of mutual outbidding in armaments, taken to the final extreme, at last bears its inevitable fruits. This, my lords, princes and statesmen, is where in your wisdom you have brought old Europe. And when nothing remains to you but to open the last great war dance—that will suit us all right.
>
> The war may perhaps push us [Marxists] temporarily into the background, may wrench from us many a position already conquered. But when you have unleashed forces which you will then no longer be able to control, things may go as they will: at the end of the tragedy you will be ruined and the victory of the proletariat will either be already achieved or at any rate inevitable.

Talk about perspectives!

Trotsky also had a profoundly dialectical understanding of war. As an example, take the following selection from the preface to *The War and the International*, which served as a textbook on imperialist war in the Soviet Union until it was banned by Stalin in 1924:

> The forces of production which capitalism has evolved have outgrown the limits of nation and state. The national state, the present political form, is too narrow for the exploitation of these productive forces. The natural tendency of our economic system, therefore, is to seek to break through the state boundaries.
>
> The whole globe, the land and the sea, the surface as well as the interior has become one economic workshop, the different parts of which are inseparably connected with each other. This work was accomplished by capitalism.

> But in accomplishing it the capitalist states were led to struggle for the subjection of the world-embracing economic system to the profit interests of the bourgeoisie of each country. What the politics of imperialism has demonstrated more than anything else is that the old national state that was created in the revolutions and the wars of [the past] has outlived itself, and is now an intolerable hindrance to economic development.
>
> The present war is at bottom a revolt of the forces of production against the political form of nation and state. [It] is the most colossal breakdown in history of an economic system destroyed by its own inherent contradictions.

This is a marvelous summing of the economic basis of imperialism and war, and of the dead end of capitalism, already foreshadowed in the *Communist Manifesto*. But Trotsky not only produced razor-sharp political analyses of the many wars he witnessed, he built the Soviet Red Army practically from scratch and led it to victory against nearly two dozen armies of counterrevolution.

However, as with so many other aspects of Marxism, it was Lenin who played a truly essential role in synthesizing and expanding on the lessons of Marx and Engels. At the time, Trotsky was formally outside Lenin's party, an advocate of unprincipled organizational unity between the Mensheviks and Bolsheviks.

It was, therefore, up to Lenin to theoretically equip and reorient his comrades in this time of unprecedented bewilderment and betrayal—in preparation for the revolutionary wave that would inevitably follow in the war's wake. Because in August 1914, the question of imperialist war was not merely theoretical, it was a matter of life and death, both politically and literally.

When the war broke out, the entire Second International had collapsed. With few exceptions, its member parties betrayed their commitment to internationalism and antimilitarism, turning their backs on the declaration made at the Basel Congress just two years earlier. Meeting in Switzerland in 1912, the assembled delegates had agreed:

> In case war should break out . . . it is [our] duty to intervene in favor of its speedy termination and with all [our] powers to utilize the economic and political crisis created by the war to arouse the people and thereby to hasten the downfall of capitalist class rule.

This was a clear call to turn the imperialist war into a class war to end capitalism. Instead, the International descended into the poisonous swamp of national chauvinism, and its members were thrown into confusion—and into the trenches.

Virtually every section bent over backwards to justify supporting "their" government against its enemies, becoming shameless apologists for the slaughter of millions of workers and peasants in uniform. As Lenin put it:

> Instead of revolutionary tactics, the majority of the Social-Democratic parties conducted reactionary tactics, went over to the side of their respective governments and bourgeoisie.

The forces of genuine Marxism were reduced to a tiny handful. It was up to comrades like Trotsky, Lenin, and Rosa Luxemburg to cut through the hypocrisy and lies. They had to swim against the stream and resist the enormous pressures and physical danger of taking a principled position against imperialist war.

The urgent task was to go back to basics to politically rearm the cadres of the party, above all, on the need for class independence and internationalism. Needless to say, there is much we can and must learn from this experience as we fight to the end the imperialist slaughters of our day.

Lenin on imperialist war

While every war is different, Lenin's analysis of World War I provides a rock-solid baseline for understanding every military conflict in the imperialist epoch, even when the fighting takes place through proxies, and not directly between the main imperialist powers.

It is important to bear in mind that most of Lenin's writings during this period were intended for the core cadres of the party, not the broader masses, which were beyond reach at that time. As he forcefully "bent the stick" against the prevailing mood of social chauvinism, he used particularly sharp language, trying to shake his comrades out of their demoralization and disorientation at the dramatic turn of events.

The tasks of revolutionaries flow first and foremost from our political perspectives, and making sense of what appeared to be a senseless slaughter was the first order of business. It's no accident that Lenin wrote his classic book, *Imperialism: The Highest Stage of Capitalism* in 1916, in the middle of the war. It, too, was part of his effort to politically rearm the party.

Another key work was "Socialism and War," published in September 1915, and distributed to the participants of the Zimmerwald Conference. Zimmerwald was a gathering of socialist and anti-war activists held in Switzerland, which laid the basis for revolutionary opposition to the war, and eventually, the founding of the Communist International.

In what follows, we will quote extensively from various works written by Lenin in this period. He was extremely careful and precise in his wording, and it can't really be improved upon.

He begins by emphasizing that we must analyze each war in its full context, and cannot simply copy-paste a position from one war to another:

> Socialists have always condemned war between nations as barbarous and brutal. But our attitude towards war is fundamentally different from that of the bourgeois pacifists . . . and of the anarchists.
>
> We differ from the former in that we understand the inevitable connection between wars and the class struggle within the country; we understand that war cannot be abolished unless classes are abolished and socialism is created; and we also differ in that we fully regard civil wars, i.e., wars waged by the oppressed class against the oppressing class, slaves against slave owners, serfs against landowners, and wage workers against the bourgeoisie, as legitimate, progressive and necessary.
>
> We Marxists differ from both the pacifists and the anarchists in that we deem it necessary historically—from the standpoint of Marx's dialectical materialism—to study each war separately.
>
> In history there have been numerous wars which, in spite of all the horrors, atrocities, distress and suffering that inevitably accompany all wars, were progressive, i.e., benefited the development of mankind by helping to destroy the exceptionally harmful and reactionary institutions (for example, autocracy or serfdom), the most barbarous despotisms in Europe (Turkish and Russian).
>
> Therefore, it is necessary to examine the historically specific features of precisely the present war.

In other words, communists are not opposed to war in the abstract, but to reactionary wars, to imperialist wars, wars intended to deepen the oppression of the masses. But we are fully in favor of wars waged by the toilers against their exploiters.

Lenin explains how, during the revolutionary rise of capitalism, the system waged a series of historically progressive wars against reactionary institutions such as the Church, the feudal autocracy, and serfdom. In his "Letter to American Workers," he includes the first and second American

32. Zimmerwald Conference, September 1915.

Revolutions among history's "immense, world-historic, [and] progressive" wars:

> The history of modern, civilized America opened with one of those great, really liberating, really revolutionary wars of which there have been so few compared to the vast number of wars of conquest which, like the present imperialist war, were caused by squabbles among kings, landowners or capitalists over the division of usurped lands or ill-gotten gains.
>
> That was the war the American people waged against the British robbers who oppressed America and held her in colonial slavery, in the same way as these "civilized" bloodsuckers are still oppressing and holding in colonial slavery hundreds of millions of people in India, Egypt, and all parts of the world . . .
>
> The American people have a revolutionary tradition which has been adopted by the best representatives of the American proletariat, who have repeatedly expressed their complete solidarity with us Bolsheviks. That tradition is the war of liberation against the British in the eighteenth century and the Civil War in the nineteenth century.

The Russian Civil War that followed the October Revolution was also a "really liberating, really revolutionary" war. But World War I was not that kind of war. It was the first global imperialist war in the modern sense of the word imperialism, a new phenomenon that had to be analyzed and understood in the heat of the moment. Lenin summed up the essence of the epoch we live in to this day as follows:

> Formerly progressive, capitalism has become reactionary. It has developed the forces of production to such a degree that mankind is faced with the alternative of going over to socialism or of suffering years and even decades of armed struggle between the "great powers for the artificial preservation of capitalism by means of colonies, monopolies, privileges and national oppression of every kind.

As he graphically put it, World War I was nothing more nor less than a:

> War between the biggest slave owners for preserving and fortifying slavery. It is not the business of socialists to help the [robbers]. Socialists must take advantage of the struggle between the robbers to overthrow them all.
>
> To be able to do this, the socialists must first of all tell the people the truth. That is at the bottom of it all, and to understand this truth, to express it, "to show things as they actually are," is the fundamental task of socialist policy as distinct from bourgeois policy, the principal aim of which is to conceal, to gloss over this truth.

And the truth is that the working class has nothing to gain and everything to lose in an inter-imperialist war, which at best, exchanges one set of oppressors for another and perpetuates the rule of capital on a world scale.

Revolutionary tactics and the fight against social-chauvinism

Flowing from his class analysis of war and imperialism, Lenin took up a number of tactical and organizational questions affecting the day-to-day work of the Bolsheviks under such conditions. As he always emphasized, communists must be implacable when it comes to questions of principle, and infinitely flexible when it comes to tactics. Although we are always guided by the need for 100% class independence, there is no one-size-fits-all approach applicable to all times, places, and conditions.

For example, he addressed situations in which it is legally impossible to speak the truth openly, as was the case in Germany and Russia during the war. As he says, this is

> No argument in favor of concealing the truth, but [rather], in favor of setting up an illegal organization and press that would be free of police surveillance and censorship."

Another tactic Lenin takes up in the context of the war, but applicable in principle at all times, is participation in bourgeois parliaments or legislatures. Whether or not to run candidates or take elected positions in the first place must be determined on a case-by-case basis. But once such a position is taken, the following must be borne in mind: "While it is natural for the bourgeoisie to try to hoodwink the people, how should socialists in parliament conduct themselves?"

As always, Lenin goes to the heart of the matter:

> There are different kinds of parliamentarism. Some utilize the parliamentary arena in order to win the favor of their governments, or, at best, to wash their hands of everything. Others utilize parliamentarism in order to remain revolutionary to the end, to perform their duty as socialists and internationalists even under the most difficult circumstances.

> The parliamentary activities of some bring them into ministerial seats; the parliamentary activities of others bring them to prison, to exile, to penal servitude. Some serve the bourgeoisie, others—the proletariat. Some are social-imperialists. Others are revolutionary Marxists.

In just two sentences, Lenin contrasted the "national-liberal labor" policy of the opportunist-reformists to a genuine revolutionary policy:

> Whoever justifies participation in the present war perpetuates imperialist oppression of nations. Whoever advocates taking advantage of the present embarrassments of the governments to fight for the social revolution champions the real freedom of really all nations, which is possible only under socialism.

The point about the "real freedom of really all nations" is essential, because the question of imperialism is intimately tied up with the colonial revolution and the national question, whether in peacetime or war. According to Marx and Engels: "No nation can be free if it oppresses other nations."

And as Lenin explained:

> Socialists cannot achieve their great aim without fighting against all oppression of nations. Therefore, they must without fail demand that [revolutionaries in] *oppressing* countries . . . should recognize and champion the right of *oppressed* nations to self-determination, precisely in the political sense of the term, i.e., the right to political secession. The socialist of a ruling or colony-owning nation who fails to champion this right is a chauvinist.
>
> The championing of this right, far from encouraging the formation of small states, leads, on the contrary, to the freer, fearless and therefore wider and more widespread formation of very big states and federations of states, which are more beneficial for the masses and more fully in keeping with economic development.

> The socialists of *oppressed* nations must, in their turn, unfailingly fight for the complete—including organizational—unity of the *workers* of the oppressed and oppressing nationalities. The idea of the juridical separation of one nation from another—so-called "cultural-national autonomy"—is reactionary.

Above all, Lenin made clear that there is no "progressive" bourgeois in the imperialist epoch, and mercilessly attacked the social-chauvinists who justified "their own" ruling class's imperialist actions and ambitions:

> Social-chauvinism is advocacy of the idea of "defense of the fatherland" in the present war. Further, this idea logically leads to the abandonment of the class struggle during the war, to voting war credits, etc.
>
> Actually, the social-chauvinists are pursuing an anti-proletarian, bourgeois policy; for actually, they are championing not "defense of the fatherland" in the sense of fighting foreign oppression, but the "right" of one or other of the "great" powers to plunder colonies and to oppress other nations.
>
> The social-chauvinists repeat the bourgeois deception of the people that the war is being waged to protect the freedom and existence of nations, and thereby they go over to the side of the bourgeoisie against the proletariat.

Trotsky echoed this when writing about the colonial revolution in the "Manifesto of the Second Congress of the Communist International," adopted by the Comintern in August, 1920:

> The toilers of the colonial and semicolonial countries have awakened. In the boundless areas of India, Egypt, Persia, over which the gigantic octopus of British imperialism sprawls—in this uncharted human ocean vast internal forces are constantly at work, upheaving huge waves that cause tremors in the City [of London]'s stocks and hearts.

> In the movements of colonial peoples, the social element blends in diverse forms with the national element, but both of them are directed against imperialism. The road from the first stumbling baby steps to the mature forms of struggle is being traversed by the colonies and backward countries in general through a forced march, under the pressure of modern imperialism and under the leadership of the revolutionary proletariat . . .
>
> The socialist who aids directly or indirectly in perpetuating the privileged position of one nation at the expense of another, who accommodates himself to colonial slavery, who draws a line of distinction between races and colors in the matter of human rights, who helps the bourgeoisie of the metropolis to maintain its rule over the colonies instead of aiding the armed uprising of the colonies; the British Socialist who fails to support by all possible means the uprisings in Ireland, Egypt and India against the London plutocracy—such a socialist deserves to be branded with infamy, if not with a bullet, but in no case merits either a mandate or the confidence of the proletariat.

In short, social-chauvinism is the consummation of petty-bourgeois opportunism. It is the application of class collaborationism to foreign policy. In Lenin's words:

> Not a single Marxist has any doubt that opportunism expresses bourgeois policy within the working-class movement, expresses the interests of the petty bourgeoisie and the alliance of a tiny section of bourgeoisified workers with "their" bourgeoisie against the interests of the proletarian masses, the oppressed masses.

In the relatively peaceful and prosperous decades leading up to the war, the workers' leaders in countries like Germany and France had gotten more than a bit comfortable. They rubbed elbows with the ruling class, and

33. V. I. Lenin.

34. Karl Kautsky.

> Converted the utilization of bourgeois legality into subservience to it, created a tiny stratum of bureaucrats and aristocrats within the working class, and drew into the ranks of the Social-Democratic parties numerous petty-bourgeois "fellow travelers."
>
> The war accelerated this development and transformed opportunism into social-chauvinism, transformed the secret alliance between the opportunists and the bourgeoisie into an open one.
>
> Opportunism and social-chauvinism have the same ideological-political content: collaboration of classes instead of class struggle, renunciation of revolutionary methods of struggle . . . Opportunism has "matured," is now playing to the full its role as emissary of the bourgeois in the working-class movement.

As Lenin explains, Karl Kautsky and his followers were the main architects of this betrayal:

> By means of obvious sophistry they rob Marxism of its revolutionary living spirit; they recognize *everything* in Marxism *except* revolutionary methods of struggle, the preaching of and preparation for such methods, and the training of the masses precisely in this direction.
>
> [For Kautsky and co.] The International is merely a "peacetime instrument" . . . that in peacetime we live like brothers, but in wartime we . . . call upon the German workers to exterminate their French brothers, and vice versa.

No wonder Rosa Luxemburg wrote that "since August 4, 1914, German Social-Democracy has been a stinking corpse." And with it, the Socialist International as a whole.

This is why, as early as 1915, Lenin proclaimed the need for a Third International, even when the active forces of revolutionary Marxism were scattered to the four winds. As he wrote in "Socialism and War":

> Hard as the struggle may be, in individual cases, against the opportunists who predominate in many organizations, peculiar as the process of purging the workers' parties of opportunists may be in individual countries, this process is inevitable and fruitful. Reformist socialism is dying; regenerated socialism "will be revolutionary, uncompromising and insurrectionary," to use the apt expression of the French Socialist, Paul Golay.

Class war versus class collaboration and pacifism

In May of 1915, in the dark, early days of the war, Karl Liebknecht secretly printed a leaflet titled, "The Main Enemy is at Home!" In it, he urged the workers to absorb the lessons of the first ten months of the war and to "learn everything, don't forget anything!" As he wrote:

35. Karl Liebknecht, Berlin, 1911.

> The main enemy of the German people is in Germany: German imperialism, the German war party, German secret diplomacy. This enemy at home must be fought by the German people in a political struggle, cooperating with the proletariat of other countries whose struggle is against their own imperialists.

Already, during Christmas 1914, there had been fraternization between the troops, as depicted in the 2005 film, *Joyeaux Nöel*. Recognizing the threat this represented, the generals clamped down ferociously on the units involved. But the underlying sentiment of solidarity between the workers and peasants remained beneath the surface, even if they wore different uniforms and sang songs in different languages. Although not possible at all times or in all conditions, Lenin clearly understood the revolutionary implications, especially as the war got closer to ending:

> The capitalists either sneer at the fraternization of the soldiers at the front or savagely attack it. Through lies and slander, they try to make out that the whole thing is "deception" of the Russians by the Germans, and threaten—through *their* generals and officers—punishment for fraternization.
>
> From the point of view of safeguarding the "sacred right of property" in capital and the profits on capital, such a policy of the capitalists is quite correct. Indeed, if the proletarian socialist revolution is to be *suppressed* at its inception, it is *essential* that fraternization be regarded the way the capitalists regard it.
>
> The class-conscious workers, followed by the mass of semi-proletarians and poor peasants guided by the true instinct of oppressed classes, regard fraternization with profound sympathy. Clearly, fraternization is a path to peace. Clearly, this path does not run through the capitalist governments, through an alliance with them, but runs *against* them. Clearly, this path tends to develop, strengthen, and consolidate fraternal confidence between the workers of different countries.
>
> Clearly, this path is *beginning to wreck* the hateful discipline of the barrack prisons, the discipline of blind obedience of the soldier to "his" officers and generals, to his capitalists (for most of the officers and generals either belong to the capitalist class or protect its interests). Clearly, fraternization is the revolutionary initiative of the *masses*, it is the awakening of the conscience, the mind, the courage of the oppressed classes; in other words, it is a rung in the ladder leading up to the socialist proletarian revolution.
>
> Long live fraternization! Long live the *rising* worldwide socialist revolution of the proletariat!

It was in this overall context that Lenin raised the slogan: "Convert the imperialist war into civil war." In other words, convert the imperialist war between nations into a revolutionary war between classes. This is the essential meaning of the slogan: "no war but the class war!"

As Lenin explained:

> Civil war is just as much a war as any other. He who accepts the class struggle cannot fail to accept civil wars, which in every class society are the natural, and under certain conditions inevitable, continuation, development and intensification of the class struggle. That has been confirmed by every great revolution. To repudiate civil war, or to forget about it, is to fall into extreme opportunism and renounce the socialist revolution . . .
>
> The representatives of the [American] bourgeoisie understand that for the sake of overthrowing Negro slavery, of overthrowing the rule of the slave owners, it was worth letting the country go through long years of civil war, through the abysmal ruin, destruction, and terror that accompany every war. But now, when we are confronted with the vastly greater task of overthrowing capitalist *wage*-slavery, of overthrowing the rule of the bourgeoisie—now, the representatives and defenders of the bourgeoisie, and also the reformist socialists who have been frightened by the bourgeoisie and are shunning the revolution, cannot and do not want to understand that civil war is necessary and legitimate.

As we've seen, Lenin had to push back hard against the tide of nationalist, chauvinist patriotism summed up by the slogan "defense of the fatherland," which initially infected many advanced workers. To this end, he developed the policy of revolutionary defeatism, which takes the question of class independence in both domestic and foreign policy to its logical conclusion: "During a reactionary war a revolutionary class cannot but desire the defeat of its government."

The basic idea is that, instead of falling into support for "your" bourgeoisie in an inter-imperialist war, you should explain to the advanced workers that the defeat of "your" own imperialism would be the best outcome for the working class as a whole. Did this mean that Lenin was "for" German imperialism, or that he wanted Russia to be occupied and brutalized by the Kaiser's armies?

Marxists view all processes in nature and society dialectically, not in black-and-white, either-or dichotomies. Far from attempting to deny or banish contradiction from reality, we embrace and seek to understand it. Flowing from our uncompromising commitment to class independence, we are under no obligation to choose between "lesser evils," either in politics or in an inter-imperialist conflict.

The idea that "the enemy of my enemy is my friend" is an overly simplistic and undialectical trap disguised as "common sense." As Lenin once said: "Every abstract truth, if it is accepted without analysis, becomes a mere phrase."

For example, just because modern-day Russian imperialism is the enemy of US imperialism does not mean Putin and his gangsters are our friends. This is because he is also the enemy of our friend, the Russian working class. The position of revolutionary communists is clear. Just as the capitalists always side with each other against the workers when their interests are threatened, we always take the side of the exploited and oppressed of all countries, against the exploiters and oppressors of all countries. *Always.*

Lenin's revolutionary defeatism was aimed at shaking the party out of its shock and awe at the collapse of the International and to ground them in a class perspective. As he explained, while an Allied military victory would strengthen tsarism and postpone the hour of revolutionary liberation, its defeat would lead inevitably to a collapse of the regime and unleash a period of revolution. This is precisely what had happened in 1905 after the tsar's armies were humiliated in the Russo-Japanese War. As Lenin argued:

> Both the advocates of victory for their governments in the present war and the advocates of the slogan "neither victory nor defeat" equally take the standpoint of social-chauvinism. A revolutionary class cannot but wish for the defeat of its government in a reactionary war, cannot fail to see that its military reverses facilitate its overthrow.
>
> Only a bourgeois who believes that a war started by the governments must necessarily end as a war between governments and wants it to end as such, can regard as "ridiculous" and "absurd" the idea that the Socialists of *all* the belligerent countries should wish for the defeat of *all* "their" governments and express this wish. On the contrary, it is precisely a statement of this kind that would conform to the cherished thoughts of every class-conscious worker, and would be in line with our activities towards converting the imperialist war into civil war . . .
>
> The opponents of the defeat slogan are simply afraid of themselves when they refuse to recognize the . . . inseparable link between revolutionary agitation against the government and helping bring about its defeat.

Again, Lenin wasn't addressing the masses at this time, who naturally feared German imperialism, even if they didn't like the tsar or the war. Later, he advocated far broader slogans such as "Peace, Land, and Bread!" to mobilize the masses against the war and for the socialist revolution. This is a classic example of the art of developing slogans and transitional demands. What is necessary and appropriate in a particular context and audience may be entirely inappropriate and even reactionary in another.

After the fall of the tsar, Alexander Kerensky's bourgeois government wanted to continue the war against German imperialism on behalf of the Allies. Many honest workers and Bolsheviks were duped by his appeals to "defend the revolution." However, the revolution was still at the bourgeois-democratic stage, meaning that the war was still being waged on an imperialist basis:

> Revolutionary defensism must be regarded as the most important, the most striking manifestation of the petty-bourgeois wave that has swept over "nearly everything." It is the worst enemy of the further progress and success of the Russian revolution.
>
> Those who have yielded on this point and have been unable to extricate themselves are lost to the revolution. However, the masses yield differently from the leaders, and they extricate themselves in a different way, through a different course of development and by different means.
>
> Revolutionary defensism is, on the one hand, a result of the bourgeoisie's deception of the masses, a result of the trusting lack of reasoning on the part of the peasants and a section of the workers. On the other hand, it is an expression of the interests and viewpoint of the small proprietor, who is to some extent interested in annexations and bank profits, and who "sacredly" guards the traditions of tsarism, which demoralized the Great Russians by making them do a hangman's work against other peoples.
>
> What is required of us is the *ability* to explain to the masses that the social and political character of the war is determined not by the "good will" of individuals or groups, or even of nations, but by the position of the *class* which conducts the war, by the class *policy* of which the war is a continuation, by the *ties* of capital, which is the dominant economic force in modern society, by the *imperialist character* of international capital, by Russia's dependence in finance, banking and diplomacy upon Britain, France, and so on. To explain this skillfully in a way the people would understand *is not easy*; none of us would be able to do it at once without making mistakes.

> But this, and only this, must be the aim or, rather, the message of our propaganda. The slightest concession to revolutionary defensism is *a betrayal of socialism*, a complete renunciation of *internationalism*, no matter what fine phrases and "practical" considerations may be used to justify it.

Once the Bolsheviks stood at the head of a government representing the workers and poor peasants, however, its class content was transformed, and the revolutionary war they waged against the landlords, capitalists, and imperialists was absolutely justified and progressive, despite the death and devastation that accompanies every war.

Yet again, class independence is our "true north." Determining the essential class content of any situation is the starting point for drawing correct conclusions and pointing the way forward. All things being equal, if a backwards, colonial country is being bullied or invaded by an imperialist power, we defend it without hesitation against imperialist aggression, even if it is ruled by bourgeois reactionaries. This was the case when the US invaded Iraq in 1990 and again in 2003.

And if a workers' state were being attacked by an imperialist power, we would side unconditionally with the workers' state, even if it was degenerated or deformed, and even if we had our own criticisms of its leadership. This was the case when Nazi Germany invaded the Soviet Union and when American imperialism carpet-bombed North Vietnam. It is also the basis for our decades-long defense of the Cuban Revolution against imperialist sabotage and aggression.

Lenin also takes up the question of pacifism, and in particular, the abstract demand for "disarmament."

> The Kautskyite advocacy of "disarmament," which is addressed to the present governments of the imperialist Great Powers, is the most vulgar opportunism, it is bourgeois pacifism, which

> *actually*—in spite of the "good intentions" of the sentimental Kautskyites—serves to distract the workers from the revolutionary struggle. For this advocacy seeks to instill in the workers the idea that the present bourgeois governments of the imperialist powers are *not* bound to each other by thousands of threads of finance capital and by scores or hundreds of corresponding *secret treaties* (i.e., predatory, plundering treaties, preparing the way for imperialist war).

Whether their intentions are honest or not, what pacifists fail to understand is that militarism and war are not the result of "bad" policies by "bad" individuals or governments. Despite their lofty promises and pretensions, international bodies like the United Nations are dominated by the main imperialist powers. They are rooted in class society and cannot serve as impartial arbiters or decree world peace.

Nonetheless, Lenin was careful to differentiate between the healthy pacifism of the masses and the pacifism of those who would give cover to the ambitions of "their" own bourgeoisie.

> The sentiments of the masses in favor of peace often express incipient protest, anger and consciousness of the reactionary character of the war. It is the duty of all Social-Democrats to utilize these sentiments. They will take a most ardent part in every movement and in every demonstration on this ground; but they will not deceive the people by conceding the idea that peace without annexations, without the oppression of nations, without plunder, without the germs of new wars among the present governments and ruling classes is possible in the absence of a revolutionary movement.
>
> Such a deception of the people would merely play into the hands of the secret diplomacy of the belligerent governments and facilitate their counterrevolutionary plans. Whoever wants a

> lasting and democratic peace must be in favor of civil war against the governments and the bourgeoisie . . .
>
> "Disarmament" means simply running away from unpleasant reality, not fighting it . . .
>
> Marxism is not pacifism. It is necessary, of course, to fight for the speediest termination of the war. But only if a *revolutionary* struggle is called for does the demand for peace acquire proletarian meaning. Without a series of revolutions, so-called democratic peace is a philistine utopia.
>
> The purpose of a real program of action would be served only by a *Marxist* program, which gave the masses a full and clear explanation of what has occurred, which explained what imperialism is and how to combat it, which openly stated that it was opportunism that led to the collapse of the Second International, which openly called for the building of a Marxist International without and *against* the opportunists.
>
> Only such a program as would show that we have confidence in ourselves, confidence in Marxism, that we proclaim a life-and-death struggle against opportunism would sooner or later ensure for us the sympathy of the genuine proletarian masses.

Lenin pulled no punches when explaining how workers could successfully turn the imperialist war into a class war:

> An oppressed class that does not strive to learn to use arms, to acquire arms, only deserves to be treated like slaves. We cannot, unless we have become bourgeois pacifists or opportunists, forget that we are living in a class society from which there is no way out, nor can there be, save through the class struggle. Our slogan must be: arming of the proletariat to defeat, expropriate and disarm the bourgeoisie.
>
> We are not in favor of a bourgeois militia; we are in favor only of a proletarian militia. Therefore, "not a penny, not a man," not

> only for a standing army, but even for a bourgeois militia. We can demand popular election of officers, abolition of all military law, equal rights for foreign and native-born workers, with free election of [military] instructors paid by the state, etc.
>
> Only under these conditions could the proletariat acquire military training for itself and not for its slave owners; and the need for such training is imperatively dictated by the interests of the proletariat. These are the only tactics possible for a revolutionary class, tactics that follow logically from, and are dictated by, the whole objective development of capitalist militarism.
>
> Only after the proletariat has disarmed the bourgeoisie will it be able, without betraying its world-historic mission, to consign all armaments to the scrap heap. And the proletariat will undoubtedly do this, but only when this condition has been fulfilled, certainly not before.

Again, as always, it comes down to class independence, in all things, at all times.

In the Guidelines on the Organizational Structure of Communist Parties adopted by the Third Congress of the Comintern in 1921, the communist attitude toward arming the workers is elaborated further:

> The proletariat rejects in principle and combats with the utmost energy all military institutions of the bourgeois state and of the bourgeois class in general. On the other hand, it utilizes these institutions to give the workers military training for revolutionary battles.
>
> Therefore, it is not against the military training of youth and workers but against the militaristic order and the autocratic rule of the officers that intensive agitation should be directed. Every possibility for the proletariat to get weapons into its hands must be exploited to the fullest.

36. Our Own Kind of Military Training!—Barton.
Socialist Appeal. August 1940.

This was the basis for Trotsky's Proletarian Military Policy during World War II, which was carried out brilliantly by Ted Grant and his comrades in Britain in the early 1940s, and discussed in some detail in the article "Marxism Versus Sectarianism."

However, let us never forget that, as explained in Part One of this book, the power of imperialism is ultimately rooted in its control over finance capital. Without money, the capitalists and their states can't wage war.

When we speak of "arming the masses," therefore, it is the *masses* that are the key to the equation, not the *arms*. If we do not succeed in winning the majority *politically*, then all the arms in the world will not make a revolution. First and foremost, revolutionary communists must strive to arm the masses with *ideas*. Only then can we paralyze the capitalist economy, bring the war machine to a halt, and pose the question: Who really runs society?

Lenin was a brilliant dialectical materialist, but he was also a realist. He knew that unless and until global capitalism was ended, even greater horrors would follow. As he wrote even before the Russian Revolution:

> We do not wish to ignore the sad possibility—if the worst comes to the worst—of mankind going through a *second* imperialist war, if revolution does not come out of the present war, in spite of our efforts.

Of course, there was a revolutionary wave after World War I, and it did end capitalism, but only in one country, Russia. Due to its material backwardness and prolonged isolation—which resulted from a lack of revolutionary leadership and the failure of the socialist revolution in the more advanced capitalist countries—we saw the rise of Stalinism and fascism. Despite Lenin's best efforts, the world did, in fact, have to endure another world war, even bloodier than the first.

To end war, end capitalism!

The task of Marxists today is to learn the lessons of history, the lessons of Lenin. Ending imperialism will require a prolonged and arduous fight. But the hardships we will face will be far outweighed by the prize we seek to win: a world of permanent peace, dignity, and superabundance for all. As Lenin soberly put it, we must "think about and reflect on the fierce class struggle and class wars needed to achieve that beautiful future."

Rosa Luxemburg wrote the following lines from prison in the Spring of 1915. They are even more resonant today, after a further century of imperialist bloodletting:

> Friedrich Engels once said: "Bourgeois society stands at the crossroads, either transition to socialism or regression into

> barbarism." What does "regression into barbarism" mean to our lofty European civilization? Until now, we have all probably read and repeated these words thoughtlessly, without suspecting their fearsome seriousness.
>
> A look around us at this moment shows what the regression of bourgeois society into barbarism means. This world war is a regression into barbarism. The triumph of imperialism leads to the annihilation of civilization. At first, this happens sporadically for the duration of a modern war, but then when the period of unlimited wars begins it progresses toward its inevitable consequences.
>
> Today, we face the choice exactly as Friedrich Engels foresaw it a generation ago: either the triumph of imperialism and the collapse of all civilization as in ancient Rome, depopulation, desolation, degeneration—a great cemetery. Or the victory of socialism, that means the conscious active struggle of the international proletariat against imperialism and its method of war. This is a dilemma of world history, an either/or; the scales are wavering before the decision of the class-conscious proletariat.
>
> The future of civilization and humanity depends on whether or not the proletariat resolves manfully to throw its revolutionary broadsword into the scales. In this war imperialism has won. Its bloody sword of genocide has brutally tilted the scale toward the abyss of misery. The only compensation for all the misery and all the shame would be if we learn from the war how the proletariat can seize mastery of its own destiny and escape the role of the lackey to the ruling classes.

As for Lenin, his revolutionary optimism was boundless and his defiance of world imperialism in both words and deeds was unmatched. In June of 1918, the Russian proletariat was in the midst of a desperate civil war against the forces of counterrevolution. The German Army had occupied much of Ukraine, the Japanese had seized Vladivostok, the Czech Legion had proclaimed a government in the Volga, British troops had landed in Murmansk, and the American imperialists had launched their own "expedition" to snuff out the young Soviet republic. It was literally a question of life or death, socialism or barbarism. Despite the incredible odds he and his comrades faced, Lenin made this inspiring appeal in his "Letter to American Workers":

> Despite this, we are firmly convinced that we are invincible, because the spirit of humankind will not be broken by the imperialist slaughter. Humanity will vanquish it. And the first country to *break* the convict chains of the imperialist war was *our* country. We sustained enormously heavy casualties in the struggle to break these chains, but we *broke* them. We are *free from* imperialist dependence, we have raised the banner of struggle for the complete overthrow of imperialism for the whole world to see.
>
> We are now, as it were, in a besieged fortress, waiting for the other detachments of the world socialist revolution to come to our relief. These detachments *exist*, they are *more numerous* than ours, they are maturing, growing, gaining more strength the longer the brutalities of imperialism continue. The workers are breaking away from their social traitors . . . Slowly but surely the workers are adopting communist, Bolshevik tactics and are marching towards the proletarian revolution, which alone is capable of saving dying culture and dying humankind.
>
> In short, we are invincible, because the world proletarian revolution is invincible.

Capitalism, imperialism, and the horrors of war inherent to this system need not be the endgame for our species. As Leon Trotsky succinctly put it: "There is only one way of avoiding war—that is the overthrow of this society."

Part 3: When US Imperialism Invaded Soviet Russia

In the summer of 1918, the Russian Revolution was at a crossroads. Tsar Nicholas and the Provisional Government had been overthrown, one after another, and the new Soviet power had appealed to the world's war-weary masses for a "just and democratic peace . . . without annexations and reparations." But the First World War still raged, and the counterrevolution was gaining momentum.

In March of that year, German imperialism had imposed the Treaty of Brest-Litovsk on the Soviet Republic, leading to a loss of 34% of its population, 54% of its industrial land, 26% of its railways, and 89% of its coalfields. Under the pretense of keeping Russian munition stores out of German hands, British troops landed at Murmansk on the very next day.

Russia's former "allies" were out for blood, keenly aware of the threat the revolution posed to world capitalism. Winston Churchill was adamant that Bolshevism had to be "strangled in its cradle." Wave upon wave of imperialist "expeditions" followed, with 21 military contingents from 16 countries joining the counterrevolutionary efforts of the proto-fascist White Armies.

Surrounded and outgunned, the communist cause seemed hopeless. But the Russian masses had something none of the imperialist armies had: the indomitable spirit of revolution and genuine liberation.

To be sure, there were countless acts of military brilliance and civilian sacrifice by the Soviet people. However, the Bolsheviks' primary weapon was *political.* They systematically addressed the invaders' troops on a *class basis*, appealing for proletarian unity against their common exploiters. Time and again, the morale of the imperialists' rank-and-file soldiers was so undermined that they eventually had to be withdrawn.

And although most Americans are utterly unaware of it, the US also sent troops to fight the Red Army, from August 1918 to April 1920. In a 1984 speech addressed to the people of the Soviet Union, that Cold Warrior *par excellence*, Ronald Reagan, declared that "our sons and daughters have never fought each other in war." But they had fought. And American troops had also mutinied.

Imperialist hypocrisy

In April 1917, the US had declared war on Germany. By entering the war at such a late stage, Woodrow Wilson and the American ruling class hoped to "mop up" after years of slaughter. There was also the small matter of nearly $10 billion in loans made to the Allies during the war, which would have been jeopardized in the event of a German victory. It was also no coincidence that they entered the fray just weeks after the February Revolution, which brought down the tsar and threatened to take Russia out of the war on the Eastern Front.

The Americans' stated aim was to defeat the kaiser while ensuring stability and cutting across the threat of a Europe-wide revolution. But by October of that year, events in Russia had taken a far more dangerous turn as far as the interests of imperialism and the capitalist system were concerned: the Bolsheviks were in power.

Shortly after taking the reins, Lenin issued his famous decrees on Peace, Land, and Nationalities, and Trotsky published the Allies' secret plans to carve up the world among themselves. This put pressure on Wilson, who was cynically posing as a "peace loving" president.

On January 8, 1918, Wilson issued his Fourteen Points, outlining US imperialism's vision for a "new world order." Along with liberal rhetoric about peace and democracy, point eight addressed Russia specifically:

> The evacuation of all Russian territory and such a settlement of all questions affecting Russia as will secure the best and freest cooperation of the other nations of the world in obtaining for her an unhampered and unembarrassed opportunity for the independent determination of her own political development and national policy and assure her of a sincere welcome into the society of free nations under institutions of her own choosing; and, more than a welcome, *assistance also of every kind that she may need* and may herself desire. The treatment accorded Russia by her sister nations in the months to come will be the acid test of their good will, of their comprehension of her needs as distinguished from their own interests, and of their intelligent and unselfish sympathy." (My emphasis)

However, what kind of treatment was to be accorded, and to which Russians, wasn't specified—though Wilson's multiple military interventions against Mexico during its ongoing revolution offered some clues. At the same time these lofty words were issued, contingency plans to snuff out the Soviet Republic were already in motion. As the US Ambassador to

37. The Dogs of the Entente—Viktor Deni, 1919.
Uncle Sam, France, and Britain hold the leashes of the White generals Denikin, Kolchak, and Yudenich.

France put it, "Three or four Japanese or American divisions are enough to put an end to the Bolsheviks."

And according to historian William A. Williams, "Intervention as a consciously anti-Bolshevik operation was decided upon by American leaders within five weeks of the day Lenin and Trotsky took power."

The Bolsheviks were seen as coup mongers, representing only a minority of the Russian people. Edgar Sisson, an officer for the US Committee on Public Information stationed in Petrograd, Russia, reported to Woodrow Wilson that "the present leaders of the Russian Bolshevik government were installed by Germany."

David Rowland Francis, the last US ambassador to tsarist Russia, wrote to the Secretary of State saying he had "evidence that the Soviet government submits to German demands without protest and am almost convinced that Lenin and possibly Trotsky are pliable tools if not responsive German agents."

As is so often the case with imperialist invaders—whether through naiveté or pure cynicism—the Americans believed they would be welcomed as liberators and that the local population would rise in revolt against the Bolsheviks. As Ambassador Francis wrote to Washington, "Information from all sources demonstrates dissatisfaction with the Soviets and indicates that [an] Allied intervention would be welcomed by [the] Russian people."

On July 17, 1918, Wilson agreed to a "limited military intervention." By August 3, the US government publicly stated that it was in full accord with the other imperialist powers with their Russian intervention policy.

But the imperialists woefully underestimated the depths of the revolution—and the heroism and determination of the Soviet masses.

Finding a pretext

The US government set in motion operational plans for a series of military expeditions to the Soviet Republic. Publicly, they claimed that this was to keep strategic ports and arms depots out of the hands of the Germans. But their real aim was to keep these from the Bolsheviks.

US imperialism had other motives as well. Japanese imperialism was on the rise, and the West's "Open Door" to the East was under threat. The first contingent of Japanese troops had already landed at Vladivostok on April 5, 1918. But how to justify American military intervention in Eastern Siberia, which was thousands of miles from the German Imperial Army? The answer came in the form of the Czech Legion.

During the war, 70,000 Czech and Slovak soldiers had volunteered to fight with the tsarist army against the Central Powers in exchange for independence from the Austro-Hungarian Empire. But with the tsar gone and the Bolsheviks in power, they were left stranded in Russia—a seasoned and sizable foreign army in the midst of the revolution. They began moving slowly eastward on the Trans-Siberian Railway, hoping to evacuate the country via Vladivostok and travel by sea to rejoin the Allies' side in Western Europe.

However, in May 1918, after a series of minor clashes, they went into open revolt against the Bolshevik regime, occupying several important cities along the key transportation artery. This put them objectively in the camp of counterrevolution, and the White Armies seized on the chaos to set up a series of anti-Bolshevik governments across Siberia.

As Trotsky wrote at the time:

> The Soviet power entertains the most friendly feelings toward the mass of the Czechoslovak workers and peasants, who are the brothers of the Russian workers and peasants. However, the Soviet power cannot tolerate a situation in which the Czechoslovaks, confused by reactionary scoundrels, White Guards and foreign agents, have seized railway stations by armed force and used violence against the Soviets, as happened at Novo Nikolayevsk.
>
> The Military Commissariat has issued an order for immediate and unconditional disarmament of all Czechoslovaks and shooting of those who resist by force the measures taken by the Soviet power. At the same time, the Military Commissariat again declares and confirms, in the name of the Government as a whole, that the Soviet power entertains the most friendly feelings towards the Czechoslovaks and, for its part, will do everything necessary to enable them to leave Russia in the shortest possible time. But this depends on their complete and unconditional surrender of all arms and strictest submission to the instructions of the People's Commissariat for Military Affairs.

But they did not disarm.

The standoff between the Soviet power and the Czech Legion was the excuse the Americans had been looking for to intervene. The Czechs were anti-Bolshevik, anti-German, anti-Japanese, and the most formidable fighting force in the region at the time. This was precisely the cover US imperialism needed to pursue its policy of active support for "reputable and sound elements of order."

Doughboys and Polar Bears

The US invasion of Soviet soil began on August 15, 1918, with 3,000 troops disembarking at Vladivostok. This was the beginning of what one US Army historian called "one of the most unique military adventures of the 20th century." All told, nearly 9,000 American troops—nicknamed "doughboys" due to their dust-covered uniforms—would serve on that front, having been transferred mainly from the occupation of the Philippines.

Then, on September 4, roughly 5,000 troops from the American Expeditionary Force, North Russia—better known as the "polar bears"—landed at Arkhangelsk, a key port on the White Sea with a direct railway line to Petrograd.

The first order of business was the creation of an International Police Force composed of troops from 12 nations under the command of a Russian-born American officer, Major Samuel Ignatiev Johnson. The next task was to ensure the Trans-Siberian Railway remained operational so the Czechs could reconsolidate their forces.

Of course, officially speaking, none of this had anything to do with intervening in the Civil War already raging between the Reds and the Whites. Nor did it have anything to do with counterbalancing the Japanese—who had responded to the landing of US troops by beefing up their own contingent to 72,000—a clear message as to their claim on the Far East.

38. American soldiers from the 31st Infantry near Vladivostok, Russia, April 27, 1919.

The Allied imperialists of Great Britain, France, Canada, and Australia had also dispatched tens of thousands of troops to Siberia. For their part, the Reds were roughly 15,000 strong on this front, including some German-Austrian POWs who had defected to join the communist cause.

The White Armies represented the forces of reaction in Russia. Financed and supported by the imperialists, they represented the interests of the big landowners, the Orthodox Church, and the capitalists. They were willing to restore the pre-Bolshevik status quo by any means necessary.

The proto-fascist warlord Alexander Kolchak organized the armies of counterrevolution in the Far East, along with Anton Denikin in Southern Russia, and Nikolai Yudenich in the Northwest. Under the Allies' protective aegis, Kolchak declared himself "Supreme Ruler of Russia" and head of the Russian State, in opposition to the rule of the Bolsheviks. His

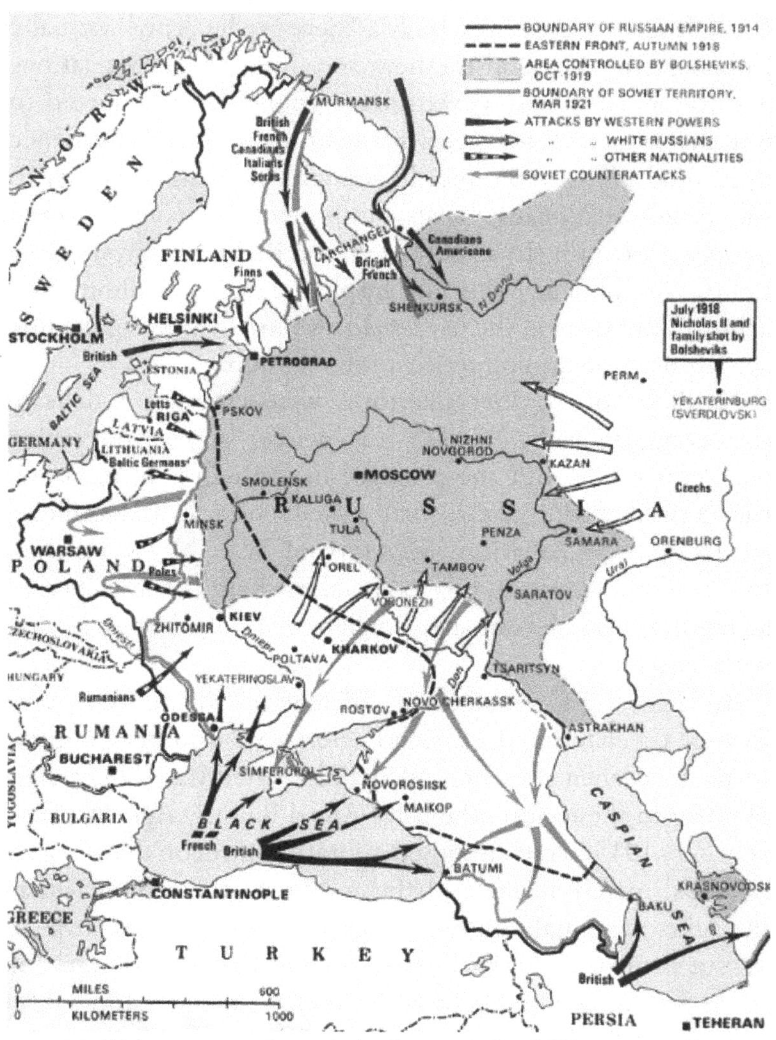

39. Troop movements in the Russian Civil War, 1919–21.

was a horrifying regime of pogroms, torture, executions, and forced labor.

On the other hand, the Red Army represented the forces of revolution—the working class and the mass of poor peasants.

Leon Trotsky successfully built a "new model army" virtually from scratch to defend the new, socialized property relations and the revolutionary government. Though he was forced to rely on former tsarist officers with technical skills and experience that could not be reproduced overnight, he ensured loyalty to the revolutionary cause by appointing political commissars to oversee every unit. In a short span, the Red Army grew into a tightly disciplined, politically inspired force of millions that achieved miracles on the battlefield, eventually turning the tide against reaction and imperialist intervention.

Needless to say, the Americans were entering a delicate situation. Officially, the US was neither at war nor allied with either side. But the presence of thousands of boots on the ground during a civil war risked political and military escalation. The American Secretary of War, Newton Baker, told William Graves, the US general in charge of the Siberian adventure, "Watch your step; you'll be walking on eggs, loaded with dynamite."

In theory, the Americans' "defensive" operations were focused on enabling the Czech Legion's exit from the country. In practice, their presence aided and abetted the White reign of terror in the region. The Inter-Allied Railway Agreement of February 1919, which imposed military control on the Siberian railways, merely formalized the reality on the ground—that the Allies were maintaining supply lines for Kolchak's troops. White control over the railways allowed them to attack or starve anyone not on board with Kolchak's dictatorship.

Some 250 American soldiers were sent to defend the Souchan mines, located 75 miles northeast of Vladivostok. These shafts provided much of the coal used to operate the railways in Eastern Russia—an essential resource for the counterrevolution. One of the Allies' first acts had been to reinstate the mine's former manager, who had been run out of the area by the workers. Another 2,000 Americans were stationed 1,700 miles west of Vladivostok to guard another vital railway node. Thousands more took up positions at other strategic locations on the rail lines.

Though he played the charade of "noninterference" and "neutrality" in public, General Graves was unambiguous as to his role in cables to Washington: "We are making this condition [Kolchak's dictatorship] possible by our presence here . . . As I see this question, we become a party, by guarding the railroad, to the actions of this governmental class."

All of this led inevitably to a series of clashes with Red Army troops, as well as with the growing ranks of pro-Bolshevik guerillas and even White Cossacks opposed to the presence of foreign interlopers.

Red partisan attacks on rail freight, track, and bridges increased throughout March and April. By May, Graves decided that to maintain order, American troops would be given official license to pursue the guerrillas who were harassing Kolchak. A summer of skirmishes, attacks, and combat patrols into the surrounding countryside followed, often alongside White Russian and Japanese troops.

In June, the Battle of Romanovka saw the Reds launch a surprise attack on an American army camp, resulting in 24 Americans dead and 25 wounded. Five days later, the US Ambassador to Japan traveled to Kolchak's capital at Omsk. While not officially recognizing him as the official leader of Russia, he took a "sympathetic interest in Kolchak's organization and activities."

However, the ambassador estimated an additional 40,000 US troops would be needed to ensure Kolchak's victory and stymie Japanese encroachment on the region. But this was impossible.

Many American soldiers were more sympathetic to the Reds than to the Whites and were horrified by Kolchak's cruelty. On October 1, 1919, US soldiers had been arrested and flogged by Kolchak's Cossacks—seemingly no one was exempt from their brutality.

Similar scenes of fighting and eventual demoralization took place around Arkhangelsk, where the "polar bears" were stationed and placed under the control of the British. Let's not forget that most of these operations took place after World War I officially ended on November 11, 1918. The Americans, British, and Canadians fought alongside the Whites against the Reds in the Battle of Tulgas on Armistice Day itself. Yet the occupation of parts of Soviet Russia continued—so much for Wilson's "nonintervention."

Internationalist appeals

The Reds did not only respond militarily, but politically, appealing to the invading troops on the basis of proletarian internationalism. On August 20, 1918, Lenin wrote his famous "Letter to American Workers." Brimming with internationalism and packed with prescient insights into US history, politics, and its coming role in the world revolution, it is a must-read for communists today. Appeals were also directed to the workers of Europe.

Lenin was a supreme theoretician and strategist. But he was an equally skilled tactician and, of course, a fervent internationalist. He always saw the Russian Revolution as merely one component in the world revolution, and he was under no illusions that it could survive in isolation. As he explained:

> We are counting on the inevitability of the international revolution. But that does not mean that we count upon its coming at some

40. "Be on Guard!"—Dmitry Moor, 1921.
Leon Trotsky, leader of the Red Army.

> definite, nearby date . . . We know that revolutions cannot come neither at a word of command nor according to prearranged plans.
>
> We know that circumstances alone have pushed us, the proletariat of Russia, forward, that we have reached this new stage in the social life of the world not because of our superiority but because of the peculiarly reactionary character of Russia. But until the outbreak of the international revolution, revolutions in individual countries may still meet with a number of serious setbacks and overthrows.

Given its economic and military might and the weight of its working class, Lenin understood that the US was a vital key for that worldwide process—and this remains the case today.

In fact, the ideas outlined in his letter are more relevant today than ever.

In it, he adopted an honest, frank, and open tone, laying bare the revolution's many problems and shortcomings while pointing to its infinite potential and the cynical hypocrisy of those who sought to drown it in blood:

> In the Soviet Republic there arises before us a new world, the world of socialism. Such a world cannot be materialized as if by magic, complete in every detail, as Minerva sprang from Jupiter's head.

He also displayed his rich knowledge of the "revolutionary tradition in the life of the American people," referencing the American Revolution, the US Civil War, and Eugene Debs. By highlighting the class divisions in American society, he sought to drive a wedge between the American workers and their exploiters. He counterposed the "American plutocrats" to the "revolutionary proletariat of America" and called on them to perform the important task of ending the intervention. The real enemy, after all, is at home.

As he explained:

> [The US imperialists] have made the greatest profits. They have made all, even the weakest countries, their debtors. They have amassed gigantic fortunes during the war. And every dollar is stained with the blood that was shed by millions of murdered and crippled men, shed in the high, honorable, and holy war of freedom.

In simple yet profound terms, he explained the class roots of the war and the foreign intervention against the Soviets, making it abundantly clear that both the Germans and the Allies were criminally responsible for the horrific slaughter. Far from pliable tools or agents of the kaiser, the Bolsheviks were

German imperialism's mortal enemies, as evidenced by the terms of Brest-Litovsk.

He condemned all the imperialists with the most vivid language imaginable:

> The dead body of bourgeois society cannot simply be put into a coffin and buried. It rots in our midst, poisons the air we breathe, pollutes our lives, clings to the new, the fresh, the living with a thousand threads and tendrils of old customs, of death and decay.

Declining morale

Outnumbered and unwelcome, many of the American workers and farmers in uniform had growing doubts about their role in Russia and chafed under the command of the British in Arkhangelsk. An American officer summed up the flagging mood among the troops:

> They stated that they were drafted to fight Germany, not the Bolsheviks. That they had been sent here to guard supplies and not carry on aggressive warfare; that after the signing of the Armistice with Germany their job was finished and if the government wanted them to stay on and fight Bolshevism it should say so and announce some definite policy regarding Russia."

Another informed America's top general, John "Blackjack" Pershing, that:

> The morale of our troops has been low since the signing of the Armistice with Germany. The men and some of the officers seem unable to understand why they should be kept in Russia after fighting has stopped with Germany.

Due to their familiarity with cold weather, most of the "polar bears" stationed in North Russia came from the Upper Midwest. Once the Armistice was official, Chicago,

Detroit, and Wisconsin newspapers increased the pressure to bring the troops home. Some even reprinted soldiers' letters describing the harsh conditions they faced in full, in defiance of government censorship. A cartoon published in the *Chicago Tribune* depicted two American soldiers in Arkhangelsk asking each other, "Say, when did we declare war on Russia?"

An editorial in the same paper wrote:

> Our men are dying for a cause, the purpose of which they are no more certain than we in America. America has not declared war on Russia, but Americans are killing Russians or are being killed by them.

The American troops were subjected to a constant stream of proletarian internationalist appeals from the Soviets—who added that the occupiers faced certain destruction if they remained on Russian soil. The imperialists' presence was also used to rally the Russian peasantry to the side of the revolution.

One leaflet depicted Uncle Sam and British capitalists holding the leashes of White leaders. The American Red Cross noted, "The presence of the Allied Expedition in North Russia constitutes one of the strongest pillars of the Bolshevik government."

As one of the direct participants recalled:

> When a man's own home paper printed the same story [as did Bolshevik propaganda] of the million men advancing on Archangel with bloody bayonets fixed, and told the horrible hardships the soldiers endured . . . the doughboy's spirit was depressed.

Political pressure grew to end the expedition, with Republican members of Congress and senators spearheading the charge. The vote on the bill was dead-even along party lines, with the Democratic vice president breaking the tie in favor of prolonging the adventure.

After this failed vote, morale among the soldiers plummeted even further. On March 30, 1919, a tipping point was reached when a sergeant in North Russia ordered four enlisted men to load their sleds and move to the front. They refused, and a general meeting of the men was called. According to a certain Lieutenant May, the soldiers complained that "They had never been supplied with an answer as to why they were there, but the Reds were trying to push them into the White Sea and that they were fighting for their lives."

Mutinous mood

While there are conflicting accounts about what happened next, the *Washington Post* published an article on April 11 titled "US Troops Mutiny on Archangel Front." The article reported that after four soldiers had refused to go to the front, 250 more soldiers had been insubordinate and predicted that a "general mutiny" was possible if the troops were not withdrawn immediately. These reports eventually made it back to the "polar bears" in Russia, driving spirits down even further.

At least some American soldiers had concluded that the British, who had overall command of the operation, dreamed of outright conquest—something that has been subsequently confirmed. As one wrote in his diary, "There were no supplies. Actually, the British wanted to occupy and conquer the state of North Russia in order to obtain the pine from the forests."

Fears that US troops might not obey orders from British officers grew. As one American commander wrote, "Grave doubts were expressed by many of our officers that orders for aggressive operations would be obeyed."

The mood of the Russian peasants in the occupied regions was clearly swinging in favor of the Reds. The October Revolution had given land to the peasants, but wherever the Whites took control, they ruthlessly restored the former landowners, backed by a regime of terror. It was easy to decide which side had their best interests at heart.

Meanwhile, Trotsky's titanic effort to build a Red Army was achieving wondrous results. Even US military intelligence had to concede this: "Within the last two months, the whole Bolshevik forces have been reorganized, and a serious attempt is being made to create a large, well-disciplined army on a European model."

As the Bolsheviks gained momentum, worries that the occupiers would be overrun intensified. Allied positions were regularly hit with long-range artillery, and the intelligence services reported that "[the] enemy is systematically accumulating troops on all fronts with the view of a general offensive before the thaw."

One American commander, General Stewart, urgently wrote to the Secretary of War: "The enemy are becoming more numerous on all fronts and are more active. The allied command is small, and we have no reserves."

The final battle in North Russia occurred near the village of Bolshie Ozerki on April 2, 1919. By then, the US troops had run out of numbers, weapons, supplies, and morale. That June, as soon as navigation reopened on the White Sea, American troops began their withdrawal, with British soldiers sent in to replace them. Soon after, the Bolsheviks overran those positions and retook Murmansk and Arkhangelsk.

On April 1, 1920, the last US troops pulled out of Siberia. A combined 424 Americans had died in combat or due to disease or frostbite in North Russia and Siberia.

Internationalism in action

The Bolsheviks' fight against US imperialism did not stop at Russia's borders. Lenin's letter was smuggled into the USA and published in a slightly abridged form in December 1918

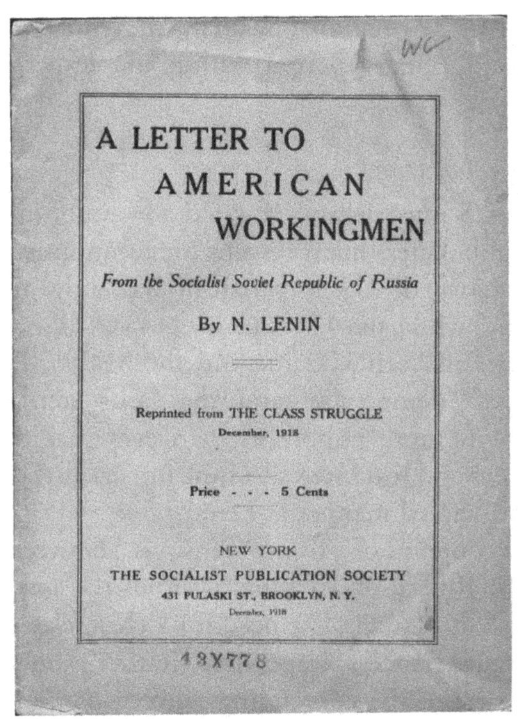

A LETTER TO
AMERICAN
WORKINGMEN

From the Socialist Soviet Republic of Russia

By N. LENIN

Reprinted from THE CLASS STRUGGLE
December, 1918

Price - - - 5 Cents

NEW YORK
THE SOCIALIST PUBLICATION SOCIETY
431 PULASKI ST., BROOKLYN, N. Y.
December, 1918

41. Pamphlet of "Letter to American Workers"—V. I. Lenin, 1918

in the New York magazine *The Class Struggle* and the Boston weekly, *The Revolutionary Age.* Instrumental in getting the letter published in the US was none other than John Reed, the author of *Ten Days That Shook the World.*

From there, the letter made its way into the bourgeois press in the US, France, Britain, and Germany. In the US, in particular, it became a focal point for the revolutionary left, serving as a de facto foundational document for the embryonic communist movement and helping to raise opposition to Wilson's armed intervention against the revolution.

Here, we see the fruits of Lenin's proletarian internationalism in action. Facing the threat of destruction from all sides, he appealed to the workers of the world on a class basis, without the slightest hint of national chauvinism, with a view toward building revolutionary parties within the imperialists' own borders.

For world revolution

The fate of US imperialism's ill-fated adventure in the young Soviet Republic offers many lessons for communists today.

The hypocrisy of US imperialism has only grown since 1918. Today, while the US and its NATO allies fund wars and atrocities in both Ukraine and the Middle East—all in the name of "democracy" and the "self-determination of nations"—it is more important than ever that communists expose the lies and real interests of the imperialists, in the same bold and principled manner as Lenin.

In the context of rising tensions between Western imperialism, Russia, and China, with all the instability and "proxy wars" this entails, the need for a clear, class-based, and internationalist stance is imperative. Rather than siding with one or another of the contending powers, communists must appeal to workers everywhere to fight their own imperialists and join forces for the victory of the world socialist revolution.

Over 100 years since the US invaded Russia, the potential for world revolution has never been greater, and we have every right to share Lenin's inexhaustible confidence in the world working class:

> Let the "socialist" snivelers croak, let the bourgeoisie rage and fume, but only people who shut their eyes so as not to see, and stuff their ears so as not to hear, can fail to notice that all over the world the birth pangs of the old, capitalist society, which is pregnant with socialism, have begun. Our country, which has temporarily been advanced by the march of events to the van of the socialist revolution, is undergoing the particularly severe pains of the first period of travail.

> [But] we have every reason to face the future with complete assurance and absolute confidence . . . We are entitled to be proud and to consider ourselves fortunate that it has come to our lot to be the first to fell in one part of the globe that wild beast, capitalism, which has drenched the earth in blood, which has reduced humanity to starvation and demoralization, and which will assuredly perish soon, no matter how monstrous and savage its frenzy in the face of death.

Timeline

July 1609–Aug. 1701	Beaver Wars, also known as the Iroquois Wars
July 1636–Sep. 1638	Pequot War
1675–76	King Philip's War
May 1763–Oct. 1766	Pontiac's War
April 1775–Sep. 1783	Revolutionary War, the First American revolution
Aug. 1786–Feb. 1787	Shays's Rebellion
Sep. 1787–June 1788	US Constitution ratified
June 1798–July 1798	Alien and Sedition Acts passed
April 1803	The Louisiana Territory purchased from France

Dec. 1823	The Monroe Doctrine announced, a foreign policy framework rejecting further European colonization and intervention in the Americas
May 1830	Indian Removal Act signed into law by President Andrew Jackson
1831–March 1839	Forced displacement of over 60,000 Native Americans. Thousands of Native Americans and slaves die on the Trail of Tears
Dec. 1835–Aug. 1842	Second Seminole War
March 1845	Texas annexed by the US
April 1846–Feb. 1848	Mexican-American War
June 1846	Oregon Territory acquired from Great Britain
April 1861–April 1865	The American Civil War, the second American revolution, ends slavery and paves the way for the unfettered development of capitalism in the US
April 1865–March 1877	Post–Civil War Reconstruction launched to reincorporate the Southern states back into the Union. Progress made toward ensuring the rights of the freedmen and greater racial integration across the South, but tragically aborted. The Compromise of 1877 marks the end of Reconstruction, followed by a period of counterrevolution, Jim Crow, and white supremacist terror
March 1867	Alaska purchased by the US from Russia
June 1876–Oct. 1876	Great Sioux War and the Battle of the Little Bighorn

Sep. 1873– May 1874	The Panic of 1873 triggers an economic depression that lasts half a decade
July 1877	The Great Railroad Strike
May 1886– June 1886	Haymarket Riot
Feb. 1898	The USS *Maine* sunk in Havana, used as a pretext for the Spanish-American War
Aug. 1898	Hawaii annexed
April 1898– Aug. 1898	Spanish-American War
May 1899– July 1902	Philippine-American War
July 1902	Cuba formally released from US control, but remains a de facto colony of the US
Nov. 1903– Jan. 1914	Panama Canal built
Dec. 1904	The Roosevelt Corollary to the Monroe Doctrine announced by President Theodore Roosevelt, asserting the US duty to intervene militarily in Latin America
Aug. 1912– Jan. 1933	US occupation of Nicaragua

July 1914– Nov. 1918	WWI breaks out in July of 1914, an imperialist war over the redivision of the world. Great Britain and France, as the older, more established capitalist states, possesses the majority of the colonies, while Germany, arriving later on the scene of capitalist development but with a rapidly growing economy, has fewer colonial possessions. This contradiction could only be solved through war, with the imperialists dragging the entire world into a bloody slaughter. In April of 1917, the US enters the war on the side of the allies
August 1914	Panama Canal completed
July 1915– Aug. 1934	US occupation of Haiti
March 1917	US purchases the Virgin Islands from Denmark
June 1919	Treaty of Versailles signed
Nov. 1917– Jan. 1920	The first Red Scare follows the Russian, German, and other revolutions. Threatened by these events, the US ruling class unleashes blatant political and physical attacks on labor rights, civil liberties, and free speech
Dec. 1928	Banana Massacre, Colombia
April 1924– Oct. 1924	Last Apache raid into US territory
Oct. 1929– 1941	The Great Depression, an economic slump that begins with the collapse of the stock market

March 1933–June 1936	The New Deal implemented by President Franklin D. Roosevelt to stabilize the capitalist system and stave off revolution. These reforms do not end the economic slump, and it takes munitions production for WWII to pull the US economy out of the depression
May 1934–Aug. 1934	The Minneapolis Teamsters Strike, West Coast Longshore Strike, and Toledo Auto-Lite Strike, led by communists, socialists, and anarchists, sweeps across the US and lays the basis for industrial unionism in the US and the formation of the Congress of Industrial Organizations (CIO)
Aug. 1935	The National Labor Relations Act, better known as the Wagner Act, establishes the National Labor Relations Board (NLRB) to cut across rising militant class struggle and channel it toward a supposedly impartial federal labor board
Nov.1935	Congress of Industrial Organizations (CIO) formed
Sep.1939–Sep. 1945	World War II; the US joins the side of the allies December 1941
Sep. 1940	Destroyers-for-Bases deal made between the US and the UK
March 1941	Lease-Lend Act
July 1944	Bretton Woods Conference. The International Monetary Fund (IMF) and the International Bank for Reconstruction and Development (IBRD), the forerunner of the World Bank, created. The Bretton Woods system established, fixing national currencies to the US Dollar, in turn tied to the gold standard. Following the global economic crisis, the Bretton Woods Agreement collapses in the 1970s

Aug. 1945	On August 6 and 9, 1945, the US detonates atomic bombs on the Japanese cities of Hiroshima and Nagasaki, killing between 150,000 and 246,000 people
Sep. 1945	Korea partitioned along the 38th parallel, with the Soviet Union occupying the North and the US occupying the South
May 1945–Oct. 1946	The largest strike wave in US history
1945–1973	The postwar economic boom, driven by European reconstruction, expansion into new markets following the colonial revolutions, and other factors, registers an unprecedented upswing in the capitalist system that lasts for almost three decades
1945–1960	During this period of colonial revolution, three dozen new states in Asia and Africa achieve autonomy or total independence from colonial rule
July 1946	The Philippines granted nominal independence from the US, but forced to grant 99-year leases to the US military for several military bases
March 1947–Dec. 1989	Cold War
March 1947–Dec. 1957	Second Red Scare and McCarthyism
June 1947	The Labor Management Relations Act, better known as Taft-Hartley, passed. It prohibits political strikes and wildcat strikes along with jurisdictional strikes, bans the closed shop, and requires union officers to affirm they were not not communists. It also empowers the president to prevent strikes considered a threat to national security. Taft-Hartley remains in effect today

April 1948–Dec.1951	Marshall Plan
April 1949	North Atlantic Treaty Organization (NATO) founded as a military alliance including the US, Canada, and several Western European countries, to confront the Soviet Union
Oct. 1949	Chinese Revolution throws off the yoke of imperialism and abolishes capitalism and landlordism. From the beginning, it is a deformed workers' state with a bureaucratic caste running society. On the basis of the planned economy and the nationalized means of production, the Chinese economy develops immensely in the following decades
June 1950–July 1953	Korean War
June 1954	United Fruit calls in the CIA to overthrow President Jacobo Árbenz in Guatemala
March 1957	European Economic Community (EEC) founded
Jan. 1959–Dec. 1959	Cuban Revolution
Nov.1960	CIA involved in the military coup which overthrows President José María Velasco Ibarra in Ecuador
April 1961	Bay of Pigs Invasion
Oct. 1962	Cuban Missile Crisis
July 1963	The US supports a military coup against President Carlos Julio Arosemena Monroy of Ecuador
April 1964	The US government provides military support to the coup against social democrat President João Goulart, establishing a military dictatorship in Brazil

March 1965	First US ground troops deployed in Vietnam
Aug. 1965–March 1973	Anti–Vietnam War Movement
Aug. 1971	The US government supports a right-wing military coup in Bolivia
Jan. 1973–March 1973	Withdrawal of US troops from Vietnam
Sep. 1973	The US supports the coup against democratically elected President Salvador Allende; General Augusto Pinochet establishes a military dictatorship in Chile
Oct. 1973	Beginning of the energy crisis
Nov. 1973–March 1975	Crisis of the world economic slump, marking an end to the postwar boom
March 1976	US backs military coup in Argentina
Dec. 1978	The Chinese bureaucracy opens China up to limited foreign investment and sets up private firms. The bureaucracy has no fully worked out plan at this point, but these initial concessions marks the beginning of the long process leading to capitalist restoration
Aug. 1981	The Professional Air Traffic Controllers Organization (PATCO) strike crushed by President Ronald Reagan. Over 11,000 workers fired, banned from federal service for life, and PATCO decertified
Nov. 1989	Fall of Berlin Wall
Dec. 1989	US invasion of Panama
Dec. 1991	Collapse of the Soviet Union

Jan 1991–Feb. 1991	Gulf War; Iraq invaded by an alliance of Western imperialists led by the US
1992	North American Free Trade Agreement (NAFTA) signed
Feb. 1993	The European Union created
Sep. 1994–March 1995	US intervention in Haiti
Jan. 1995	World Trade Organization founded
March 1999	Czechia, Hungary, and Poland join NATO
March 1999–June 1999	NATO bombs Yugoslavia
Sep. 2001	9/11 terrorist attacks
Oct. 2001	Patriot Act signed into law
Oct. 2001	US invades Afghanistan
Dec. 2001	China joins the WTO
Feb. 2003	Mass protests against planned invasion of Iraq in cities around the world. Some of the first anti-war protests to occur before the outbreak of hostilities
March 2003–May 2003	Iraq invaded
2004	Expansion of NATO to include Bulgaria, Estonia, Latvia, Lithuania, Romania, Slovakia, and Slovenia
Nov. 2004–Jan. 2005	"Orange Revolution" in Ukraine
May 2006	"A Day without Immigrants" mass protests around the US on May Day

Sep. 2014–Feb. 2015	Minsk agreements signed between Russia and Ukraine
2016	Trans-Pacific Partnership signed; Trump withdraws in 2017
July 2020–Aug. 2021	Withdrawal of the last US troops from Afghanistan
2022	Russia invades Ukraine

Image Credits

Barton, Socialist Appeal: Image 36

Flickr, via:
- FDR Presidential Library and Museum: Image 23
- Tuija Aalto: Image 26
- Ilya Varlamov: Image 24

Lonet S: Images 1, 15

Kelly Martin / kmartindesign.com for David Vine, *The United States of War: A Global History of America's Endless Conflicts, from Columbus to the Islamic State* (University of California Press, 2020): Image 18

Robert Minor, *The Daily Worker*: Image 30

US Army Photograph: Image 14, 25
The appearance of US Department of Defense (DoD) visual information does not imply or constitute DoD endorsement.

Wikipedia Commons, via:
- Acroterion: Image 21
- William Morris: Image 2
- Jonathan McIntosh: Image 29
- Unknown photographer, Reproduction by Lear 21: Image 22

All other images are in the public domain

Notes

What Is Imperialism?

page 3 McCarthy, Daniel. "This Is Why Trump Won." *New York Times*, November 6, 2024.

3 Friedman, Thomas L. "Foreign Affairs Big Mac I." *New York Times*, December 8, 1996.

5 Burns, William J. "Spycraft and Statecraft." *Foreign Affairs* 103, no. 2, January 30, 2024.

6 Gates, Robert M. "The Dysfunctional Superpower." *Foreign Affairs* 102, no. 6, September 29, 2023.

6 Harman, Jane, Eric Edelman, John M. Keane, Thomas G. Mahnken, Mara Rudman, Mariah Sixkiller, Alissa Starzak, and Roger Zakheim. *Commission on the National Defense Strategy*. US Government Publishing Office, July 2024.

6 JPMorgan Chase & Co., "JPMorgan Chase Third-Quarter 2024 Results." 2024.

6 *Global Risk Agenda 2024*. Verisk Maplecroft, July 2024.

7 Ahn, JaeBin, Benjamin Carton, Ashique Habib, Davide Malacrino, Andrea Presbitero, and Dirk Muir. *Geoeconomic Fragmentation and Foreign Direct Investment*. World Bank, May 2023.

7 Ritchie, Deborah. "The Changing Face of FDI." *Global Finance*, May 10, 2024.

8 Marx, Karl. *A Contribution to the Critique of Political Economy*, Moscow: Progress Publishers, 1977.

10 3rd Viscount Palmerston, Henry John Temple. "Speech at House of Commons." Speech, London, March 1 ,1848.

10 Churchill, Winston, "War Speech, 1939 at the House of Commons." Speech, London, September 3, 1939. America's National Churchill Museum.

10 Leonard Wood to Elihu Root, January 13, 1900, *Leonard Wood Papers*, Manuscript Division, Library of Congress

11 Butler, Smedley D. *War Is a Racket*. Round Table Press, 1935.

11 Marx, Karl, and Friedrich Engels. "The Communist Manifesto." Essay. In *Marxist Classics* Vol. 1. New York City, NY: WR Books, 2017.

13 Trotsky, Leon. *The Balkan Wars (1912–13): The War Correspondence of Leon Trotsky*. Pathfinder Press, 1981.

13 Trotsky, Leon. "Lenin on Imperialism." *Fourth International* Vol. 3, No. 1 (1942): 19–21.

14 Trotsky, Leon. "The Transitional Program," in *Marxist Classics* Vol 1. New York City, NY: WR Books, 2017.

17 Lenin, VI. *Imperialism: The Highest Stage of Capitalism*. London: Wellred Books, 2014.

18 Ibid.

19 Ibid.

20 Ibid.

22 Marx, Karl. *Capital: A Critique of Political Economy*, Vol. 1. Translated by Ben Fowkes, edited by Ernest Mandel. London: Penguin Books, 1990

23 Ibid.

24 Ibid.

24 Lenin, VI. *Imperialism: The Highest Stage of Capitalism*. London: Wellred Books, 2014.

25 Ibid.

26 Ibid.

26 Trotsky, Leon. "Lenin on Imperialism." *Fourth International* Vol. 3, No. 1 (1942) 19–21.

From Colony to Colossus: The Meteoric Rise of US Imperialism

page 33 Washington, George. "Washington's Farewell Address." Speech, Washington, D.C., 1796.

34 Jefferson, Thomas. Thomas Jefferson to Archibald Stuart, January 25, 1786, National Archives.

35 Jefferson, Thomas. "First Inaugural Address." Speech, Washington, D.C., 1801. National Archives.

37 Portales, Diego. Quoted by Uribe, Armando, *El Libro Negro de la Intervención Norteamericana en Chile*. México: Siglo XXI Editores, 1974.

38 Polk, James K. "War Message to Congress." Speech, Washington D.C., 1846. Miller Center.

39 Grant, Ulysses S. *Personal Memoirs of Ulysses S. Grant: Volumes One and Two*. New York City, NY: Open Road Integrated Media, 2014.

39 Thoreau, Henry David. *On the Duty of Civil Disobedience*. London: The Simple Life Press, 1903.

41 John O'Sullivan, "Annexation," *The United States Magazine and Democratic Review*, Volume 17, 1845.

43 Lenin, VI. *Imperialism: The Highest Stage of Capitalism*. London: Wellred Books, 2014.

44 Hayes, Rutherford B. *The Diary and Letters of Rutherford B. Hayes, Nineteenth President of the United States*. Edited by Charles Richard Williams. Columbus, Ohio:Ohio State Archaeological and Historical Society, 1922.

45 Beveridge, Albert. Quoted in Zinn, Howard. *A People's History of the United States: 1492–2001*. New York: HarperCollins, 2003.

47 Kipling, Rudyard. "The White Man's Burden," *The New York Sun*, 1899.

48 Twain, Mark. From *The New York Herald*, 1900.

49 James, William. "On the Philippine Question." *Report of the Anti-Imperialist League Annual Meeting*, 1903.

50 Immerwahr, Daniel. *How to Hide an Empire: A History of the Greater United States*. Farrar, Straus and Giroux, 2019.

51 Shafter, William. Chicago News, 1899. Quoted in Francisco, Luzviminda. "The First Vietnam : The U.S.-Philippine War of 1899," *Bulletin of Concerned Asian Scholars*, 1973.

55 Taft, William Howard. "Fourth Annual Message." Speech, Washington D.C., 1912. Miller Center.

60 Trotsky, Leon. "Europe and America." *Fourth International* Vol. 4, No. 1, 1943.

62 Chamberlain, Joseph. "Speech to the Colonial Conference." Speech, London, 1902.

63 Trotsky, Leon. "Disarmament and the United States of Europe." *Fourth International* Vol. 6, No. 5, 1945 : pg 62, 63.

68 Mason, J.W., "The Economy During Wartime." *Dissent* Fall 2017, 2017.

69 Ibid.

71 Stephenson, Neil. *Cryptonomicon*. New York City, NY: Avon, 1999.

73 Marx, Karl, and Friedrich Engels. "The Communist Manifesto." in *Marxist Classics* Vol 1. New York City, NY: WR Books, 2017.

75 Patton, George. Quoted by Coleman, Phillip. *Cannon Fodder: Growing up for Vietnam*. New York City, NY: Paragon House Publisher, 1987.

The Postwar Boom and the Restoration of Capitalism

page 79 Wedemayer, Albert, Letter to U.S. Army Chief of Staff George C. Marshall. China: 1942, quoted in Ronald H. Spector, "After Hiroshima: Allied Military Occupations and the Fate of Japan's Empire, 1945–1947", *Journal of Military History*, Volume 69, Number 4, 2005.

80 Marshall, George. "For the Common Defense: Biennial Report of the Chief of Staff, July 1, 1943 to June 30, 1945," *The War Reports*, 1947.

81 Roosevelt, Eleanor. Quoted in Perkins, Sam. "Why World War II Soldiers Mutinied after V-J Day." *HISTORY*, 2018.

81 Garcia, Daniel Eugene. "Class and Brass: Demobilization, Working Class Politics, and American Foreign Policy between World War and Cold War." *OUP Academic*, 2010.

84 Eugenio, Laurinne Jamie. "The Mass Emigration of Filipino Nurses to the United States." *Harvard International Review*, 2024.

84 "Caribbean Lost 70% of Highly-Skilled Population – CDB Rep." *Guyana Times*, 2018.

84 Pérez, Carlos Andrés. Quoted in Ali, Tariq. "A Beacon of Hope for the Rebirth of Bolívar's Dream." *The Guardian*, 2006.

85 Perkins, John. *Confessions of an Economic Hit Man*. Ebury Press, 2007.

86 Stieglitz, John. Quoted in Cassidy, John. "Master of Disaster." *The New Yorker*, 2002.

87 Dulles, Allen. Quoted in Wiener, Tim. *Legacy of Ashes: A History of the CIA*. Doubleday, 2007.

92 Trotsky, Leon. "Trade Unions in the Epoch of Imperialist Decay." *Fourth International* Vol. 2, No. 2. 1940.

94 Bowman, James. "The Invention of the War Machine." *The New Atlantis*. 2014.

100 Grant, Ted. "Will There Be a Slump?" 1960.

101 Dwight, Eisenhower D. "Farewell Address." National Archives and Records Administration. 1961.

104 McNamara, Robert. Interview with CNN, The National Security Archive, 1996.

105 Summers, Harry G. Quoted in Allen, Charles. "Assessing the Army Profession." *Parameters: The US Army War College Quarterly* 41, No. 3. , 2011.

111 Trotsky, Leon. "Twenty Years of Stalinist Degeneration." *The Bulletin of the Russian Opposition*. 1938.

112 Boot, Max. "Reagan Didn't Win the Cold War." *Foreign Affairs*. 2024.

114 Bush, George H.W. "Address Before a Joint Session of the Congress on the State of the Union." George H.W. Bush Presidential Library & Museum: 1991.

115 Jacques, Martin. "We are globalised, but have no real intimacy with the rest of the world." *The Guardian*, 2006.

117 "Strobe Talbott Memo to Secretary Christopher and Tony Lake: Handling Yeltsin." National Security Archive, 1994.

117 Clinton, Bill. "Memorandum of Telephone Conversation between Clinton and Yeltsin." National Security Archive, 1994.

117 Kórdhunov, Maxim. Mikhail Gorbachev: I am against all walls. *Russia Beyond*, 2014.

118 Brzezinski, Zbigniew. *The Grand Chessboard: American Primacy and its Geostrategic Imperatives*. New York: Basic Books, 1997.

118 Matlock, Jack F. "I Was There: NATO and the Origins of the Ukraine Crisis." *Responsible Statecraft*, February 15, 2022.

120 McConnell, Scott. "George Kennan's Internal Exile," *Modern Age: A Conservative Review*, July 15 2023.

Imperialism Today: Dynamite in the Foundations

page 124 Kennan, George. "Letter to an American," *The New Yorker*, September 24, 1984.

124 Kristol, William and Robert Kagan. "Toward a Neo-Reaganite Foreign Policy," *Foreign Affairs*, 1996.

126 Greenberger, Robert S. and Karby Leggett. "Bush Dreams of Changing Not Just Regime but Region," *The Wall Street Journal*, March 21, 2003.

127 Congressional Research Service. Congress, *Civilian Control of the Military, and Nonpartisanship*. Congressional Research Service, June 2020.

129 Trump, Donald. Interview. By Maria Bartiromo. *Fox News Sunday Morning Futures*, 2024.

129 Posse Comitatus Act of 1878, 18 U.S.C. § 1385, 1878.

129 Insurrection Act of 1807, 10 U.S.C. § 254, 1807.

129 Bertrand, Natasha and Haley Britzky. "Pentagon officials discussing how to respond if Trump issues controversial orders." *CNN*, November 8, 2024.

131 Sophocles. *Three Theban Plays: Antigone; Oedipus the King; Oedipus at Colonus*. Translated by Robert fagles. New York, NY: Penguin Books, 1984.

132 Von Tunzelmann, Alex. *Indian Summer: The Secret History of the End of an Empire*. Hew York City, NY: Henry and Holt, 2007.

133 US Department of State. *Report by the Policy Planning Staff.* Feburary 24, 1948.

138 Doshi, Rush, Jessica Chen Weiss, James B. Steinberg, Paul Heer, Matt Pottinger, and Mike Gallagher. "What Does America Want From China?" *Foreign Affairs* 103, no. 4, May 30, 2024.

141 Dulles, John Foster. Interview. By James Shepley. *Time*, 1956.

143 Daniels, Joe and Steven Bernard. "South America's 'made in China' megaport prepares to transform trade." *Financial Times*, November 13, 2024.

145 Lee, Kuan Yew, Graham T. Allison, Robert D. Blackwill, and Ali Wyne. *Lee Kuan Yew: The Grand Master's Insights on China, the United States, and the World.* Cambridge, MA: The MIT Press, 2013.

145 Blackwill, Robert D. "Trump's Foreign Policies Are Better Than They Seem." *Council on Foreign Relations*, April 2019.

147 Nietzsche, Friedrich, and Gary J. Handwerk. *Human, All Too Human.* Vol. 2. Stanford, California: Stanford University Press, 1997.

147 Washington, George. "1793 State of the Union Address." Speech. December 3, 1793. The Avalon Project.

148 Eaglen, Mackenzie. "10 Ways the US Is Falling Behind China in National Security." American Enterprise Institute, August 29, 2023.

149 Biden, Joe. "Remarks by President Biden on Russia's Unprovoked and Unjustified Attack on Ukraine." Speech, Washington, D.C. February 24, 2022.

150 Roth, Andrew and Pjotr Sauer. "Andrei Belousev: Putin picks trusted technocrat to run defense ministry." *The Guardian*, May 14, 2024.

151 Vershinin, Alex. "The Attritional Art of War: Lessons from the Russian War on Ukraine." The Royal United Services Institute for Defence and Security Studies, March 18, 2024.

154 Beaver, Wilson and Jim Fein. "America Must Remedy Its Dangerous Lack of Munitions Planning." The Heritage Foundation, February 26, 2024.

155 Levantovscaia, Kathryn. "Overstretched and undersupplied: Can the US afford its global security blanket?" *New Atlanticist*, January 5, 2024.

156 Einsenhower, Dwight D. *Crusade in Europe*. New York City, NY: Doubleday, 1948.

159 Wicker, Roger. "America's Military Is Not prepared for War—or Peace." *The New York Times*, May 29, 2024.

160 Jones, Seth. "China Is Ready For War." *Foreign Affairs*, October 2, 2024.

162 Kissinger, Henry. *Diplomacy*. New York City, NY: Simon & Schuster, 1994.

163 Brzezinski, Zbigniew. *The Grand Chessboard: American primacy and its geostrategic imperatives*. New York: Basic Books, 1997.

164 Fong, Clara and Lindsay Maizland. "China and Russia: Exploring Ties Between Two Authoritarian Power." Council on Foreign Relations, March 20, 2024.

164 Bradsher, Keith. "China Is Striking Deals to Cement Its Role as Asia's Trade Hub." *The New York Times*, September 24, 2024.

167 Draghi, Mario. Quoted in Gross, Jenny and Patricia Cohen. "Europe's 'Reason for Being' at Risk as Competitiveness Wanes, Report Warns." *The New York Times*, September 9, 2024.

169 Kissinger, Henry, 1968, quoted in Buckley, William F. *United Nations Journal: A Delegate's Odyssey*. New York, Putnam, 1974.

170 Trump, Donald. Interview. By Cook, Nancy, Joshua Green, Mario Parker, and Brad Stone. *Bloomberg Businessweek*, July 16, 2024.

171 Machiavelli, Niccolò. *Discourses on Livy*. Oxford University Press, USA, 2009.

171 Nixon, Richard, Quoted by Haldeman, H.R. with Joseph DiMona. *The Ends of Power*. New York: Times Books, 1978.

172 Sinaceur, Marwann, and Larissa Z. Tiedens. "Get Mad and Get More Than Even: When and Why Anger Expression Is Effective in Negotiations." *Journal of Experimental Social Psychology* 42, no. 3, May 2006.

172 Trump, Donald. Speech. Wheeling, VA, September 19, 2018.

175 Le Monde with AFP. "The full transcript of Putin's speech: 'It is not Russia but the US that has destroyed the system of international security.'" *Le Monde*, November 21, 2024.

177 Putin, Vladimir. Quoted in Soldatkin, Vladimir and Guy Faulconbridge. "Putin praises Trump, says Russia is ready for dialogue." *Reuters*, November 7, 2024.

178 Engels, Friedrich. "Preface to 'On the Question of Free Trade.'" In Marx and Engels *Collected Works*, Vol. 26, New York City, NY: International Publishers, 1990.

179 Doi, Noriyuki. "Trump election spurs new surge in China chip stocks." *Nikkei Asia*, November 16, 2024.

180 Jinping, Xi, Quoted in "Promote steady improvement and growth in China-US relations through the right way forward: Global Times editorial." *Global Times*, November 7, 2024.

181 Sullivan, Joe. "A BRICS Currency Could Shake the Dollar's Dominance." *Foreign Policy*, April 4, 2024.

182 Trump, Donald, Quoted by AP News, "Trump likens buying Greenland to 'a large real estate deal.'" *AP News*, November 18, 2019.

Imperialism in Latin America and the World Revolution

page 185 Roosevelt, Franklin Delano. "Good Neighbor Policy, 1933." Speech, March 4, 1933. U.S. Department of State.

186 Dulles, John F. "Secretary of State John F. Dulles, Radio Address, 1954." Speech, June 1954. UMBC: University of Maryland, Baltimore County.

188 Trump, Donald. Quoted in Rodriguez, Sabrina. "Trump's North American Trade Deal Starts Now. Here's What to Expect." *Politico*, July 20, 2020.

189 Bacon, David. "The Maquiladora Workers of Juárez Find Their Voice." *Portside*, December 3, 2015.

189 Schumer, Charles. "Senator Chuck Schumer and Robby Mook Discuss Campaign 2016." Speech, Philadelphia, July 28, 2016. C-Span.

190 Vocht, Shan Van. "Socialism and Nationalism." *James Connolly: Socialism and Nationalism* (1897), January 1897.

190 "Foreign Direct Investment in Latin America and the Caribbean." United Nations ECLAC, July 10, 2023.

191 Zhang, Minlu. "China's Trade with Mexico, FDI on the Rise." World - *Chinadaily.com.cn*, August 22, 2024.

192 "Menendez, Risch, Rubio, Kaine Introduce Resolution Recognizing 9th Summit of the Americas, Hosted by U.S.: United States Senate Committee on Foreign Relations." Foreign Relations Committee, March 17, 2021.

193 Faller, Craig. Quoted in Roy, Diana. "China's Growing Influence in Latin America." Council on Foreign Relations, June 15, 2024.

194 Ibid.

196 Sharma, Ruchir. "Immigration Crackdowns Are Good Politics but Bad Economics." *Financial Times*, January 14, 2024.

196 "The Cost of Immigration Enforcement and Border Security." American Immigration Council, August 14, 2024.

199 Ibid.

200 Dullens, Allen W. "Statement by Mr. Allen W. Dulles to the Senate Foreign Relations Committee." General CIA Records, May 31, 1960.

202 Jones, Edgar L. "One War is Enough." *The Atlantic*, May 1945.

204 Trotsky, Leon. "Marxism in Our Time." *Labor Action*, Vol. 10, No. 43, October 28, 1946.

206 Office of the Director of National Intelligence, *Annual Threat Assessment of the U.S. Intelligence Community*, Office of the Director of National Intelligence, February 5, 2024.

207 Trotsky, Leon. "Marxism in Our Time." *Labor Action*, Vol. 10, No. 43, October 28, 1946.

A Marxist Primer on Imperialist War

page 210 Trotsky, Leon. *My Life*. London: Wellred Books, 2018.

211 Lenin, VI. "May Day and The War." In Lenin. *Collected Works* Vol. 36. Moscow: Progress Publishers, 1971.

212 Bismark, Otto von. "Blood and Iron." Speech. 1862.

213 Sherman, William. *Memoirs of General W. T. Sherman.* New York City, NY: Library of America, 1990.

213 Trotsky, Leon. "The Transitional Program." Essay. In *Marxist Classics* Vol 1. New York City, NY: WR Books, 2017.

216 Grant, Ted. "Arms race, war in the 1980s— 'Politics by other means.'" *Militant International Review* 29, 1985.

217 Clausewitz, Carl von. *On War.* Translated by J. J. Graham. Wordsworth Classics of World Literature. Ware, England: Wordsworth Editions, 1997.

218 Trotsky, Leon. "A Fresh Lesson." *The New International* IV, no. 12, 1938.

219 Engels, Friedrich. *Origins of the Family, Private Property, and the State.* London: Wellred Books, 2020.

220 Engels, Friedrich. *Anti-Dühring.* London: Wellred Books, 2017.

221 Engels, Friedrich. "Introduction to Borkheim." 1888.

222 Trotsky, Leon. *The War and the International.* Chicago: International Socialist Review, 1918.

224 "Manifesto of the International Socialist Conference at Zimmerwald." In Lenin. *Selected Writings: On Imperialist War.* London: Wellred Books, 2024.

224 Lenin, VI. "Socialism and War." In Lenin. *Selected Writings: On Imperialist War.* London: Wellred Books, 2024.

226 Ibid.

227 Lenin, VI. "Letter to American Workers." In Lenin. *Collected Works* Vol. 28. Moscow: Progress Publishers, 1965.

228 Ibid.

229 Lenin, VI. "Bourgeois Pacifism and Socialist Pacifism." In Lenin. *Selected Writings: On Imperialist War.* London: Wellred Books, 2024.

230 Ibid.

230 Lenin, VI. "The Socialist Revolution and the Right of Nations to Self-Determination." In Lenin. *Collected Works,* Vol. 22. Moscow: Progress Publishers, 1964.

231 "Socialism and War." In Lenin. *Selected Writings: On Imperialist War.* London: Wellred Books, 2024.

231 Trotsky, Leon. "Manifesto of the Second Congress of the Communist International." In *The First Five Years of the Communist International* Vols 1 & 2. London: Wellred Books, 2020.

232 "Socialism and War." In Lenin. *Selected Writings: On Imperialist War*. London: Wellred Books, 2024.

233 Ibid.

235 Liebknecht, Karl. "The Main Enemy Is At Home!" In *Selected Speeches and Essays*. Translated by John Wagner. Berlin, 1952.

236 Lenin, VI. "The Significance of Fraternisation." In Lenin. *Collected Works* Vol. 24. Moscow: progress Publishers, 1964.

237 VI, Lenin. "The Military Programme of the Proletarian Revolution." In Lenin. *Collected Works* Vol. 23, Moscow: Progress Publishers, 1964.

239 "Socialism and War." In Lenin. *Selected Writings: On Imperialist War*. London: Wellred Books, 2024.

240 VI, Lenin. "The Tasks of the Proletariat in Our Revolution (Draft Platform for the Proletarian Party)." Lenin. *Collected Works* Vol. 26, Moscow: Progress Publishers, 1964.

241 VI, Lenin. "On the Disarmament Slogan." In Lenin. *Collected Works* Vol. 23, Moscow: Progress Publishers, 1964.

242 "Socialism and War." In Lenin. *Selected Writings: On Imperialist War*. London: Wellred Books, 2024.

243 VI, Lenin. "The Military Programme of the Proletarian Revolution." In Lenin. *Collected Works* Vol. 23, Moscow: Progress Publishers, 1964.

244 Third Congress of the Comintern 1921, Guidelines on the Organizational Structure of Communist Parties, on the Methods and Content of their Work. 1921.

246 VI, Lenin. "The Military Programme of the Proletarian Revolution." In Lenin. *Collected Works* Vol. 23, Moscow: Progress Publishers, 1964.

246 Luxemburg, Rosa. "The Junius Pamphlet." Translated by Dave Hollis. Politische Schriften, first published 1916.

248 Lenin, VI. "Letter to American Workers." In Lenin. *Collected Works* Vol. 28. Moscow: Progress Publishers, 1965.

248 Trotsky, Leon. "Some Questions on American Problems." *Fourth International* Vol. 1, No. 5, 1940.

When US Imperialism Invaded Soviet Russia

page 249 Lenin, VI. "Decree on Peace." In Lenin. *Collected Works* Vol. 26. Moscow: Progress Publishers, 1964.

251 Wilson, Woodrow. "Fourteen Points." Speech. Washington, D.C., 1918.

252 Fuller, JV. "The Ambassador in France (Sharp) to the Secretary of State." P*apers Relating to the Foreign Relations of the United States* Vol. 2, US Government Printing Office, 1932.

252 Williams, WA. "American Intervention in Russia, 1917–1920." *Studies on the Left*, No.3, 1963.

253 Fuller, JV. "The Ambassador in Russia (Francis) to the Secretary of State." *Papers Relating to the Foreign Relations of the United States* Vol. 2, US Government Printing Office, 1932.

254 Trotsky, Leon. "Communique of the People's Commissariat for Military Affairs." *Leon Trotsky's Military Writings* Vol. 1. Translated by Brian Pearce. 1923.

255 Williams, WA. "American Intervention in Russia, 1917–1920." *Studies on the Left*, No. 3, 1963.

261 Lenin, VI. "Letter to American Workers." In Lenin. *Collected Works* Vol. 28. Moscow: Progress Publishers, 1965.

262 Ibid.

263 Ibid.

263 *Historical Files of the American Expeditionary Force, North Russia, 1918–1919*, US National Archives and Records Administration, M924, Roll 1.

264 Ibid.

265 Habib, D, *Playing Into the Hands of Isolationists: Woodrow Wilson's Russian Policy, 1918–1920*, San Jose State University, 1995

265 Otoupalik, H, *Quartered in Hell: The Story of the American North Russia Expeditionary Force 1918–1919*. Doughboy Historical Society, 1982.

266 *Historical Files of the American Expeditionary Force, North Russia, 1918–1919*, US National Archives and Records Administration, M924, Roll 1.

267 Ibid.

268 Lenin, VI, "Prophetic Words." Lenin. *Collected Works* Vol. 27, Moscow: Progress Publishers, 1965,

Titles by Wellred Books

Wellred Books is a publishing house specialising in works of Marxist theory. Among the titles we publish are:

Anti-Dühring, Friedrich Engels
Bolshevism: The Road to Revolution, Alan Woods
Chartist Revolution, Rob Sewell
China: From Permanent Revolution to Counter-Revolution, John Peter Roberts
The Civil War in France, Karl Marx
Class Struggle in the Roman Republic, Alan Woods
The Class Struggles in France, 1848-1850, Karl Marx
The Classics of Marxism: Volumes One & Two, Various authors
Colossus: The Rise and Decline of US Imperialism, John Peterson
Dialectics of Nature, Friedrich Engels
The Eighteenth Brumaire of Louis Bonaparte, Karl Marx
The First Five Years of the Communist International, Leon Trotsky
The First World War: A Marxist Analysis of the Great Slaughter, Alan Woods
Germany: From Revolution to Counter-Revolution, Rob Sewell

Germany 1918-1933: Socialism or Barbarism, Rob Sewell
History of British Trotskyism, Ted Grant
The History of Philosophy: A Marxist Perspective, Alan Woods
The History of the Russian Revolution: All Volumes, Leon Trotsky
The History of the Russian Revolution to Brest-Litovsk, Leon Trotsky
The Ideas of Karl Marx, Alan Woods
Imperialism: The Highest Stage of Capitalism, VI Lenin
In Defence of Lenin, Rob Sewell & Alan Woods
In Defence of Marxism, Leon Trotsky
Ireland: Republicanism and Revolution, Alan Woods
'Left-Wing' Communism: An Infantile Disorder, VI Lenin
Lenin and Trotsky: What They Really Stood For, Alan Woods & Ted Grant
Lenin Selected Writings, VI Lenin
  On Imperialist War
  On the National Question
  The Revolutions of 1917
Marxism and Anarchism, Various authors
Marxism and the USA, Alan Woods
Materialism and Empirio-criticism, VI Lenin
My Life, Leon Trotsky
The Origin of the Family, Private Property & the State, Friedrich Engels
The Permanent Revolution and Results & Prospects, Leon Trotsky
Permanent Revolution in Latin America, John Roberts & Jorge Martin
Reason in Revolt, Alan Woods & Ted Grant
Revolution and Counter-Revolution in Spain, Felix Morrow
The Revolution Betrayed, Leon Trotsky
The Revolutionary Legacy of Rosa Luxemburg, Marie Frederiksen
The Revolutionary Philosophy of Marxism, John Peterson (Ed.)

Russia: From Revolution to Counter-Revolution, Ted Grant

Spain's Revolution Against Franco, Alan Woods

Stalin, Leon Trotsky

The State and Revolution, VI Lenin

Ted Grant: The Permanent Revolutionary, Alan Woods

Ted Grant Writings: Volumes One and Two, Ted Grant

Thawra hatta'l nasr! - Revolution until Victory!, Alan Woods & others

What Is Marxism?, Rob Sewell & Alan Woods

What Is to Be Done?, VI Lenin

Women, Family and the Russian Revolution, John Roberts & Fred Weston

Writings on Britain, Leon Trotsky

To make an order or for more information, visit marxistbooks.com, email sales@marxistbooks.com or write to Wellred Books, PO Box 1575, New York, NY 10013.

www.ingramcontent.com/pod-product-compliance
Ingram Content Group UK Ltd.
Pitfield, Milton Keynes, MK11 3LW, UK
UKHW021949140325
456288UK00005B/229

9 798218 554880